YALE PUBLICATIONS IN RELIGION, 1

David Horne, editor

Published under the direction of the Divinity School

St. Ignatius and

Christianity in Antioch

by VIRGINIA CORWIN

New Haven

YALE UNIVERSITY PRESS, 1960

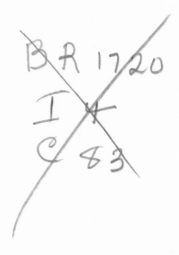

Preface

THE THEOLOGY of St. Ignatius of Antioch was wrought in struggle, not in the study. His letters, written on the road to his death in Rome, show him still inextricably engaged with life, and give clear evidence of the vitality of his work as bishop. He was deeply rooted in Christian loyalties—deeply enough to die for his faith—but at the same time he was so much in conversation with his generation that his own beliefs were shaped by that dialogue. Even to-day his thought has a vigor and freshness wholly lacking in most of the documents that have survived from the early second century. He revered St. Paul, but he had no hesitation in differing from him.

Because controversy was so central in his life the discoveries of the Essene library at Qumran and the light thrown on gnosticism by the Valentinian *Gospel of Truth* from the collection at Chenoboskion are of special importance for understanding him. The years from 80 to 150 have been singularly inaccessible to scholars, and these discoveries add immensely to our knowledge of the varieties of religious thought current in that period. Some of the Christians in Antioch seem to have been of Essene origin, and others in the church were exponents of a docetic form of gnosticism. Jews and Gnostics differed widely on the nature of God and man and the world, and Christian theology had to be developed and clarified in the face of this conflict.

Ignatius himself has been interpreted by some scholars as profoundly gnostic, but this book takes issue with that position. He was without doubt influenced by the Docetists—for instance in their conception of revelation—but he stood steadfastly against them in most respects. The current debate as to whether gnosticism antedates Christianity, and whether it played the major role in the development of Christianity that some scholars believe, can be settled only on the basis of detailed investigation of the writings and men of the early period, and it may be hoped that a

new study of St. Ignatius will be of help in that task. His own
freedom, and what he reveals of the thought of his docetic opponents, suggest that in his time there was no clear-cut single
movement that could be defined as gnostic, certainly not of a
Mandaean sort, but that there were, rather, varieties of thought
which could more properly be called proto-gnostic. His struggle
to find norms, and to decide what in truth could be called Christian, discloses him to have been a significant leader.

His view of the church was as important as his theology. He
saw men as divided inwardly and alienated from one another
and from God. Only in the church, he believed, could life be
found, because life was the divine gift. There, uniquely, men
and women could learn to live in community, and slowly experience the healing of their separateness.

The new materials that we have to work with have increased
our resources for understanding the period but have not done
away with our perplexities. It will be long before there is significant agreement about their meaning, and in the meantime writing about the early second century must be in part conjecture.
No book can escape those difficulties.

The debt I owe to my predecessors in Ignatian studies is tre-
mendous, though I have tried to indicate where the positions
with which I disagree are to be found. The quotations from Ignatius are freshly done, but since the variety of ways in which a
Greek phrase can be taken is understandably limited, my translations must sometimes sound like echoes. Quotations from the
Bible are in general from the American Revised Version, published by Thomas Nelson and Sons.

In the libraries where I have worked I have learned a new
article of belief—in the Communion of Scholars. To those libraries, where I have been given courtesies without number, I
express my thanks: especially to the great Sterling Library at
Yale, to the Cambridge University Library, and in season and
out of season to the Neilson Library at Smith College.

I am grateful to the Governors of the John Rylands Library
of Manchester for permission granted me to quote from the
Odes and Psalms of Solomon, edited by Rendel Harris and Al-
phonse Mingana; and to the American Philosophical Society

for permission to reproduce, in somewhat modified form, the plan of the city of Antioch in the article by Charles R. Morey, "The Excavation of Antioch-on-the-Orontes," published in the 1936 volume of the Proceedings of the Society.

To Wellesley College I am grateful chiefly for many intangibles, but also for the pleasantly tangible gift of the Fanny Bullock Workman Scholarship, which made possible some of the work on this book. I thank the Ford Foundation for the grant which has helped to pay for its publication.

Finally, special thanks must go to three of my friends who have given me encouragement and that rarer gift, criticism. For all of them this has meant precious time taken from their own writing. Carl H. Kraeling, who directed the Yale doctoral dissertation that was the first stage of my Ignatian study, Paul Schubert, and Robert L. Calhoun have all read the manuscript in different stages of its development. My thinking has been stimulated and clarified by their knowledge.

V. C.

Northampton, Massachusetts
December 1959

Contents

Maps of St. Ignatius' journey across Asia Minor, of Syria, and of Antioch appear on pages 15, 33, and 35 respectively.

Abbreviations

THE conventional abbreviations have been used for biblical references, except that in cases where confusion is possible N.T. is sometimes added, e.g. N.T. Rom.—in contradistinction to *Rom.*, which means Ignatius, *Epistle to the Romans.*

Abr.   Philo, *De Abrahamo*
Adv. haer.   Irenaeus, *Against Heresies*
Ant.   Josephus, *Antiquities of the Jews*
Anth. Pal.   *Anthologia Palatine* (or *Graeca*)
BA   *Biblical Archaeologist*
Barn.   *Epistle of Barnabas*
BASOR   *Bulletin of the American Schools of Oriental Research*
Bell.   Josephus, *Jewish Wars*
CAH   *Cambridge Ancient History*
CDC   Cairo *Damascus Document* (R. H. Charles, *Apocrypha and Pseudepigrapha*)
Conf.   Philo, *De confusione linguarum*
Contr. Ap.   Josephus, *Contra Apion*
Corp. Herm.   *Corpus Hermeticum*
DSD   *Dead Sea Manual of Discipline* (Cave I, Qumran)
Eph.   Ignatius, *Epistle to the Ephesians*
ERE   Hastings, *Encyclopedia of Religion and Ethics*
Excer. Theod.   *Excerpta ex Theodoto*
Fug.   Philo, *De fuga et inventione*
GG   Bartsch, *Gnostisches Gut und Gemeindetradition bei Ignatius*
Hab. Com.   Habakkuk *Commentary* (Cave I)
Heres   Philo, *Quis rerum divinarum heres*
Hermas, *Mand.*   Hermas, *The Shepherd: Mandates*
HTR   *Harvard Theological Review*
HUCA   *Hebrew Union College Annual*
JBL   *Journal of Biblical Literature*
JR   *Journal of Religion*
JTS   *Journal of Theological Studies*
Jub.   *Jubilees* (R. H. Charles)
Mag.   Ignatius, *Epistle to the Magnesians*
Mig.   Philo, *De migratione Abrahami*
Mos.   Philo, *De vita Mosis*
Mut.   Philo, *De mutatione nominum*

Opif.   Philo, *De opificio mundi*
Phld.   Ignatius, *Epistle to the Philadelphians*
Plant.   Philo, *De plantatione*
Poly.   Ignatius, *Epistle to Polycarp*
Poly. Phil.   Polycarp, *Epistle to the Philippians*
Post.   Philo, *De posteritate Caini*
Qol.   *Qolasta* (Lidzbarski, *Mandäische Liturgien*)
RB   *Revue biblique*
Ref.   Hippolytus, *Refutation of All Heresies*
Relig. Untersuch.   Schlier, *Religionsgeschichtliche Untersuchungen zu*
                                den Ignatiusbriefen
Rom.   Ignatius, *Epistle to the Romans*
Smyr.   Ignatius, *Epistle to the Smyrnaeans*
Som.   Philo, *De somniis*
Spec.   Philo, *De specialibus legibus*
Test. Asher, Gad, Jos., etc.   *Testaments of the Twelve Patriarchs*
                                (R. H. Charles)
Tral.   Ignatius, *Epistle to the Trallians*
Virt.   Philo, *De virtutibus*
ZNTW   *Zeitschrift für die neutestamentliche Wissenschaft*

Sɪɢʟᴀ used are in general those of Lightfoot, *Apostolic Fathers,* 2d ed., Pt.
II, Vol. 2, pp. 3–6:
G   The original Greek version
L   Latin Version
S   Syriac Version
Σ   Syriac Abridgment
A   Armenian
B   Berlin Papyrus (see C. Schmidt and W. Schubert)
C   Coptic
g   Greek of the Long Recension
l   Latin of the Long Recension
Sₘ   Syriac Acts

PART ONE

The Situation

1.   The Letters and the Man

THE LETTERS written by Ignatius have a rare advantage, among early Christian writings, in being fixed in place, even if not precisely in time. We do not know accurately the year in which they were written and must remain content with holding that it was probably between A.D. 108 and 117,[1] in other words in the last years of the reign of the emperor Trajan or possibly in the earliest years of Hadrian.

The place reference is definite, however. We know that their author was bishop of Antioch in Syria. He wrote to five of the churches in western Asia Minor and to the great Roman church, as he was being taken up to Rome by a guard of soldiers to face a death sentence. The problems of the Asia Minor churches are constantly under discussion, and in consequence the letters are often treated primarily as sources for church history in Asia Minor, even to the extent of identifying an "Asia Minor theology." It is fortunate for our knowledge of early Christian history that they reveal so much about practical problems in the cities in western Asia Minor, but what is fundamental is Ignatius' own thought, theological and ecclesiastical. It was the result of years of experience in Antioch, and the letters primarily reveal a form of Christianity that was of Syria, not Asia Minor.

It is a rare luxury to know the provenance of writings from the early church. *I Clement* and some of St. Paul's letters can be used as sources for the history of one or another of the

1. Eusebius, in the *Chronicon*, places the martyrdom in A.D. 108, but his methods of dating are not reliable. A. von Harnack, *Die Chronologie der altchristlichen Litteratur bis Eusebius* (2 vols. Leipzig, 1897–1904), *1*, 381–406, argues for a date between 110 and 117, or possibly in the early years of Hadrian, before 125. He here abandons his earlier position set forth in *Die Zeit des Ignatius*, Leipzig, 1878. J. B. Lightfoot prefers a date between 100 and 118: *The Apostolic Fathers*, Pt. II, *S. Ignatius and S. Polycarp* (2d ed. London, 1889), 2, 435–72.

3

churches; however interesting it would be to know in which of
the great churches the four canonical gospels were written, we
must be satisfied with a combination of more or less precise
reference, carefully checked tradition, and skillful inference.
Any reconstruction of the problematical and fascinating years
in the history of the churches before 150 must depend on similar
methods. It is therefore difficult to overestimate the advantage
of being able to date or place any given piece of evidence. In
the Ignatian letters, which have that marked advantage, we can
trace at least the outlines of thought in one of the most important churches at the very beginning of the second century,
and see the mind of its vigorous leader at work.

There are excellent studies of Ignatius' thought, and references to him are legion in histories of the church and of Christian thought; nevertheless the letters have not achieved the
full importance they deserve. This is partly because they have
always been overshadowed by the more systematic writings of
St. Paul and the author of the Fourth Gospel, partly because
the long controversy about their genuineness has quite un-
justifiably caused hesitation about them even up to the present.

Eusebius [2] knew seven Greek letters written by Ignatius: to
the churches in Ephesus, Magnesia, Tralles, Philadelphia, and
Smyrna in the Roman Province of Asia; to the church in Rome;
and to Polycarp of Smyrna. Fortunately for later scholars Eusebius quotes from *Rom., Smyr.,* and *Poly.* These seven letters,
uninterpolated, exist in Greek, Latin, and Armenian versions,
with fragments in Coptic and Syriac. The letters were extensively interpolated, probably in the fourth century, and presumably at the same time five other letters were added to them,
bearing the name of Ignatius and addressed to the churches in
Tarsus, Antioch, and Philippi; to Hero, traditionally his successor at Antioch; and to one Mary of Cassabola. A letter from
Mary to Ignatius was also included. This so-called Long Recension exists in Greek and Latin only. Probably in the eleventh
or twelfth centuries, but certainly before the middle of the
thirteenth, four Latin letters appeared, purporting to be a correspondence between Ignatius and St. John and Ignatius and the

2. *Ecclesiastical History* 3.36.

Virgin Mary; but these letters, although popular, disappeared quickly from serious consideration.

In 1623 Vedelius of Geneva separated the Eusebian seven from the five others, which he recognized as spurious. He saw that even the seven original letters had suffered interpolation, but he could not establish the early text. Ussher in his edition of 1644 distinguished the limits of the original letters by using two Latin MSS of the uninterpolated letters which he discovered. He had inferred their existence because quotations made by Robert Grosseteste and two fourteenth-century English writers tallied with quotations from Eusebius and Theodoret, instead of with the Long Recension. This discovery, however, established the text only of the Latin version, not of the Greek of the original. Two years later in 1646 Voss published the Greek version of all but *Romans,* which was finally published by Ruinart in 1689. Thus at the end of the seventeenth century the claims of the Long Recension seemed to have been disposed of.

In 1845 Cureton published his *Antient Syriac Version of the Epistles of Saint Ignatius to St. Polycarp, the Ephesians and Romans,* a collection known as the Short Recension, because it has a smaller number of letters and because these lack phrases, sentences, and even long sections that appear in the text of the uninterpolated seven, which now came to be known as the Middle Recension. The letter to the Ephesians, for instance, is perhaps a third of its length in the Middle Recension. Cureton's thesis was that the genuine form of the letters had at last been discovered, and that Eusebius himself had not been certain of the authenticity of all that he cited. This view had some popularity for a while, but in the opinion of most scholars the independent editions of Zahn in 1876 and of Lightfoot in 1885 established the Middle Recension as original.[3]

3. The main editions are: T. Zahn ed., *Ignatii et Polycarpi, Epistulae, Martyria, Fragmenta* (Patrum Apostolicorum Opera, Fasc. II, ed. O. de Gebhart, A. von Harnack, and T. Zahn), Leipzig, 1876; Lightfoot, *The Apostolic Fathers,* Pt. II; F. X. Funk, *Patres Apostolici* (2d ed. 2 vols. Tübingen, 1901), Vol. 1, more conveniently available in the edition of K. Bihlmeyer, *Die apostolischen Väter,* Tübingen, 1924.

More recent discoveries have added new textual material. The Berlin

Relative agreement on this matter was not enough, however, to satisfy all scholars that the letters were the authentic writings of Ignatius. Debate began in the sixteenth century, and has continued almost to the present time, as to whether the situation envisaged in the letters and the ideas expressed there could possibly be those of an early second-century bishop. The earlier discussions not infrequently displayed skepticism based on an a priori position. [Critics, for instance, attacked the genuineness of the letters on the ground, important to early Protestants, that the monarchical episcopate did not exist in the early years of the second century. Others argued that the heretical thought of Ignatius' opponents is that of the developed gnostic systems and therefore cannot be dated before the time of Marcion or close to the middle of the second century. Most scholars took their stand on unbiased grounds, but there were some whose position against the episcopate or for a particular theory of Christian origins made their case suspect.

Lightfoot and later writers have done valuable service by showing that at least a part of the opposition on these points arose from a misunderstanding of the letters. Lightfoot [4] argued convincingly that Ignatius does not assume that the episcopate exists everywhere among the churches, nor does he justify it for the full-fledged doctrinal reasons which later became general. Neither is his picture of the false teaching that of the later gnostic systems, but something far less developed, and in significant ways rather different.]

Papyrus 10581 containing *Smyr.* 3.3–12.1 in Greek was published by C. Schmidt and W. Schubart, *Altchristliche Texte,* Vol. 1, Berlin, 1910. A Coptic fragment from the Sammlung Papyrus Erzherzog Rainier K9416–9421 contains *Tral., Phld.,* and *Rom.* as far as 5.2, with the exception of 3.3. See C. Wessely, *Neue Materialien zur Textkritik der Ignatiusbriefe,* Vienna, 1913. Wessely believes that it and MS Borg. 248 (published by Lightfoot) belong together. K. Lake, *The Apostolic Fathers,* Vol. 1 (London, 1925), takes account of all but the last-named textual discovery.

There are many modern translations, e.g. C. C. Richardson, *Early Christian Fathers,* Philadelphia, 1953; J. A. Kleist, *The Epistles of St. Clement of Rome and St. Ignatius of Antioch,* Westminster, Md., 1946.

4. *St. Paul's Epistle to the Philippians* (8th ed. London, 1888), pp. 181 ff.; *Apostolic Fathers, 1,* 373–82, 395–99. The older scholarship is discussed in full by Lightfoot in *Apostolic Fathers.*

Since Lightfoot's time [5] there have been two attempts to explain the letters as written in part at least by others than the bishop of Antioch. Völter, writing in 1892 and again in 1910, believed that Ignatius wrote only the epistle to the Romans, and that the six other letters are to be attributed to Peregrinus Proteus, the hero of Lucian's satire. He held that the epistle of Polycarp to the Philippians was the work of a forger, writing to guarantee the genuineness of all seven letters. Völter's thesis was conclusively refuted by Rackl, in his *Christologie des heiligen Ignatius,* where he argued that *Romans* is closely related to the six other letters, and that what we know about Peregrinus Proteus does not coincide with the views of the letters.

Delafosse, in *Lettres d'Ignace d'Antioche* (1927), holds that the largest part of the letters was written by a Marcionite bishop named Theophorus, sometime between A.D. 135 and 188, probably more specifically in the interval between 160 and 180. They were worked over between 190 and 211 by a Catholic Christian, who knew and used the writing of Irenaeus. It was the Catholic forger who constructed the fictitious figure of Ignatius, the bishop of Antioch, compounding it of the Marcionite Theophorus and a Catholic named Ignatius who was martyred at Philippi. The name of this Philippian Ignatius appears in the letter of Polycarp written not long before the Polycarp's martyrdom in A.D. 166.[6]

The argument of Delafosse is more imaginative than convincing. In order to uncover the original document supposedly

5. Only the longer studies of Ignatius will be cited here: T. Zahn, *Ignatius von Antiochien,* Gotha, 1873; D. Völter, *Die ignatianischen Briefe,* Tübingen, 1892; D. Völter, *Polykarp und Ignatius,* Leiden, 1910; E. von der Goltz, *Ignatius von Antiochien als Christ und Theologe,* Leipzig, 1894; M. Rackl, *Die Christologie des heiligen Ignatius von Antiochien,* Freiburg, 1914; W. Bauer, *Die Briefe des Ignatius von Antiochia und der Polykarpbrief,* Tübingen, 1920; H. Delafosse, *Lettres d'Ignace d'Antioche,* Paris, 1927; H. Schlier, *Religionsgeschichtliche Untersuchungen zu den Ignatiusbriefen,* Giessen, 1929; C. C. Richardson, *The Christianity of Ignatius of Antioch,* New York, 1935; H.-W. Bartsch, *Gnostisches Gut und Gemeindetradition bei Ignatius von Antiochien,* Gütersloh, 1940 (cited as *GG*).

6. Delafosse, *Lettres,* p. 35.

written by Theophorus it is necessary to identify large parts of
the letters as coming from the Catholic redactor. In some
letters whole paragraphs are removed, and there is scarcely a
page without excisions. All references to the "true" incarnation
are deleted, and that is not a doctrine carried by a peripheral
phrase or two but is the theological heart of the letters. It is a
bold method of dealing with a text. Not only are there dele-
tions, but passages are taken in isolation, as for example when
the reference to *one* God in *Mag.* 8 is interpreted as denying
the dual existence of the Good God and the evil Creator of
Marcion's thought, instead of proclaiming the unity of the
Father and Christ, an idea that appears again and again.

The motive suggested for the work of the redactor is insufficient: he wishes the backing of the great Polycarp for the
fictional character he is creating. In order to effect that, he
takes the name of the Ignatius who in Polycarp's letter to
the Philippians is martyred at Philippi and uses it for a bishop
of Antioch. And instead of making a new start he chooses the
infinitely harder task of reworking the so-called Marcionite
letters to make them anti-Marcionite. Even though the letters
present difficulties of interpretation of their own, there is nothing so difficult or complicated as this reconstruction. Finally,
we conclude that the parts of the letters presumably written
by Theophorus are not distinctively Marcionite. It is a theory
which for all its ingenuity can hardly be taken seriously. In the
view of most scholars the attacks upon the genuineness of the
letters have not proved convincing, and the most reasonable
thesis is that they really were written by Ignatius the bishop
of Antioch.

Since Polycarp's letter to the Philippians is the only early
witness to their genuineness, the status of this letter is extraordinarily important. But a crucial difficulty immediately appears, for an apparent contradiction in it has forced many of
the radical scholars to discard it as spurious, and with it all
early witness to the Ignatian letters vanishes. In chapter 9
Polycarp seems to assume the death of Ignatius as already accomplished, and begs the church to have faith that he and other
martyrs including Paul are already with the Lord, whose suf-

fering they have shared. In chapter 13, on the other hand, Polycarp professes ignorance of the fate of Ignatius and asks for any definite news of him and his companions which the church in Philippi may have. Scholars have met the difficulty in a variety of ways: some have held that Polycarp's letter was spurious or has suffered interpolations, others that the apparent contradiction arises from a misunderstanding wholly natural when the Greek was translated into Latin.[7] This last solution, originally presented by Pearson, has been held by many later scholars, including Lightfoot.

Recently Harrison in his book *Polycarp's Two Epistles* has made an important contribution to Ignatian studies by proposing a solution more satisfactory than any previous ones.[8] As the title suggests, he maintains that there are parts of two letters in what is usually considered one. Chapter 13 follows after a chapter that has all the marks of a conclusion except the final farewell formula. Chapter 13, therefore, and perhaps 14, Harrison believes to be part of a letter written shortly after Ignatius had left Philippi, in answer to one that enclosed the letter sent by the Philippian church.[9] This earlier letter had asked Polycarp to send on to Philippi copies of the letters of Ignatius. Chapters 1 to 12, however, were written at some time in the third decade of the second century, when all the churches knew of the martyrdom. Harrison believes that the false teachers at Philippi who appear in chapters 1 to 12 are clearly later than those of the Ignatian period, and are holding Marcionite doctrines. He has worked out the solution with great care, and it fits so well into what we know of the circumstances that it is hard to see why it has not been suggested earlier. This thesis removes one very serious ground for uncertainty about the Ig-

7. From the last sentence of *Poly. Phil.* 13 to the end of the letter only the Latin version is extant. Zahn, *Ignatius von Antiochien*, p. 290, and Lightfoot, *Apostolic Fathers*, *1*, 588 f., hold that *de his, qui cum eo sunt* had behind it something like καὶ περὶ τῶν μετ' αὐτοῦ and that the introduction of a time reference is therefore an error of the translator.

8. See P. N. Harrison, *Polycarp's Two Epistles to the Philippians* (Cambridge, 1936), pp. 25–72, for the history of the criticism of Polycarp's letter to the Philippians.

9. Ibid., esp. pp. 15 f., 107–20, 155–206.

natian letters. It establishes witness to the existence of a collection of Ignatian letters made by Polycarp himself at the time
of Ignatius' martyrdom, a collection that probably comprised
all but the letter to the Roman church. Lake has pointed out [10]
that Polycarp could not have had ready access to this letter, and
it is the one letter which has in fact had a rather different textual history from the others.

Not all parts of Harrison's thesis seem equally cogent, but
not all the details are essential for its establishment. It must be
said that the echoes of Ignatius' phrases that he finds in Polycarp's letter [11] are not so easy to explain when we remember
how many years had elapsed since Polycarp had sent on the
letters. Even if, with Harrison, one assumes that Polycarp refreshed himself by rereading the letters, it is hard to see why
he should hope that the Philippian church would recognize the
allusions. Harrison maintains, rather unconvincingly, that the
echoes of Ignatius' writing make better sense if chapters 1 to
12 were written at the later date, because Polycarp knows that
the Ignatian letters are thoroughly familiar to his readers, as
they would not have been had they been enclosed with the
covering letter. This assumes that the Philippian church knew
them by heart, an unlikely supposition. Nevertheless, the main
point of the book is made successfully, and one may reasonably
hold that Polycarp knew Ignatius' letters.

After the controversy over the genuineness of the letters began to die down, the question that moved into the center of
attention concerned the relation of Ignatius' thinking to other
circles of contemporary and earlier thought. Successive discoveries of new materials have increased our knowledge of the
early period and have made new studies necessary. Von der
Goltz' monograph, *Ignatius von Antiochien als Christ und
Theologe*, preceded the discovery of most of the new documents
and concentrated on Ignatius' relation to Paul and the Fourth
Gospel. Richardson's book, the *Christianity of Ignatius of*

10. *Apostolic Fathers, 1,* 280 f.
11. *Polycarp's Two Epistles*, pp. 163–65; cf. Lightfoot, *Apostolic Fathers,
1,* 599.

Antioch, excellent as many of the separate studies are, practically ignores the work of Schlier, *Religionsgeschichtliche Untersuchungen zu den Ignatiusbriefen,* which preceded it by seven years, and fails to discuss Ignatius' relation to gnosticism and the *Odes of Solomon.*

It is the influence of gnostic thought [12] that has been for a quarter of a century the focal point of Ignatian study. Bousset inaugurated this phase of the study of religions in the Hellenistic world, Reitzenstein developed for it a characteristic method, and Bultmann and many others have furthered it. Schlier's work is the most important for Ignatius, although it seems to me unsatisfactory in its major conclusions. In the opinion of all the scholars of the religious-historical school (*Religionsgeschichtlicheschule*) there stands in the background of Ignatius' thought an Iranian myth that has resulted in a complex group of influences—a pre-Valentinian form of gnosis, the fully articulated myth of the Mandaean redeemer, and various sorts of Syrian-Christian gnosis, some of which have already penetrated the Christian world-view and preaching. Ignatius is also the heir of the original Christian proclamation. Schlier believes that this gnostic influence is very strong—so strong, indeed, that it practically explains Ignatius' theology. He finds evidence of it in the view of Christ as a descending and ascending redeemer, in the conception of church members as *pneumatikoi* who are by nature redeemed and ontologically related to Christ, and in Ignatius' conception of the meaning of his own

12. The general argument for the radical influence of gnosticism is to be found widely, perhaps in classical expression in W. Bousset, *Hauptprobleme der Gnosis,* Göttingen, 1907; R. Reitzenstein, *Das iranische Erlösungsmysterium,* Bonn, 1921, and *Die hellenistischen Mysterienreligionen,* 3 Aufl., Leipzig, 1927; R. Reitzenstein and H. H. Schaeder, *Studien zum antiken Synkretismus,* Leipzig, 1926; H. Jonas, *Gnosis und spätantiker Geist,* Göttingen, Vol. 1, 1934. Vol. 2, 1954. For the argument that gnostic influence is early see esp. R. Bultmann, *Das Evangelium des Johannes* (Göttingen, 1952), pp. 6–14; "Der religionsgeschichtliche Hintergrund des Prologs zum Johannes-Evangeliums," in *Eucharisterion,* Pt. II, Göttingen, 1923; *Theology of the New Testament* (New York, Vol. 1, 1951, Vol. 2, 1955), *1,* 164–83.

martyrdom. Schlier holds, of course, that the earlier Christian preaching also informs Ignatius' thought, but it is difficult to discover that he gives it much weight.]

Schlier's book has brought much contemporary material into juxtaposition with Ignatius' thought, and his study is suggestive and interesting. It shares, however, many of the difficulties of the work of other religious-historical writers influenced by Reitzenstein, since Schlier used the same methods. Their primary interest is in individual figures and motifs of myth, which they find in different religions, but a difficulty arises because they tend to assume that the whole myth was known whenever a phrase suggests an aspect of it. That this is sometimes the case is of course true, but it is not always so, and it can never be assumed. Parallels become less convincing when they exist only in documents which in their present form come from a considerably later period and which must undergo drastic source analysis to establish an "early" stratum, and this difficulty emerges in many of Schlier's examples. Furthermore, the method is almost by definition atomistic, presenting concepts isolated from the total scheme in which alone they have meaning. Schlier declares that he does not intend to examine Ignatius' whole theology, but it is precisely this which must be done to evaluate his parallels drawn from gnostic writings. As we shall argue in later chapters, it is very difficult to agree with Schlier in his belief that the phrases that *might* be evidence, for instance, of the descending and ascending redeemer figure are in fact to be so understood, especially when one tries to relate them to the whole scheme of thought in the letters. Phrases which at first sight might seem to belong to various kinds of gnostic thought are present, but not the structure of thought, although Ignatius was unquestionably influenced by contemporary interests and approaches to problems, some of which may be described as gnostic.

More recently another important study also maintains the essential gnosticism of Ignatius, although its thesis is developed quite differently from that of Schlier. Bartsch in his *Gnostisches Gut und Gemeindetradition bei Ignatius von Antiochien* uses methods of the religious-historical school but has a broader in-

terest than Schlier in the whole structure of Ignatius' theological position. He criticizes Schlier's view that the gnostic
redeemer figure is to be found in Ignatius' thought and holds
instead that gnostic influence has penetrated primarily in the
idea of the unity of God and the whole complex of notions
characteristic of the Hellenistic mystery cults. He believes it
possible to distinguish three strata in Ignatius' theology: the
ungnosticized deposit of early Christian preaching, an indirect
gnosticism mediated through Johannine circles, and a quite
direct gnostic influence on Ignatius himself. This approach is
not wholly unlike the one used here, which like any historical
study must try to identify possible sources for insufficiently
assimilated notions, but Bartsch's single-minded interest in
gnostic ideas leads him to miss other circles of thought. As we
shall try to show in Chapters 5 and 9, the important notion of
the unity of God has a wider historical background than
Bartsch grants, and it seems more likely that a partially gnostic
background can be presumed for the notion of the revelation of
the unknown God than for the conception of the one God.

The most recent addition to our knowledge of early Christianity is the group of manuscripts, both complete and fragmentary, from the Essene library, especially the *Manual of
Discipline,* the *Damascus Document,* and the *Habbakuk Commentary.* Their discovery deepens our knowledge of the
thought-world of Ignatius, the Fourth Gospel, and the *Odes of
Solomon,* and has the additional advantage of indicating one
avenue, at least, by which the pseudepigraphic writings of *I
Enoch, Jubilees,* and, by a less direct connection, the *Testaments of the Twelve Patriarchs* [13] could have become accessible
to Christians of the late first century. The little churches in
Antioch and the other cities were clearly the possessors of
thought from very different kinds of backgrounds, in accordance with which one or another group within them tried to
interpret the meaning of the events of the life and death of

13. *The Testaments of the Twelve Patriarchs* has not been found at
Qumram, but it resembles the thought of the others so closely that it is
difficult to avoid the conclusion that there was an historical connection,
perhaps after A.D. 70. See below, p. 71 n.

Christ. The present study will set forth the conviction that
Ignatius cannot adequately be interpreted as gnostic. Although
he has indubitably been influenced in part by the content of
gnostic thought, he was probably more profoundly influenced
by some of their approaches to theological problems, notably
the need for revelation, and by their freedom in using myth.
He does not, in my opinion, share their dualism. He certainly
knew a gnostic Docetism in Antioch, as he knew also a Judaizing group, who seem to have been, as we shall try to show in
the next chapter, an Essene-Christian group. He shares with
the latter their respect for written and institutional authority,
though he differs from them in the interpretation of the Old
Testament books. It is in this lively setting that his theology is
hammered out; and in spite of the fragmentary phrases in
which we meet it, we shall see that it has more unity than is
sometimes recognized. At the same time the study of the thought
of Ignatius will inevitably make us sharply aware of the problems of the early Christian churches in Antioch, and by inference in other cities, in a period when diversity, not uniformity,
was the rule.

We shall first concern ourselves with the external situation
presented in the letters, and it will be apparent how coherent
and natural it is. The little side allusions present a series of
subtle agreements, altogether too spontaneous and complex to
be easily sustained self-consciously by a forger. Ignatius as a
prisoner condemned to death was brought across the great roads
of Asia Minor in the custody of Roman soldiers—his "wild
beasts," of whom he writes that they "become worse as they are
well treated" (*Rom.* 5.1). Others, probably victims of the same
persecution, had preceded him (*Rom.* 10.2). The road he might
well have been expected to travel, the main highway across
southern Asia Minor,[14] ran out to Ephesus, where parties of

14. See Map 1. See also T. R. S. Broughton, "Roman Asia Minor," pp.
861–68, in T. Frank, *Economic Survey of Ancient Rome,* Vol. 4, Baltimore,
1938. Eusebius, *Ecclesiastical History* 3.36, believes he preached all across
Asia Minor. *Rom.* 5.1 is sometimes interpreted as implying that he had
gone by ship from Antioch to a southern port like Attalia, but the reference

1. St. Ignatius' Journey across Asia Minor

prisoners or travelers would take ship to go either direct to Italy or on up the coast. He describes the Ephesian church as the "highroad of those about to become martyrs for the sake of God" (*Eph.* 12.2). But near Laodicaea his guards must have turned north and west to Philadelphia and later to Smyrna, where they apparently stayed some time.

Word of his arrival may have been carried down from Smyrna to the churches in Ephesus and Magnesia and Tralles, all of which sent delegations of their leading men; or perhaps, more likely, the message was sent west from Laodicaea. Ignatius describes the situation truly when he writes to the Romans that the churches receive him "not simply as one passing through, since even those which did not naturally lie on my way went from city to city to anticipate my arrival" (*Rom.* 9.3). It is clear that he is receiving special honor. In Philadelphia and in Smyrna he had stayed long enough to preach to groups (*Phld.* 7), to learn the problems of the churches there, and in Smyrna, at least, long enough to become well acquainted with different individuals and family groups. This may not, however, have been more than a few days in each place. His guards evidently allowed him a certain degree of freedom, for he had no lack of visitors, who, we must suppose, ministered to his physical comfort (*Smyr.* 9.2, *Mag.* 15, *Eph.* 2.1) as well as sharing with him in a fellowship "of the Spirit" (*Eph.* 5.1).

The churches in the cities through which he had not passed he knew only by report, but they had sent responsible representatives who discussed with him their community problems. From Tralles only Polybius the bishop had made the trip, and he did not stay until the departure of Ignatius (*Tral.* 1.1). From Magnesia the young bishop Damas (*Mag.* 2, 3) had brought with him the presbyters Bassus and Apollonius, and Zotion, a deacon. Ephesus, the nearest of the three cities, had understandably enough sent a slightly larger group, made up of the

---

to sea travel may equally apply to the voyages across the Aegean and the Adriatic which lay ahead. Rheus Agathopus, accompanied by the deacon from Cilicia, had "followed" Ignatius, and this implies a land trip, if they went through Cilicia.

bishop Onesimus,[15] a deacon named Burrhus, and Euplus, Fronto, and Crocus (*Eph.* 1, 2) of whose positions we are told nothing. Before leaving Smyrna, Ignatius wrote to all three of the cities to thank them for sending representatives and to establish them in the Christian faith. He also wrote to the church at Rome, a letter very different from the others, since its subject was different. He begs the Roman church in very moving argument not to try to have his sentence repealed. Shortly after writing this he must have left Smyrna, for we may suppose that his dating of the letter to Rome, on the ninth day before the Kalends of September—that is, August 24 (*Rom.* 10.3)—indicates his intention of giving the Roman church some idea of when to expect him. It is the only letter that bears a date, and it is the only one in which time was significant. This is the kind of circumstance a forger is unlikely to have invented.

Whether the party left for Troas by road or by coasting vessel and how long they stopped there we have no idea. With him went Burrhus, the deacon of Ephesus, whose trip was financed jointly by the churches in Ephesus and Smyrna "as an expression of honor," as Ignatius writes to the Philadelphians (11.2). One cannot help wondering whether there is not a shadow of reproach that the Philadelphian church had not done something of the same sort when he was taken on from their city. As part of his general task of easing the rigors of the prisoner's life Burrhus served as secretary (*Phld.* 11.2, *Smyr.* 12), and it seems obvious that he must later have been the one to take back the letters to the churches in Philadelphia and Smyrna and to Polycarp. Kindly messages relayed from the church at Troas make it probable that they had offered Ignatius the same sort of hospitality and fellowship he had received in Smyrna (*Smyr.* 12.1), but of it we have no details.

What was responsible for the change of mood in the letters written at Troas is the arrival of Philo, a deacon from Cilicia, and Rheus Agathopus, an "elect man, who has said farewell to this life" and was following Ignatius from Syria, as he writes

15. J. Knox, *Philemon among the Letters of Paul* (Chicago, 1935), pp. 50–56, considers Bishop Onesimus identical with the slave Onesimus of the Epistle to Philemon.

(*Phld.* 11.1). Rheus Agathopus brought news from Antioch that
the disturbances that had weighed so heavily upon the mind
of Ignatius (*Eph.* 21, *Mag.* 14, etc.) had come to an end, and
that peace reigned. He writes of the "God-given freedom from
care" (*Poly.* 7.1). The whole tone changes; instead of begging
the churches to pray for the church in Syria, as he had been
doing earlier in the letters from Smyrna, he writes with relief
to urge the churches in Philadelphia and Smyrna to send
ambassadors to Antioch to rejoice with them, as the churches
nearer Antioch have already done (*Phld.* 10.2, *Poly.* 8.2). He
later laid the same charge upon the church in Philippi (*Poly.
Phil.* 13.1). It is upon this note of relief that the letters end,
and silence follows. We know that he and his guards left Troas
hurriedly (*Poly.* 8.1) for Neapolis in Macedonia, whence they
went through Philippi (*Poly. Phil.* 9) and so presumably on over
the great trunk road to Dyrrachium, where they would take
ship for Brundisium and go by land up to Rome. But past that
point we have nothing except the report that he was martyred.

It is apparent that this is an elaborate situation, supported
by a great many individually insignificant but interlocking
facts. Cross references bear out the unity and, we must suppose, the genuineness of the letters. For example, the tone of
the concluding paragraphs of the letters written from Troas
is different from those written earlier, since the anxiety has
been lifted. Rheus Agathopus has brought the good news of
peace. Philo and he followed hard on Ignatius' heels through
Philadelphia and Smyrna and report cordial receptions there,
although they had encountered difficulties earlier (*Phld.* 11.1,
Smyr. 10). The references to Burrhus are subtly different in the
letters to Philadelphia and to Smyrna, and suggest Ignatius'
awareness that the two churches have different knowledge
about him. Ignatius thanks the Smyrnaeans because they, with
the Ephesians, have sent Burrhus on (*Smyr.* 12.1), and says that
he is taking down the very letter they will read, and that he
has "in all ways" refreshed Ignatius. To the Smyrnaean Christians, who know the deacon, it makes sense to write praising
him as a "pattern of the ministry of God" (ibid.), whereas the
letter to Philadelphia, where Burrhus is presumably not known,

naturally enough contains no personal reference, and refers to him only as the person taking down the letter (*Phld.* 11.2), adding that his presence is an evidence of the kindness of the Ephesian and Smyrnaean churches. Again, in Smyrna Ignatius knew well various groups of people to whom he sent messages. Only one of them, Alce, receives a message both in the general church letter and in the one written to Polycarp. That is the kind of natural and inconsequential difference we might expect from a person writing letters to a large group whom he remembers pleasantly, whereas a forger would be less free and probably more obvious about tying the letters together. The spurious letter to Antioch, for example, tries to convince the reader by sending greetings from the bishops of all the cities, whether or not the persons named could have been present at the time of writing.

These are slight but telling examples of the delicate and subtle consistency with which the situation is presented. It is not conclusive evidence, but such as it is it buttresses confidence that the letters are genuine. Detailed study of the theology will not show quite so unified a structure, but in its own way it adds even more surely to our conviction that we are in the presence of very early Christian thought.

The letters may seem unimpressive at first glance, but one must grant that the trying circumstances under which they were written would account in large measure for their lack of coherence and form. The writing is broken, marred occasionally with uncompleted sentences and above all lacking in connected argument. Nowhere is there development of ideas in measured, logical sequence. Everywhere, on the contrary, the mind of the writer passes quickly from one suggested and only half-explicated point to another. To admit all that we have said is not, however, to dispose of the letters as inconsequential, even in matters of style. There is a brilliance of metaphor, an economy of phrase, an urgency of spirit that expresses itself in the swift sentences, as though the writer knew that time was short. It is not surprising that the more moving of the passages, especially those expressing Ignatius' readiness for martyrdom, should have been quoted again and again. Norden has said that the letters are the "most glorious thing that has come to us from that period." [16]

They bear the clear marks of having been written under external as well as internal pressure. Since they were dictated not only in the presence of one or more of the Roman soldiers but possibly with other prisoners and various members of the visiting delegations or of the churches in Smyrna or Troas sitting by, one can see that interruption would be the rule rather than the exception, and that development of ideas would be impossible. They are written in two groups: four from Smyrna and three from Troas. Although the soldiers doubtless had other things to do than to guard this provincial being sent up to the capital to die in the games, we cannot suppose that they would have delayed at any point longer than was necessary. The letters to Ephesus, Magnesia, and Tralles could not have been written immediately upon arrival at Smyrna, since the delegations from the other cities would hardly have been there, and it is likely that at least *Romans* was written just before departure. Since it has been estimated that the trip from Smyrna to Troas by sea would have taken perhaps three or four days,[17] and that if they went by land seven or eight days might have been necessary,[18] it is plain that all the letters may have been written within a week's time—at most within two weeks. The shortness of this interval may account in part for the general similarity of the letters, and even more telling is the fact that the letters to Ephesus, Magnesia, and Tralles were written within a day or so of each other, and possibly at one sitting. Full recognition of that fact would modify somewhat the emphasis that has been placed on Ignatius' determination to buttress the position of the bishops. There is no question that he felt strongly on the

16. E. Norden, *Die antike Kunstprosa*, 2 (Leipzig, 1898), 510 f. For all the awkwardness of language, Norden describes the style as showing "nicht den Eindruck, als ob sich dies aus dem Unvermögen des Syrers erklärte, in griechischer Sprache sich klar und gesetzmässig auszudrücken . . . ist es vielmehr die innere Glut und Leidenschaft, die sich von den Fesseln des Ausdrucks befreit."

17. W. M. Ramsay, "Roads and Travel (in the New Testament)," Hastings *Dictionary of the Bible*, 5 (1904), 386.

18. Cf. Harrison, *Polycarp's Two Epistles*, pp. 111 f.

matter, and we shall discuss its importance below, but he has sometimes been presented [19] almost in caricature as one obsessed by the idea of the episcopate. It is an annoying fact, even in the twentieth century, that letters written in swift succession are apt to bear strong resemblance to each other, as the same ideas press themselves upon the mind in similar phrases. Ignatius, writing under circumstances that weakened the chance to concentrate, must also have been a victim of this irritating trick of the mind.

It is likely that temperament as well as circumstance accounts for the running character of the thought and the lack of developed presentation of ideas. Ignatius declares that he preached "in the Spirit" (*Phld.* 7.1), and the letters as a whole reveal a vigorous, impulsive, energetic nature. He is impatient with the more phlegmatic Polycarp and urges him to "be more diligent" and to hold more meetings (*Poly.* 3.2, 4.2). It is this sort of person who might well be swept along from idea to idea as he dictated, touching lightly on each and moving on quickly to a new emphasis or new figure of speech.

To acknowledge the lack of careful development of ideas is not in the least to suggest that the letters are without clear and vigorous thought. They etch in sharp lines the thought of the leader of a great church and the triumphant and moving confession of a sensitive person. The purposes of the writer stand out sharply. He wants to thank the churches for what they have done for him, either in sending delegates or in caring for him during his visits. He writes also to warn seriously against the danger of the factions formed around false teachers, and urges unity with the bishop as a practical means of meeting the danger. He is concerned with this, however, for more fundamental reasons than a mere theory of polity, as we shall see later, for he believes that the very nature of the Christian life and the relation of man to God is threatened by divisions. It is the quality of life in the churches and the heretical beliefs that threaten it that concern him most, and he urges Christians to hold fast to the essentials of Christian faith and life. Finally, he writes either to beg them to pray for the Antioch church or,

19. E.g. B. H. Streeter, *The Primitive Church* (London, 1929), pp. 173 ff.

later, to send ambassadors to Syria to rejoice with the Antioch Christians after peace has been restored.

Although Ignatius writes about objective matters, he never succeeds in wholly forgetting his personal predicament, and it faces the reader of the letters in all its stark reality. Ignatius, perhaps six weeks or so before we first see him in Smyrna, had started the weary march across Asia Minor in the summer heat as a prisoner. He had been condemned in a local trial in Antioch, and the end of the journey was to be death, perhaps in the great Flavian Colosseum.[20] He has frequently been re- proached for his preoccupation with his fate, and the almost morbid way in which in the letter to the Romans he seems to delight in the martyrdom ahead. "I long for the beasts made ready for me . . . I will even tease them to devour me promptly" (*Rom.* 5.2). But there has been less recognition of the subtle play of forces that would have made it difficult to be matter of fact about the fate that lay ahead.

In the first place it must have been horrible beyond measure to anyone cursed, as Ignatius evidently was, with imagination. A passage in his letter to the Romans runs over the number of brutal forms in which death might meet him, all of which he tries to nerve himself to face. "Fire, cross, struggles with wild beasts, cuttings, tearing in pieces, racking of bones, mangling of limbs, crushing of my whole body, cruel tortures of the devil —let them come upon me, only may I attain to Jesus Christ" (*Rom.* 5.3). Even if the Christians in the Roman church gave what strength they could, if the sentence was death in the games one would at the end stand alone before the pitiless brutality of the public ranged rank above rank in the great Colosseum or in some smaller stadium. No wonder the early Christians have a vivid sense of "the world" that is against them. And the experience of dying might be mercifully brief or it might be drawn out in ghastly manner. It would have

---

20. The Roman and Antiochene Acts both say that he was killed "in the amphitheater." H. Delahaye, in "L'Amphithéâtre Flavien et ses en- virons," *Analecta Bollandiana, 16* (1897), 221, 250 f., points out that there were other places in Rome than the Colosseum where the martyrdom might have occurred.

taken an insensitive nature not to dread such a fate when one
encountered it in imagination, even if when the time came it
could be faced with courage.

The letter to the Romans is shot through with a kind of
bravado, but the reasons for it are wholly natural: Ignatius was
afraid that his courage might not be equal to the test. This fear
is reflected in all the letters in various ways, but particularly
in his appeal for prayers: "Pray for me also . . . that I may be
granted the lot which I am set to obtain, that I be not found
reprobate" (*Tral.* 12.3).[21] He does not write to the Roman
church to try to have his sentence changed; he says that if they
succeed, it will be only an "unseasonable kindness" (referring
perhaps to the proverb "an unseasonable kindness is no different from hostility").[22] He is not sure that his decision will endure, even though it is made in the unwavering conviction that
by dying as a martyr he will attain unto God. "Even though
when I come I myself entreat you, do not listen to me, but
rather be persuaded by this which I write you: for in the midst
of life I write to you in love with death" (*Rom.* 7.2). This fear
of the unsteadiness of his own courage is the mood from which
he recoils when he declares his desire for death. The exaggera-
tions of his words represent not morbidity, the brooding of self-
hate and contempt for life, but the fear that he might betray
his dearest convictions. Indirect witness is borne to this fear by
the fact that one of the qualities he most covets is ὑπομονή, endurance.

The conflict is heightened by his belief that in spite of the
result of his trial he still has a slight measure of freedom. He
evidently knows that it is at least possible the Roman church
will have enough influence to get him off. If what has been
inferred of the high position of some in the Roman church
late in Domitian's reign was still true fifteen or twenty years
later,[23] it would not be surprising if influence sometimes might

21. Translation from Lake, *Apostolic Fathers.* The allusions are obscure.
22. Lake's note on *Rom.* 4 suggests this.
23. In spite of the suspicious circumstance of the banishments of two
Flavia Domitillas to islands in the Mediterranean, the report of Christianity in high places in Rome during the late years of Domitian seems

have been used effectively. If he does not throw his weight against such a course, he will have tacitly accepted the result. His freedom lies in the choice either of being silent and accepting what happens or of taking responsible action ahead of time in accordance with his convictions. It is the second alternative that he has chosen. But because there is choice—or he believes that there is—his lack of steadiness is the more moving. It is a brave man who is revealed in the letters, but he is nothing if not realistic about himself. He believes wholeheartedly that "it is good to set to the world, facing toward God" (*Rom.* 2.2), and that "near the sword is near to God, with the wild beasts is with God" (*Smyr.* 4.2). But he knows that as the end looms, his courage may fail. He therefore writes to close the matter once for all. In the letter to the Romans we see the pitiless self-revelation of a man choosing death in his mind, but wincing in his body: "Ask strength alone for me, both inward and outward, that I may not only say it but also will it, that I may not only be called a Christian but also be discovered to be one. For if I be discovered to be one I shall then be able to be so called" (*Rom.* 3.2).

Although there are admittedly moments of exaggerated urgency, it is strange that such a conflict is ever represented as morbid. When such depth of personal experience and so much of importance to the church under persecution hung on his ability to maintain his determination, it would be the more remarkable if he could have written without emotion. Nevertheless, this is a choice made on principle, not impulse. We shall not see it in full perspective until we fill in the outlines of his total belief.

Another of the factors that stand just in the background of the letters is his anxiety over the church in Antioch. He asks

---

credible. Charges of "atheism" and the "adoption of Jewish customs" (Cassius Dio, *History* 67.14), coupled with the existence of the cemetery of Domitilla, and Eusebius' (*Ecclesiastical History* 3.18.4) report of "Christianity" in those circles all fit together. This is not final proof, but it suggests that Ignatius' idea that the church might have influence had some basis in fact. Cf. *Ecclesiastical History*, ed. H. J. Lawler and J. E. L. Oulton, 2 (London, 1928), 88 f., on III.18.4.

for prayers for his church, as simply and as often as he asks for prayers for himself. "Remember me in your prayers, that I may attain unto God, and remember also the church in Syria" (*Mag.* 14). And when the news comes of its peace, he writes with relief to Polycarp of the "God-given freedom from care" (*Poly.* 7.1). What had happened in Antioch before he was taken prisoner we do not know, but as a result of it he had been condemned. It has usually been assumed that the difficulty in the church that gave him such anxiety was persecution by the imperial government. Harrison has made the illuminating suggestion that since the word used for the return of peace (εἰρηνεύειν) is used only of the achievement of internal harmony, it is more likely that what was worrying Ignatius was internal dissension in the church.[24] Harrison even surmises that perhaps the persecution and the internal struggles were connected, and that some disaffected persons had involved Ignatius with the authorities. It is possible, though it can be only a matter of speculation; we simply do not know why he was condemned. But there *is* other evidence that indicates that the Antioch church had been rent by party fights, and that Ignatius had been contending with "false teachers."

In the first place it is difficult to understand otherwise Ignatius' complex sense of both failure and authority.[25] On the one hand as he passes through the churches Ignatius speaks with an unself-conscious authority. He warns the Trallians that if they do not heed it, the very fearlessness of his writing will "be a witness against them" (*Tral.* 12.3). He speaks to the Philadelphian church "with a great voice—the very voice of God" (*Phld.* 7.1). He writes the entire letter to Polycarp in a mood of affectionate but authoritative guidance, although it is

24. *Polycarp's Two Epistles,* pp. 83, 94 f. See also G. Kittel, *Theologisches Wörterbuch* (Stuttgart, 1933), εἰρήνη, εἰρηνεύω, for the emphasis on inward peace. H. de Genouillac, *L'Église chrétienne au temps de St. Ignace d'Antioche* (Paris, 1907), p. 203, argues for a combination of near-schism and resulting public disturbance for which the bishop was arrested.

25. This is discussed in every study of Ignatius. For a psychological interpretation see Streeter, *The Primitive Church,* pp. 163 ff. For the view that Ignatius sees himself as excluded from the "redeemed church" as conceived by the gnostics see Schlier, *Relig. Untersuch.,* pp. 153–57.

directed to a man already of considerable maturity,[26] with whom he had quickly reached an astonishing degree of spiritual understanding. All the delegations from the churches were consulting him on problems existing in their churches. Evidences of his real authority and his acceptance of it face us on every page.

There is, on the other hand, a strain of self-depreciation that runs through the letters. This has sometimes been treated as pure hyperbole, or even as a kind of deliberate insincerity. It is probable that there is in it some element of exaggeration, but the charge of conscious insincerity seems to be unwarranted. The self-depreciation appears in connection with three different ideas, two of which are related to his predicament as a prisoner and one of which is connected with his membership in the church in Antioch. In the first place he protests more than once that he is not worthy to speak as an apostle (*Tral.* 3.3, *Rom.* 4.3), for he is κατάκριτος, a condemned man. Peter and Paul were free; he is in chains. There is a real contrast here which is not to be overlooked, for Ignatius is *not* journeying through the churches, preaching freely, and having as his sole task the building up of the faithful; on the contrary he must have had daily and hourly reminders of the indignity of his status, wholly at the mercy of the rough soldiers, hurried along from city to city and dependent on the kindnesses of the churches for refreshment of all kinds. It is not strange that he contrasts himself with Peter and Paul.

In the second place his sense of unworthiness is tied up with his fear that he will not endure to the end. The anxiety that he may not be worthy (*Eph.* 3.1), that he may not at the last be perfected (*Phld.* 5.1), we have noted above. When he remembers this, he becomes for a moment self-conscious about his use of authority. It is in this connection that the charge of hyperbole is most nearly warranted, as when he writes to the Ephesian church, "I am a condemned man, you have obtained mercy; I stand in danger, you are safely established" (*Eph.* 12.1, cf. *Tral.* 13.3). But even here there seems to be a sincere

26. Polycarp died probably in 155–156 at the age of 86. He could hardly have been less than 40 when Ignatius met him.

and natural meaning expressed: his contrast is between them whose faith is not so greatly tested and himself who is in danger of failing to measure up to the heroism demanded. As he thinks of them, their state seems one of calm and safety that is enviable. He says self-confidence wars against him (*Tral.* 4.2), tempting him, for when he would speak boastfully he remembers that he has not yet run his race. Once again, this is not unhealthy self-depreciation but a realistic estimate of the predicament in which he lives. He never despises his lot; on the contrary he glories in it. He is confident that if he dies for his faith, he will become a "freedman of Jesus Christ, and will rise free in him" (*Rom.* 4.3). His bonds are "worthy of God" (*Smyr.* 11.1).[27] He was found "worthy to bear witness to the honor of God" (*Eph.* 21.2) by being sent by God's will (*Smyr.* 11.1) to face martyrdom. But the opportunity is enviable only if his courage shall be adequate to it, and he dare not assume that courage. In the light of that uncertainty, his own use of authority sometimes seems to him hollow pretense.

The third connection in which Ignatius protests his unworthiness is as a member of the Antioch church. In five of the letters, when he refers to the church in Syria he goes on to say that he is the least of the faithful there or that he is "not worthy to be called a member of it." [28] This unqualified sense of unworthiness is certainly not shown when he contrasts himself with the Christians in the Asia Minor churches; in fact, as we have seen, there is a quite understandable ground for the other expressions of his inadequacy. We shall therefore not go far wrong if we suppose that in this case, too, there is ground for his sense of failure, and that these expressions are not mere convention. There stands in the background some occurrence of special vividness, apparently not identical with his condemnation. He accepts that as "by the will of God." But he writes to the Romans that he is "ashamed to be called one of the church in Syria," for he is the "least of them," and "an untimely birth"

27. Schlier, *Relig. Untersuch.*, p. 155, considers that the "bonds" are symbols for him of his bondage to ὕλη, but as we shall see below in Chapter 6 Ignatius does not hold this view of matter.

28. *Eph.* 21.2, *Mag.* 14.1, *Tral.* 13.1, *Rom.* 9.2, *Smyr.* 11.1.

(*Rom.* 9.1). An occurrence disastrous enough to have produced such a sense of failure is more likely to have been a struggle within the church than persecution visited upon it from outside. For the former, as bishop, he would rightly have had a special sense of responsibility, and the failure to heal the breach might well have brought about the kind of self-torment he reveals. Nothing less serious can account for his self-reproach. Behind this mood of self-abnegation, then, we can probably see evidence for some serious trouble in the Antioch church, and it is natural to surmise that it was a schism.

As we saw in part above, Harrison has pointed out that the expression Ignatius uses of the recovered tranquillity in Antioch are far better understood if the church had come through the devastating bitterness of a deep split. He wants the Smyrnaeans to send a delegate to Syria to congratulate them that they have "achieved peace, have recovered their proper greatness, and that their own organic life has been restored" (*Smyr.* 11.2). The phrase referring to their "proper greatness" does not seem appropriate if it indicates merely the end of the persecution.

A slighter bit of evidence that seems to point in the same direction is the only example in the letters of real bitterness. In writing to the church in Smyrna Ignatius makes it clear that the false teachers have not yet been at work there (4.1). He tries, indeed, to put the Christians on their guard before the event that he fears may occur. The letter to Polycarp similarly shows no evidence that the church has been subjected to heretical teaching. The teachers of strange doctrine referred to (*Poly.* 3.1) are not spoken of as now at work, though their coming is entirely possible. Nevertheless, it is in the letter to the Smyrnaeans that Ignatius lets slip the hint that he might, though he will not, name these dread unbelievers who teach that Jesus was never really the incarnate Lord. He goes so far as to wish that he might not even remember them (*Smyr.* 5.2, 3). It is not easy to suppose that this intensity can have been evoked simply by word of unknown opponents reported to him during his swift journey. This dread memory and the bitterness he betrays are far more comprehensible if the false teachers are connected with events in Antioch surrounding the tragic schism there. They are only beginning to threaten Asia Minor churches, but they have been fully at work in Antioch.

Finally, the really conclusive evidence that the heresies not only were a problem in Asia Minor but were far more influential in the church in Syria is the indubitable fact that the incarnation, and the *real* and *true* birth and suffering and death of Jesus Christ, stand deeply embedded in his theology. In these letters written within a week or two during his journey as prisoner Ignatius was certainly not working out any new theology. What he was affirming was what he had been preaching and teaching in Antioch, perhaps for years. The antidocetism that is so prominent is not something hastily devised to meet a new situation, and thus only loosely related to his understanding of Christian truth. It is expressed in rhythmical strophes, which may have been hymns of the church or may be original with him but which in any case express deeply held convictions. These affirmations are warp and woof of his thinking. All of this will not be apparent until we examine with care the circle of ideas connected with the incarnation. But no event less tragic than internal dissension in the church at Antioch, not persecution from without, can account for all these facts.

Thus we conclude that however much the letters have to tell us of the situation in the churches of Asia Minor at the beginning of the second century, they cannot be adequately understood in that connection alone. Ignatius had spent a considerable period of his life—how long we do not know—in Syria. He had been enough of a leader to have been made the bishop of one of the great churches of his time. As his unexpected death loomed, breaking as he says into the midst of life, his ideas would have been fully developed and his theology rounded out. The Christianity presupposed is therefore that with which the church in Antioch was familiar, and what he writes of the function of the bishop and the nature of the church reflect, we must conclude, the concerns which he has been trying to put into practice, and from which he was taken when the persecution fell.

But since in the extant letters he has not developed these

ideas, making merely glancing references to them or bold
affirmations of them, our reconstruction of his total thinking
must be accomplished by putting together the allusive phrases
that seem to shed light on one another, and by comparing his
ideas and phrases with similar ones used by Christians and non-
Christians. It goes without saying that such reconstruction is a
delicate and difficult task, since most of the materials it must
deal with are controversial.

We are fortunate in having as much to work with as lies at
hand in the letters. They are adequate to throw considerable
light on the state of the church in Antioch at the end of the
first and the beginning of the second century. And we are also
fortunate that our witness is as vigorous and lively a person as
Ignatius. His letters are more self-revealing than any others of
the age except those of St. Paul. Certainty whether he was, as
some have surmised,[29] a convert, would be interesting to us because of our twentieth-century bent toward biography, but on
all such matters there is silence. We know nothing of the early
circumstances of his life, but we can know with extraordinary
intimacy his inner struggles and much of his hope for the Christian churches, and the ground of his faith. These concerns are
the real man.

29. E.g. Lightfoot, *1*, 28.

2. Antioch and the Christians

IGNATIUS gives very little direct information about his church in Antioch, and none at all about the city. It will be worth our while, before reconstructing what we can of the situation in the church, to recall what the great city must have been like through whose gate he departed, in the custody of the Roman soldiers, over the road running north to the Portae Syriae with his face set toward martyrdom at Rome.

We cannot assume that he had the passion of pride that led his contemporary Dio Chrysostom to rejoice when "a city becomes good-looking, when it gets more air, open space, shade in summer and in winter sunshine beneath the shelter of a roof, and when, in place of cheap, squat wrecks of houses, it gains stately edifices that are worthy of a great city." [1] His ultimate loyalties were not centered upon the city. But it is perhaps not pressing the case too far to see in his strange description of the Roman church (*Rom.* Ins.) as the one that has "the chief place in the country of the region of the Romans" a memory of the church of comparable pre-eminence in Syria. Rome as the first city of the empire would inevitably have lent importance to the Christian church there, but Ignatius greets it not as the head of all but as the outstanding church in its region. His compliments to the Roman church are exuberant but no more so than those he addressed to the Ephesian church, for both are written in a rather fulsome style. And his repeated reference to himself as the bishop of Syria [2] further suggests that both as Antiochene and as Christian bishop he was not lacking in self-confidence.

It would be strange if the city had left no mark upon the

1. *Discourses* 47.15 (trans. H. L. Crosby, Loeb edition).
2. Lightfoot holds (*Rom.* 2.2) that this is a genitive "denoting not the extent of his jurisdiction, but the place of his abode." But cf. below, pp. 44 f.

Christian church there, and upon its bishop, for it was famous throughout the empire, and the capital of all Syria. Josephus speaks of it as "a city which, for extent and opulence, unquestionably ranks third among the cities of the Roman world," [3] yielding in importance only to Rome and Alexandria. Dio Chrysostom lists it as one of four distinguished cities (Smyrna, Ephesus, and Tarsus being the others) when he considers a model for his own city.[4] It had outstripped in magnificence and size many neighboring cities of very ancient pedigree, although it was founded late—by Seleucus Nicator I in 300 B.C.—as an expression of the colonizing energy of the Macedonian empire. A few unimportant villages or foundations had previously existed on or near the site,[5] but between its natural advantages and the deliberate policy of the Seleucids and the Romans Antioch became within a century or two the dominant city east of Alexandria. Under the Romans it was the capital of the large imperial province of Syria, which at the time of Trajan [6] included Coele Syria and Commagene in addition to "Syria" in the narrow sense.

Antioch stood at the center of a network of great roads,[7] which were improved in Seleucid or Roman times, though some of them must have originated as age-old caravan routes, deflected toward the city as it grew. It is difficult to date some of the roads, and one cannot be sure that all of those listed were in existence by Trajan's time. They show, however, the central place which Antioch held in the province. One ran down from

3. *Bell.* 3.29 (trans. H. St. J. Thackeray, Loeb edition).

4. *Discourses* 40.11–12.

5. For the pre-Seleucid inhabitants of the Antioch plain see R. Dussaud, "Note additionelle aux fouilles de Minet-el-Beida et de Ras-Shamra," *Syria, 10* (1929), 297–303. Seleucus Nicator demolished the settlement of Antigoneia, moved its settlers to Antioch (Malalas, *Chronographia* viii.1), and absorbed Iopolis on Mt. Silpius.

6. In 70, Judea was detached from Syria; and in 73, Cilicia. F. Cumont, "The Frontier Provinces of the East," *CAH, 11,* 617.

7. R. Dussaud, *Topographie historique de la Syrie* (Paris, 1927), p. 479, and carte xiv, "Antioche et Edesse étaient les deux pôles du système stratégique romain," but it is likely that this was a second-century development. E. Honigmann, "Syria," in Pauly-Wissowa, cols. 1645–80.

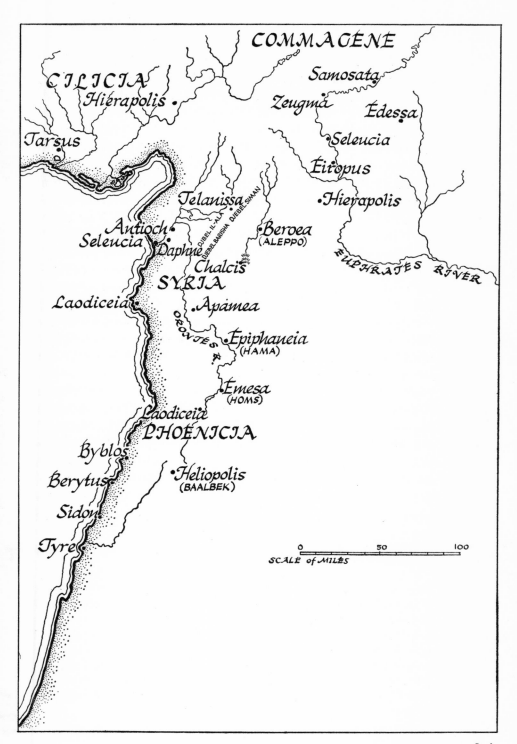

COMMAGENE

CILICIA

Hierapolis •

Samosata

Zeugma

Edessa

Tarsus

• Seleucia

Eiropus

Telanissa

• Hierapolis

Antioch •

Seleucia • Daphne

DJEBEL-IL-ALA
DJEBEL BARISHA DJEBEL SIMAN

• Beroea
(ALEPPO)

Chalcis

SYRIA

EUPHRATES RIVER

Laodiceia

• Apamea

ORONTES R.

• Epiphaneia
(HAMA)

• Emesa
(HOMS)

Laodiceia

PHOENICIA

Byblos

• Heliopolis
(BAALBEK)

Berytus

Sidon

Tyre

0   50   100

SCALE of MILES

2. Syria

the northeast, from Edessa beyond the Euphrates and on through Seleucia-Zeugma to Antioch. Another ran, roughly parallel but somewhat south of the first, from Edessa through Hierapolis and Beroea (now Aleppo), and so on to Antioch. Another came in from the southeast from Epiphaneia (now Hama) and Chalcis. Still another connected Antioch with Apamea and Epiphaneia and went on south through the Orontes Valley to Heliopolis (now Baalbek); and one ran from Antioch and Seleucia down to Laodicaea and so on down the coast through Byblos, Beirut, and Sidon to Tyre. The Royal Road through the Syrian Gates ran north and west, and over it all land traffic with Asia Minor, Greece, and Rome passed. It was the position of Antioch as the center of roads and a point of the transfer of goods that made it inevitably a kind of inland port and the metropolis of Syria.

Nothing remains on the site to suggest its appearance in the early second century of our era, and the results of the excavations, rich as they are for the fourth century, have been meager for the earlier period, although the general plan they reveal existed from the early empire at least.[8] From the remains of Gerasa, Palmyra, and Apamea one can imagine in some slight degree the city that Ignatius knew, and literary references tell something of the public buildings donated by emperors. The main avenue ran roughly northeast and southwest, parallel to the Orontes, which was deep enough at Antioch to float ocean-going vessels up from Seleucia. The river divided at the point where the city was placed, and the island in the center held the imperial palaces and the hippodrome. North of the island were suburbs, but the city proper, to the south of the river, lay just

8. See Map 3, after the plan in C. R. Morey, "The Excavation of Antioch-on-the-Orontes," *Proceedings of the American Philosophical Society,* 76 (1936), 638 f. For modern descriptions see E. S. Bouchier, *A Short History of Antioch,* Oxford, 1921; V. Schultze, *Altchristliche Städte und Landschaften, III, Antiocheia,* Gutersloh, 1930; G. Haddad, *Aspects of Social Life in Antioch in the Hellenistic-Roman Period,* Chicago, 1949. The Princeton University Excavation Report, *Antioch-on-the-Orontes,* Princeton, 1934–52, is concerned chiefly with the city of the fourth to the sixth century, but material on the earlier periods is scattered through the volumes.

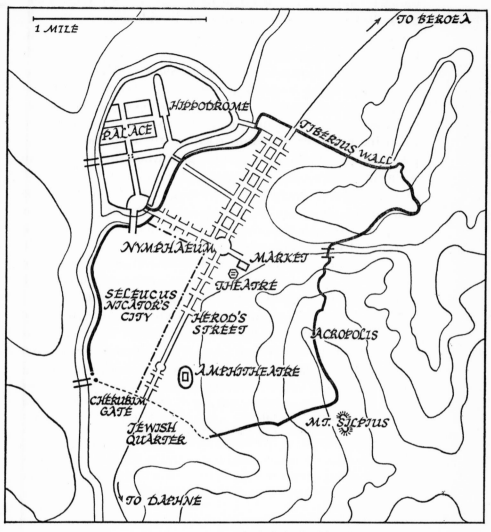

1 MILE

TO BEROEA

HIPPODROME

PALACE

TIBERIUS WALL

NYMPHAEUM

MARKET

THEATRE

SELEUCUS
NICATOR'S
CITY

HEROD'S
STREET

ACROPOLIS

AMPHITHEATRE

CHERUBIM
GATE

JEWISH
QUARTER

MT. SILPIUS

TO DAPHNE

3. Antioch in the First Century. After C. R. Morey

under the brow of two steep northerly spurs of Mt. Casius, and the walls extended some distance up its sides.

On one of the prominences was the ancient temple of Zeus Casius, and on the other stood the Acropolis. The theatre, built in the reign of Julius Caesar [9] on the slope of Mt. Silpius, the southwestern spur, was enlarged by Agrippa,[10] and again under Tiberius [11] and Trajan,[12] as the population grew. It was the place for great public meetings, such as that which gathered when the governor Mucianus tried to stir up feeling for Vespasian in a stormy meeting,[13] and again when the populace, in resentment against the Jews, met to demand that Titus rescind their privileges.[14] Baths were favorite gifts to the city; one was built on Mt. Silpius in the reign of Julius Caesar,[15] another by Agrippa [16] "outside the city," and a third and fourth were built or restored under Tiberius [17] and Gaius.[18] By the fourth century baths were available to each of the eighteen tribes, or wards, but even in the first century they were numerous enough to add to the city's reputation for luxury and magnificence.

Not far below the theater, on level ground, stood the great square market near which was the bouleterion, built in the time of Pompey [19] to take the place of the old one of Antiochus

9. Malalas, *Chronographia* 9.B.217.3. Page and line references follow the Bonn text set forth in A. Schenck von Stauffenberg, *Römische Kaisergeschichte bei Malalas*, Stuttgart, 1931. See G. Downey, "Imperial Building Records in Malalas," *Byzantinische Zeitschrift, 38* (1938), 1–15, 299–311, esp. 10, n. 3, for discussion of Malalas' view that all work done during an emperor's reign was to be ascribed to him as creator. W. Weber, "Studien zur Chronik des Malalas," *Festgabe für Adolf Deissmann* (Tübingen, 1927), pp. 40–65, believes that an ancient source that listed the buildings erected in the reign lies behind the Tiberius history.

10. Malalas, 9.222.20 f.

11. Ibid., 9.235.2.

12. Ibid., 11.276.4.

13. Tacitus, *History* 2.80.

14. Josephus, *Bell.* 7.106–11.

15. Malalas, 9.217.1.

16. Ibid., 9.222.17 f.

17. Ibid., 10.234.12.

18. Ibid., 10.243.17.

19. Ibid., 8.211 [93], following the line reference in the Dindorf ed. as set forth in Migne, *Patrologia Graeca, 97*.

Epiphanes.[20] Nearby stood the record office and the basilicas, burned in the fire of 69–70, which also took the markets.[21] Valens later built his forum a little to the east. From the group of public buildings a street ran at right angles down to the main avenue, which it crossed at a great circle where apparently the nymphaeum built in the reign of Gaius [22] stood. The main avenue was the chief contributor to the city's air of elegance; its colonnade protected throngs, promenading or shopping up and down the street, from the drenching rains in winter and the pitiless sun in the long summer,[23] and perhaps also provided, as in the smaller cities that copied it, brackets where busts and inscriptions honoring the famous could be placed. It was colonnaded and paved during or just before the reign of Tiberius, probably by the joint munificence of Herod the Great and Tiberius.[24]

The city could never be finished, for it was always subject to the ravages of severe earthquakes, two of which occurred during the reigns of Gaius and Claudius, and in A.D. 115 came a still more devastating one, which drove Trajan to spend several days in the hippodrome before it seemed safe to return to the palace.[25] The earthquakes, and the fire under Titus which Josephus mentions,[26] provided occasions for beautifying the city and opportunities for emperors or other wealthy men to show their favor. Ignatius and all his contemporaries must have watched the constant building. His use of the building metaphor of the great ramp (*Eph.* 9.1) and the ropes by which heavy

20. Ibid., 10.234.2.
21. Josephus, *Bell.* 7.54 f.
22. Malalas, 10.244.9 f.
23. Josephus mentions its advantages: *Bell.* 1.425.
24. Josephus, *Bell.* 1.425, attributes to Herod I the gift of the paved and colonnaded street. Malalas, 10.232.16, says Tiberius built two colonnades and Herod paved the road outside the city, 223.17 f. G. Downey, "Imperial Building Records in Malalas," *Byzantinische Zeitschrift, 38* (1938), 299–311, holds that Malalas is using two old sources, since the work was outside the walls until they were extended by Tiberius. The single street referred to was paved by Herod and the colonnade provided by Tiberius.
25. Cassius Dio, *History* 68.25.5 ff.
26. *Bell.* 7.54 ff.

stones were drawn into place in the walls suggests how familiar the process was to him. The city was changing decade by decade.

Very little remains by which we can reconstruct the architectural style of early second-century Antioch, although there are some survivals on the basis of which we may draw tentative conclusions. Butler has made clear that all the evidence points to the persistence of the Greek tradition, shown in the over-all proportions of buildings and in the fineness of architectural detail.[27] Thus the city must have looked in a general way like Gerasa of a rather later period, but with greater elegance and attention to classical detail. At least the public buildings probably resembled their prototypes all over the Hellenistic world. Knowledge of the domestic architecture is less certain, and no doubt the poor lived in the "cheap, squat wrecks of houses" so contemptuously described by Dio Chrysostom. The houses of the wealthy quite possibly resembled the two-storied house in Benâbil, in the northernmost tip of Djebel il-'Alâ, which is dated as early as the bi-columnar tomb monument of A.D. 132 near Sermeda.[28] Like so many of the houses in north Syria during a number of the later centuries, the long axis lies parallel to the street, and across its front run two colonnades, forming a terrace and a balcony. The lower colonnade is in Roman Ionic and the upper in the Corinthian order of a pure classic type. The well-designed decorative details show a restraint quite different from the ornateness of the third-century style of Baalbek. The tomb monuments composed of two great pillars, of which two or three examples remain, show similar restraint, as does the tomb at Babutta,[29] in the Djebel Bârîshā, where unfluted Doric capitols stand in a façade that suggests a small temple *distyle in antis*. If such restraint is to be found in small places and at a time a little later than the years of Ignatius, it

27. H. C. Butler, *Architecture and Other Arts* (New York, 1903), p. 48, considers that the monuments of these regions near Antioch "give the best idea of the classic architecture of Antioch that can now be gained. We find a graceful simplicity, an accuracy of line, a dignity of sentiment, in the monuments of the second century in this period . . ." The architecture was more Greek than Roman.

28. Ibid., pp. 59, 69 ff.

29. Ibid., p. 65.

is likely that earlier in the century in the capital the style must have been similar. Although the great public buildings of Antioch no doubt displayed greater magnificence, we may suppose that the restraint in decoration and the excellence of proportion of the temple of Zeus-Bomos [30] at Burdj Bakirha was present. The late first-century mosaics from Antioch and Daphne [31] show a similar feeling for Hellenistic standards of art in the unity of composition and realistic treatment of subjects and in the use of third dimension that they display. Although it is dangerous to argue from one art to another, all the scanty evidence suggests a fairly strong influence of the earlier Hellenistic standards in the early-second century.

With all its elegance Antioch was not without a competitor. The sacred grove of Daphne, green-shaded and cool with cascades, lay some five miles beyond the walls to the southwest and beyond the suburb of Heraclea. The gate of the Daphne road in the wall of Tiberius [32] was probably still decorated in Ignatius' time with the cherubim Titus had taken from the temple in Jerusalem. At least by the end of the first century, the mosaic-floored villas of the wealthy stretched out along the road to Daphne of the many springs, but the suburb had been a great attraction from early Seleucid times. The laurel and cypress groves, enclosing the temples of Apollo-Helios and Artemis-Atargatis and other cults,[33] provided sacred places which carried the right of asylum; [34] and as the years passed, Daphne increasingly offered opportunities to observe dramatic processions and to take part in licentious rites, although the conditions condemned in the fourth century may have been less evident in the

30. Ibid., pp. 66 ff. This temple is dated A.D. 161.

31. C. R. Morey, *The Mosaics of Antioch* (London, 1938), pp. 27–30.

32. Morey, "The Excavation of Antioch-on-the-Orontes," p. 643. G. Downey, "The Gate of the Cherubim at Antioch," *Jewish Quarterly Review*, new ser. 29 (1938–39), 167–77, points out that these cherubim could not have come from the Holy of Holies, which in Herod's temple was empty, but must have come from elsewhere in the temple or from some other source.

33. An inscription of 189 B.C. refers to "Apollo, Artemis and the other cults whose shrines are in Daphne": Bouchier, *Short History*, pp. 45 f.

34. *II Macc.* 4.33 ff.

second. Thirty-day games were celebrated, either there or in Antioch, from the time of Augustus on.[35] In fact the fame of Daphne was so great that it seems at times to have eclipsed its greater neighbor, for Antioch was on occasion described even on coins as "Antioch by Daphne," though "Antioch-on-the-Orontes" was more usual.

√ The religious activities of such a great city were extraordinarily varied. Light is shed on the history of a few of them by coins; others we know from literary or archaeological evidence. They range from worship of the great gods to little private cults. Apollo was the patron god of the early Seleucids, although under Antiochus Epiphanes he partially gave way on the coins to Zeus-Olympios,[36] and we may surmise that this change was in some way reflected in the temples in the city. Both were symbols of the aspirations of the Seleucids to be truly Greek. Malalas says that, under Tiberius, temples were built to Zeus-Capitolinus and Dionysus,[37] and reports that in the earthquake in the time of Claudius the temples of Artemis, Ares, and Herakles were badly damaged. Most of these, and other apparently Greek gods, were surely ancient oriental divinities only thinly disguised to bring them up to date, like Zeus-Hadad, to whom the great temple at Baalbek was dedicated, and Artemis-Atargatis, and Apollo-Helios-Dionysus.[38] The temple of Zeus-Casius represented on the coins of Seleucia as a tetrastyle shrine [39] containing a conical stone symbol of the deity— an interesting evidence of syncretism—may well have had its counterpart in the temple on Mt. Silpius where Trajan offered worship.[40] The Tyche of Antioch who appears on coins as early

35. Malalas, 9.225.1.

36. D. B. Waagé, *Greek, Roman, Byzantine and Crusaders' Coins* (Antioch-on-the-Orontes, 4, Pt. II, Princeton, 1952); cf. coins numbered up to 100 with, e.g., Nos. 108, 115, 116.

37. Malalas, 10.234.11, 17; 10.246.16.

38. See H. Seyrig, "La Triade Héliopolitaine et les Temples de Baalbek," *Syria, 10* (1929), 314 ff.

39. E. S. Bouchier, *Syria as a Roman Province* (Oxford, 1916), plate facing p. viii. Ammianus, *History* 22.14.4 mentions its existence in the fourth century.

40. *Greek Anthology* 6.332. Hadrian celebrated Trajan's dedication of offerings to Zeus-Casius in 106.

as the time of Tigranes, seated on a rock above the swimming river-god Orontes, seems to have had a shrine in the city,[41] and quite possibly her own city festivals. At the time of Julian rites to Adonis were celebrated,[42] and it seems more likely that this age-old Phoenician worship entered Antioch, perhaps from Byblos, early rather than late. The licentious Maiouma rites practiced in the fourth century may also have been early.[43] The goddess of Hierapolis [44] may have had a temple there, and the cults celebrating Bel or Zeus-Dolichénos,[45] imported from the East and North. Doubtless immigrant traders brought in others, as the carvings of Palmyrene gods of about 160 give evidence of a modest cult not native to Dura Europos, where they were found. Antioch drew people from many cities and countries, and one might expect them to carry their gods with them. There may also have been temples to local baalim whose sanctity had outlived their names and who remained in memory as gods of the altar, as in the contemporary temple to Zeus-Madbachos and Selamanes [46] on the summit of Djebel Shêikh Berekât, or the similar Zeus-Bomos [47] in the temple at Burdj Bakirha. Both of these stood within forty miles of Antioch, and suggest that the worship of local gods abounded—a phenomenon that would have been familiar to the bishop of the Christian church. Perhaps more familiar would be the synagogues of the city and

41. The statue of the Tyche stood within a shrine of four Ionic columns. Bouchier, *Syria,* p. 67, and plate facing p. viii.

42. Ammianus, 22.9.15.

43. See Bouchier, *Syria,* pp. 79, 83.

44. Her worship was widespread in Syria. F. Cumont, *Les Religions orientales dans le paganisme romain* (Paris, 1909), p. 154.

45. F. Cumont, *Études syriennes* (Paris, 1917), p. 257, reports a small monument to Bel, 50 km. northwest of Aleppo dated at the end of the first century A.D. Other evidences of the cult were found at Apamea and Emesa; see his p. 259. Zeus-Dolichénos was certainly worshiped as far south as Aleppo: pp. 191 ff.

46. The wall of the temenos was built from A.D. 80–120. This seems to have been a half-semitic name meaning Zeus-of-the-Altar. W. K. Prentice, *Greek and Latin Inscriptions,* Publications of an American Archaeological Expedition to Syria in 1899–1900, Pt. III (New York, 1908), pp. 104 ff., 125.

47. Butler, pp. 66 ff. The date of this temple is A.D. 161. This is fifty years later than Ignatius, but the worship is certainly older than the temple.

its suburbs; there seem to have been at least two, and quite possibly there were more.[48] Relations between Jews and non-Jews in Antioch were often strained during the latter part of the first century A.D., but we have no information specifically on the relations between Jews and Christians.

The position of Antioch rested only partly on its extent and elegance, and much more on its administrative and commercial importance. Cassius Dio comments on the great crowds [49] present during Trajan's visit in 115—soldiers, embassies from different countries, citizens with law cases in process, or present for business or sight-seeing. It had from early days been a free city. To a considerable extent this was true also of its sister cities in the Tetrapolis—Seleucia-in-Pieria, Laodicaea, and Apamea—which with Antioch formed a quadrilateral whose long sides were about sixty miles; but among them Antioch became the dominant member. One mark of independence was the right granted to them all under Antiochus Epiphanes [50] to strike coins bearing the royal effigy but lacking the royal superscription. Under the Roman emperors a large proportion of the coins used in the Near East was minted at Antioch.

From Seleucid times Antioch had possessed a council and assembly for internal administration,[51] which were recognized by Pompey when he rebuilt the bouleterion, and Julius Caesar reaffirmed its status as a free city.[52] It was partly this sense of its proud heritage that made the citizens of Antioch so vociferous in the part they played in imperial politics and local disputes. And there are evidences, various in kind and scattered, of

48. C. H. Kraeling, "The Jewish Community at Antioch," *JBL,* 51 (1932), 140 f. An old synagogue was located on the slope of Mt. Silpius. Downey has located the Kerateion, where the Jewish quarter was, outside or near the Cherubim Gate: "The Gate of the Cherubim at Antioch," pp. 176 f.; cf. Malalas, 8.207.10.

49. Cassius Dio, 68.24.

50. A. H. M. Jones, *Cities of the Eastern Roman Provinces* (Oxford, 1937), p. 251. See also Bouchier, *Short History,* appendix on the mint of Antioch.

51. Malalas, 8.205.

52. Ibid., 9.216.15. Ἐν Ἀντιοχείᾳ τῇ μετροπόλει ἱερᾷ καὶ ἀσύλῳ καὶ αὐτονόμῳ καὶ ἀρχούσῃ καὶ προκαθημένῃ τῆς ἀνατολῆς.

Antioch's influence over surrounding territory. (As in the case of other free cities there were, of course, neighboring dependent regions.) The section "belonging" in some sense to Antioch was of considerable size,[53] for a district to the east and south, including the Djebel il-'Alâ; Djebel Barisha, up to a line 20 kilometers west of Chalcis and Beroea; and on the north Telamissa in the Djebel Siman some forty-five miles northeast all used the era of Antioch beginning in 49 B.C. to date all monuments and inscriptions, although in the adjoining regions the Seleucid era was used. This must therefore be considered Antiochene territory, and its extent suggests how many villages in that highly populous area were under the control of the city. There is evidence, too, of the leadership of Antioch throughout the province of Syria, as is usual in the case of provincial capitals. From at least the earliest Roman times there was a Syrian κοινόν meeting in Antioch,[54] but at that time Phoenicia, although a part of Syria, had its own assembly. Dated soon after A.D. 86, a monument mentions the five-year meeting in Antioch of the κοινόν of Syria, Cilicia, and Phoenicia.[55] Under Trajan a coin was issued of the κοινὸν Συρίας.[56] In 119–20 an inscription records a meeting of four ἐπαρχείαι at Antioch to worship the emperor.[57]

53. The Syrian cities possessed unusually large territories as compared with Asian cities. F. Cumont, "The Frontier Provinces of the Empire," *CAH, 11,* p. 621. For the territory of Antioch see V. Kahrstedt, *Syrische Territorien in hellenisticher Zeit,* n.f., Bd. *19* (Berlin, 1926), p. 103, and map iiib. W. K. Prentice, *Greek and Latin Inscriptions* (New York, 1908), pp. 89, 106, and passim.

54. G. Fougères, "Κοινόν," *Dictionnaire des antiquités grecques et romaines,* ouvrage rédigé, *3,* 848–51. Fig. 4304 shows a coin struck for the κοινόν, dated 64 B.C., with the crowned Antioch on one side.

55. P. Guiraud, *Les Assemblées provinciales dans l'empire romain* (Paris, 1887), p. 49, with reference to the *Bull. de l'Institut Archaeologique de Rome* (1877), p. 109. The inscription is quoted by E. Beurlier, "Le κοινόν de Syrie," *Revue numismatique, 12* (1894), 288. Guiraud, p. 81, believes that the five-year κοινόν may indicate merely a specially magnificent celebration of what met more modestly every year.

56. Beurlier, pp. 288 f. For slight variations in issues struck for the κοινόν see *Antioch-on-the-Orontes, 4,* Pt. II, D. B. Waagé, *Greek, Roman, Byzantine and Crusaders Coins* (Princeton, 1952), Nos. 400, 401.

57. *Supplementum Epigraphicum Graecum* 7.847.

The four represented were Syria, Commagene with its capital
at Samosata, and Phoenicia and Coele Syria, the last two of
which were in Trajan's reign united under Tyre [58] as metropolis. It is clear that Antioch was the capital of a large territory.
There is evidence not very much later that its position provoked
imperial irritation. Spartianus says that Hadrian so hated the
people of Antioch that he wished to separate Syria in the narrow sense from Phoenicia in order that Antioch might not have
the prestige of being the metropolis for so many provinces.[59]

Since, then, there is evidence of the meeting of broadly based
provincial councils in Syria before and early in the reign of
Trajan, this all goes to strengthen the presumption that in
Ignatius' time under Trajan Antioch held administrative leadership of sorts throughout the province. Antioch citizens, by
virtue of the size of the territory actually under the control of
the city, its dominance in the Tetrapolis, and its status as provincial capital and leader among the provincial cities, had ample
reason to feel the special position of the city. The fact that the
provincial assemblies were in part for religious activities connected with worship and the games and in part for general
provincial concerns makes it not too daring to surmise that they
influenced in some degree the Christian organization [60] that in
similar fashion expected to maintain significant leadership beyond Antioch itself. The relations between village churches and
city groups may even have made necessary a far-flung organization. This development would take place most easily in a province such as Syria, where in fact as well as in name one city was

58. A. H. M. Jones, *Cities of the Eastern Roman Provinces* (Oxford,
1937), pp. 499 f., points out that popular usage and administrative practice did not always change at the same rate. The four κοινά he identifies
might continue meeting after a formal redistribution of the province.
E. Beurlier, *Le Culte rendu aux empereurs romains* (Paris, 1890), pp.
105 f., discusses variations in the relations between κοινά and provinces.

59. *Hadrian* XIII. Phoenicia had meanwhile been restored to Antioch.

60. H. deGenouillac, *L'Église chrétienne au temps de St. Ignace d'Antioche* (Paris, 1907), pp. 45 f., sees the influence of the imperial religious
organization on the Christian church but not a slavish imitation by the
church.

the undeniable leader. Such a situation would make understandable Ignatius' description of himself as bishop of Syria.[61]
One may further inquire whether the status of Antioch in its
province is not the explanation of the frequently discussed description of the Roman church as being pre-eminent "in the
country of the region of the Romans" (*Rom.* Ins.). That remains an awkward, not to say barbarous, phrase, but it suggests
just such a regional dominance as the city of Antioch and the
Antioch church possessed, and which Ignatius might take for
granted as true in that other great capital, Rome. When he describes his church Ignatius three times speaks of it as in Antioch-
in-Syria,[62] and five times as the "church in Syria." [63] It is difficult to suppose that this usage is pure hyperbole and that it does
not indicate something of the real status of the Antioch church.
✓ But if the city may well have influenced the Christian church
by its external circumstances and position of dominance, it more
surely did so by the character of the population, drawn from
many cultural groups. Greeks, Jews, Syrians, and Romans met
in its streets. Its population had been mixed from the beginning, for if Seleucus Nicator shared the convictions of Alex-
ander, intermarriage between Greeks and Syrians had been en-
couraged. The original colonists were veterans of Athenian and
Macedonian stock, and a century later Antiochus III added
Aetolians, Euboeans, and Cretans. Although the first settlers
were Greeks, it was inevitable that the city should draw Syrians
from all parts of the country, to live perhaps in the "second
quarter" of the city,[64] as merchants came in with the caravans
from cities like Beroea, fifty miles inland, or Seleucia-Zeugma
northeast on the Euphrates, or artisans drifted north from the
old cities down the Phoenician coast. Village people must often

61. See also below, p. 84.
62. *Phld.* 10.1, *Smyr.* 11.1.
63. *Eph.* 21.2, *Mag.* 14.1 *bis*, *Tral.* 13.1, *Rom.* 9.1.
64. Strabo, 16.2.4, mentions a "multitude of settlers." W. W. Tarn,
Hellenistic Civilization (London, 1927), p. 126, believes they may have
comprised a separate πολίτευμα. The second quarter might also have included the people from Antigoneia (Malalas, 8.201), founded a few years
earlier by Antigonus.

have been drawn in, as the city grew larger, from the nearby hill country where oil and wine were produced.

Perhaps the promise of freedom in the big city attracted others, like the rich Babylonian Jew who came to establish himself near Antioch in the days of Saturninus,[65] in the last decade B.C., along with a hundred relatives and five hundred mounted bowmen. There had been a Jewish community in Antioch, Josephus says,[66] from its founding, and Jews were allowed special privileges by the Seleucid kings,[67] which were maintained by the Romans. When Josephus wrote, the Jewish community of Antioch was the largest in any city in Syria.[68] By the time of Pompey, at least, there was a corporation of Roman merchants with some power in the city,[69] and we may suppose trading corporations from Delos preceded them under the Seleucids. The Roman legions quartered just north of the city had so identified themselves with Antioch by marrying there that the citizens protested vigorously when, as Vitellius was playing for the imperial power in A.D. 69, it was rumored that the Syrian legions were to be exchanged for those from Germany.[70] Apamea had been the Seleucid military stronghold, but under the Romans Antioch had clearly won pre-eminence and furthermore was perhaps turbulent enough to have been made the military center. Josephus tells us of many trips of the troops from Antioch south along the Phoenician coast to subdue revolts or otherwise to implement imperial policy.[71] As its importance increased and the population became more varied, it was inev-

65. Josephus, *Ant.* 17.2.1.

66. Ibid., 12.119; *Contr. Ap.* 2.39.

67. R. Marcus (see Josephus, *Ant.* 7, appendix C, Loeb Classical Library, Cambridge, Mass., 1943, p. 739) accepts the existence of a Jewish group from the founding but doubts that they had special privileges before the time of Antiochus Epiphanes. C. H. Kraeling, "The Jewish Community at Antioch," *JBL, 51* (1932), 137 ff., holds that only certain Jews held favorable positions from the founding, not the community as a whole.

68. Josephus, *Bell.* 7.43.

69. Caesar, *Civil Wars* 3.102.

70. Tacitus, *History* 2.80.

71. E.g. under Varus (*Bell.* 2.41.79), under Petronius (ibid. 186, 201). and under Cestius (ibid. 500).

itably attractive to new groups. By some time early in the empire it seems likely that its total population was close to a half
million,[72] though an estimate of population is in the highest
degree tentative.

It was this cosmopolitan populace of Antioch, with all its
differences of background, from which the members of the
Christian church were drawn. Almost every early report about
the city adds to the impression that the citizens were turbulent
—fierce and sudden in their loves and hatreds.[73] When Mucianus was stirring up support for Vespasian, Tacitus says the
crowd gathered together in the theater "expressed itself in extravagant adulation" and later was violent in anger at the
thought of having the legions moved.[74] Early in the agitation
against the Jews, which Josephus tells us swept Syria in the
sixties of the first century, violence was avoided in Antioch, but
about A.D. 70, when charges were brought by Antiochus the
son of the Jewish *archon* that the Jewish community was responsible for a disastrous fire, a pogrom broke out.[75] In 70 or
71 a group of the populace met Titus four or five miles outside
the city to demand that the Jewish privileges be remanded,[76]
and although he refused to act, it is clear that hatred still ran
high. It would be unlikely that the members of the Christian
church wholly escaped this excitability, especially since the
Jewish group from which many Christians must have come had

72. Chrysostom, *Homily on St. Ignatius* 4, says that at the time of
Ignatius the population was two hundred thousand, but that figure probably ignored children, slaves, and suburban dwellers. V. Schultze, *Antiocheia*, p. 152, estimates a total of 800,000. Kraeling, "The Jewish Community at Antioch," p. 136, estimates a population of between 300,000
under Augustus (following Beloch) and an ultimate size of half a million.

73. G. Haddad, *Aspects of Social Life in Antioch in the Hellenistic-
Roman Period* (Chicago, 1949), defends the characters of the Antiochenes,
and is concerned to show that they have been maligned or were at least
no worse than the populace of other cities. Not all of the references to
their character, however, can easily be accounted for as slander.

74. *History* 2.80.

75. Josephus, *Bell.* 2.479; cf. 7.46 ff. and 7.54 ff. Kraeling, "The Jewish
Community at Antioch," pp. 150 ff., holds that only one great fire can have
been involved, and that Josephus has two accounts of one event.

76. Ibid. 7.100–11.

hostile groups within itself.[77] It is no wonder that factions and disagreements marked the history of the church in its early days, and that division seemed to Ignatius the cardinal sin.

We turn now to consider in greater detail the church which grew up in the capital. Even in its earliest years there was sharp dissension. Some of those who came north after the disturbance at the time of Stephen's death preached exclusively to Jews, according to Acts 11:19, and preaching to the Greeks came only when the Hellenist Christians from Cyprus and Cyrene reached the city. The name of Nicolaus of Antioch, who was appointed among the Seven, suggests that he was a Hellenistic convert to Judaism before he became attracted to the Christian movement. Whether he returned to Antioch with the men from Cyprus and Cyrene to preach "to the Greeks also" we do not know. Paul stepped into a sharply divided church, for even his preaching was not strong enough to hold the Jewish Christians, who with Peter swung back to the observance of food laws when their consciences were worked on by the men from Jerusalem (Gal. 2:11 ff.). We tend to assume that the struggle over that and circumcision eventuated in victory in Antioch for the Hellenistic party, but actually there is silence on the matter.

We know that there was a decision against compelling uniformity in the church as a whole, for Titus did not have to be circumcized (Gal. 2:3) on the Jerusalem visit, and Paul says that he was given freedom to preach to the Gentiles, and urged only "to remember the poor," but we are not told what came of the tension in Antioch. Almost immediately after the trip to Jerusalem Paul left the city never to return, and we may wonder whether the reason for this apparent indifference to Antioch was a combination of circumstances or a disappointment because Jewish and Greek Christians fell back into relative estrangement. Obviously we simply do not know, but it is interesting to observe that factiousness plagued the church in its early days, and was again a difficulty in the time of Ignatius sixty or seventy years later.

77. So one must understand Josephus' story of the young Antiochus, *Bell.* 7.46 ff.

This characteristic of the church may be understood if we remember how large the city was, and how divided into national groups of varying size it was. From the time of its founding the second quarter was probably reserved for Syrians, and we may presume from the records that Jews congregated around their synagogues. Even within the same section of the city national groups in all likelihood tended to keep to themselves. In so divided a population there were almost inevitably several small Christian churches of different religious and perhaps social backgrounds, meeting in houses in different parts of the city,[78] and exposed to diverse influences. Their theological tendencies continued at variance because they rarely met together. Such circumstances would make understandable both the struggle over eating together in the time of Paul and Barnabas and the disagreements of docetic and Judaizing groups under Ignatius. Teachings of many kinds existed in Antioch, for the names of Menander and later of Saturninus have come to us, and they and other, unknown, teachers may well have influenced one or another of the groups within the church.

It would be interesting if we could know something of the social and economic situation of the members of the Antioch church, but on that point there is silence. We have evidence of Ignatius' judgment on social concerns, but they apply chiefly to the church in Smyrna, which he knew best of the Asia Minor churches to which he wrote. Because these are practical matters, not necessarily related to the development in theological thinking that went on throughout his preaching life, we have no right to conclude that problems in Smyrna mirror situations familiar to him at home. We can observe his responses, but not the Antiochene problems, although on a priori grounds one may suppose that he would be more likely to offer his judgment on familiar problems than on those new to him.

The presence of slave members in the Smyrna church created some tensions, and Ignatius urges Polycarp not to despise them. The comment indicates that by Ignatius' time the κοινωνία of

78. Philem. 2, N.T. Rom. 16:5, I Cor. 16:19. I am indebted to Carl Kraeling for insights relating the theological differences to the isolation of house churches.

the earliest years was an ideal not easily attained, if indeed it had ever been more than a hope. Ignatius further advises that church funds should not be used to buy freedom for the slaves, since they should use their servitude in order to obtain a "better freedom" (*Poly.* 4.3). It is obvious that some members thought otherwise, either the slaves themselves, or those of the free citizens with sensitive consciences, and that the matter was under discussion. On this point at least we may surmise both that the problem was familiar in the Antioch church (since in any great city the slave population was very large) and that Ignatius is revealing his justification of his own policy. It is not very different from the view held both by Paul [79] and the Stoics. It is significant that the Christian church was maintaining even as much fellowship as it was, in view of increasing size, which made it pertinent for Ignatius to urge Polycarp in Smyrna to "know all by name" (*Poly.* 4.2). And on this point also we can be relatively sure that the problem was one common to churches in big cities, Antioch not excepted.

The tendency in Smyrna toward asceticism may or may not have been similar to the situation in Antioch. In Smyrna, at least, the institution of "virgins called widows" (*Smyr.* 13),[80] that is familiar in Jerusalem and in some of the deutero-Pauline churches, had persisted. Perhaps the order was losing its earlier power of attraction, for Ignatius urges Polycarp not to let the widows be neglected (*Poly.* 4.1).[81] There is also a group of men who are celibates "to the honor of the flesh of the Lord," which is one phase of an ethic based on the imitation [82] of Christ (*Poly.* 5.2). Ignatius approves of them, so long as their vow of celibacy is a wholly private matter known only to the bishop. But if there is any public boasting, he holds that the whole value of continence has vanished—a stipulation ruling out the possibility

79. Col. 3:22–4:1. Philemon: W. J. Woodhouse, "Slavery (Roman)," *ERE, 11,* esp. pp. 626 f. Epictetus, *Discourses* 4.1, the essay on Freedom.

80. Lucian, *The Death of Peregrinus* 12–13, draws a satirical picture of widows waiting outside the prison to see Peregrinus.

81. Acts 6:1 notes a similar problem. It is interesting that this stands in the Antioch source.

82. See below, Chap. 8.

that an order of celibates was developing. Marriage is important and must be recognized by the church, since he urges that it be "with the consent of the bishop, that the marriage be according to the Lord and not according to passionate desire" (ibid.).

It is no exaggeration to say that the very nature of the city shaped the problems and opportunities of the church. People who were culturally and socially alien to each other had to develop a real community—a community that would at once bear witness to the faith that possessed them and become clearer about the deeper meaning of that faith.

3. The Factions in the Church

IF WE CAN know little about the social and economic background of the church in Antioch, we are on somewhat surer ground in developing a theory about the factions that were both the danger and the opportunity of the church. At least three parties seem to have been present,[1] working against one another, and on occasion breaking out into the open strife which caused Ignatius such distress. On the right was the group deeply influenced by the Old Testament, who wished to see the Christian pattern become more strongly Jewish. On the left stood the Docetists, who were the chief "teachers of strange doctrine." In the middle, we may suppose, was a center party of which Ignatius was the spokesman, agreeing in part with both of the more extreme groups but in other respects sharply distinguishing the median position from what seemed perverse in the right and left. His hope that the extremes will return indicates that it is they who hold aloof. Bauer's thesis that the majority were gnostic[2] and that the more orthodox position is in the minority can hardly be held if there were indeed several groups, and in any case Ignatius' group seems to hold the solid power of a mediating position. The two groups he treats not as clearcut heresies but as holding perverse and mistaken positions. From their own viewpoints they would be Christians who felt strongly about certain crucial points of doctrine and who made vigorous efforts to persade others to see the truth as they saw it.

Some scholars believe that the teachers of strange doctrine

1. For the view that Ignatius faces one group of false teachers see Zahn, *Ignatius*, pp. 356–99; Lightfoot, *Apostolic Fathers*, *1*, 373–77; von der Goltz, *Ignatius von Antiochien*, pp. 81 f.; Bauer, *Die Briefe des Ignatius*, pp. 238–40; *Relig. Untersuch.*, p. 109, n. 2; Bultmann, *Theology*, *1*, 171 f. For the argument for two distinct heresies see Richardson, *Christianity of Ignatius of Antioch*, pp. 51–54, 79–85; *GG*, pp. 34 f.

2. W. Bauer, *Rechtgläubigkeit und Ketzerei* (Tübingen, 1934), pp. 68 ff. Cf., against Bauer, *GG*, pp. 11 ff.

were outside the church. This view is based on the fact that Ignatius uses such vigorous language against them that it is supposed they must be fully separated. But the situation was probably less definite. In Asia Minor the Docetists were only beginning to be a threat. The Ephesian church had been on its guard and refused to give them a hearing (*Eph.* 9.1), and in Tralles and Smyrna they had not appeared in force. Ignatius begs the church in Smyrna not to allow them to speak in the church.[3] But as we have seen, Ignatius' bitter memory of them indicates that instead of being a fringe group in Antioch they were strongly entrenched, and there is evidence that both they and the Judaizers called themselves Christians. In *Mag.* 10.1, a passage that deals with the Judaizers, there is a reference to those who "are called by another name," but it is not clear that that unknown name would have been chosen by the party. After all, they "talk of Jesus Christ" (10.3). Furthermore, they evidently consider themselves within the church, since they "nominally acknowledge the bishop, but in all they do ignore him" (*Mag.* 4.1). Their position was no more ambivalent than that of the Docetists. In an introduction to a lyrical antidocetic passage Ignatius speaks of those who "carry about the name with wicked cunning" (*Eph.* 7.1), and in the Trallian letter (6.1) he says they "mingle Jesus Christ with themselves." They were evidently very free indeed in their interpretation of Christianity, but it was Christian doctrine that they were interpreting.

Not only, then, do both of the parties consider themselves Christians, but at least the Judaizers previously did belong in a full sense to the church. When Ignatius speaks of "division" and "repentance" in a single sentence (*Phld.* 8.1), the implication surely is that the division has not always existed. Eventually at least the Docetists withdrew (*Smyr.* 7.1), but the very fact that Ignatius says that they "abstain from the eucharist and from prayer" (*Smyr.* 7.1) indicates that one might have supposed that they would participate with the rest of the congregation. It is no longer possible to reconstruct the situation in detail, but the most reasonable hypothesis is that both Judaizers

3. Παραδέχεσθαι seems to imply giving them freedom for advancing their views (*Smyr.* 4.1).

and Docetists were within the church until a crisis arose, when their deep differences became clear. It is the presence of both groups within the church that made the Antioch church fertile soil for the development of theology.

The existence of parties holding somewhat divergent views does not, however, indicate that they were rigidly organized and continually in violent controversy. If we are right that the circumstance that caused Ignatius such acute suffering was an open split in the church, the rancor could evidently reach dangerous proportions; but on the other hand, Rheus Agathopus brought news that the church was again at peace, and this seems to indicate that the divisions were not irreparably deep. Perhaps the leaders had withdrawn. A somewhat open situation is suggested, rather than the struggle of obstinate groups frozen into irreconcilable opposition.

Of the two extreme parties the views of those of the "left" emerge the more clearly from the letters, and as we have seen, there is solid reason to believe that they were the chief disturbers of the peace. In one of his two uses of the word "heresy" Ignatius applies it to this group (*Tral.* 6.1); and although it is not, as in later times, sharply distinguished from a clearly defined orthodoxy, the word nevertheless carries strong condemnation. Their doctrine is "not the planting of the Father"; accepting it results in death (*Tral.* 11.1).

The doctrine Ignatius combats most vigorously is docetic, affecting their christology: the view that Christ could not be said to have borne human flesh (*Smyr.* 5), but that on the contrary he only appeared to have a fleshly body and was really ἀσώματος (*Smyr.* 2). This last assertion is one from which Ignatius recoils with horror. He further accuses them of holding that Christ was δαιμονικός—a word they might not have accepted. However repugnant to Ignatius these views might be, for the Docetists their christology meant an exalted view of his nature, which they could not conceive to have been stained by the encounter with flesh. It was because they thought of him as spiritual in origin and therefore grace-bringing that it was so important to affirm his freedom from flesh (*Smyr.* 6.2). And their christology had as a corollary some form of belief about his birth as being in appearance.[4]

The docetic teaching led to further important consequences in their thinking, for it qualified their acceptance of the passion and resurrection of Christ, since these doctrines had meaning only if the human nature was more than an appearance. This was inevitable particularly with respect to the passion. Since the passion and resurrection were absolutely central beliefs from the beginning of Christianity, this was a radical divergence. The Docetists declared that both "seemed" to take place, but they maintained that there was no real suffering and no corporeal resurrection (*Tral.* 10.1, *Smyr.* 2).

They apparently held a view of human nature characteristic of most gnostics, in which men are divided into classes, in this case only two, the *sarkikoi* and the *pneumatikoi*. Ignatius does not directly accuse them of this, but in a passage (*Eph.* 8.2) following shortly on a bitter reference to the "wild beasts" he praises the Ephesians because they do not hold a belief in such a division among men, and in an elliptical sentence he points out its inadequacy. It seems certain that the Docetists maintained the view he condemned. It would follow that those who considered themselves "spiritual" in nature would very likely be exclusive, would hold themselves above common men, and this was in fact characteristic of them, for Ignatius says that they show no concern for the ordinary unfortunates of the world (*Smyr.* 6.2)—the widow, the orphan, the poor wretch who is imprisoned or just turned loose on an unfriendly world. They are not concerned with *agape*. Furthermore they were unwilling to join with the congregations in the eucharist and prayer (*Smyr.* 7.1).

The explanation offered by the Docetists for their withdrawal from the worship of the congregation would probably be based not on their nature as *pneumatikoi* but on their objection to Ignatius' realistic doctrine of the eucharist. They assuredly did not "believe in the blood of Christ" (*Smyr.* 6.1), nor that the

4. Ignatius lays extraordinary emphasis on the fact that Christ was truly (ἀληθῶς) born (*Tral.* 9.1, *Smyr.* 1.1).

"eucharist is the flesh of our savior Jesus Christ which the Father raised up . . ." (*Smyr.* 7.1). Both involved a denial of their docetic position. They could join in some activities in the church but not in the sacrament, which affirmed so much that they denied. Their spiritualized belief could give no place to symbols that might be interpreted realistically.

One undeveloped reference Ignatius makes to their teachings probably offers the clue that explains the interrelations of the other beliefs. He says that they "hold strange views about the grace of Christ" (*Smyr.* 6.2). It would be gratifying to know precisely what the doctrines about the grace of Christ were that they taught. One can surmise that their teaching about grace was that it was linked with his coming to earth, and with nothing else.[5] As we shall see later, Ignatius shared with them the belief that the coming, the *parousia* [6] (*Phld.* 9.2), was profoundly important, but for them it may well have been the matter of unique concern.

If by his spiritual coming Christ was held to have brought grace and life, the events of his earthly life would indeed be considered of less importance. And some such interpretation must lie behind their refusal of the passion and resurrection. A docetic view taken alone is negative; it demands an affirmation before it can become a theology of salvation.

It is significant that all these doctrines led to a contempt for the Jewish writings, and it is on this point that we can hold with certainty that Ignatius stood in the center between two extremes. He says that the Docetists are not persuaded by "the prophecies nor the law of Moses, nor the gospel" (*Smyr.* 5.1). It would be interesting to know whether these Docetists that Ignatius knew held the view that the creator was a power other than the god of the Jews. It seems unlikely that this was so, for Ignatius nowhere indicates that the doctrine of creation was a matter of dispute in the church. But the Docetists were con-

5. It is possible that they held such a belief as Irenaeus (*Adv. haer.* 1.23.3) attributes to Simon Magus, that righteousness is an accidental quality, a convention of the creating angels, and is therefore irrelevant.

6. By Ignatius the word is used for the appearance on the historical scene, not the second coming.

temptuous of the beliefs of Ignatius and his followers that the prophecies of the Jews pointed to the events of the earthly existence of Christ. And this disagreement led on inevitably to the denial of the authority of the Old Testament and of "the gospel," which in this context may mean a written gospel. They claimed the right to interpret freely, and were not bound by any facts or any authority.

It is important to inquire what these opponents of Ignatius can tell us of the gnostic movement in Antioch in the early second century. It would be premature, however, to try to deal with the question now, for if we are right in declaring that Ignatius agreed with them on some points and differed with them on others, we shall be able to get their views in full perspective only after we have completed our investigation of *his* theology. We shall discuss the matter more fully in the chapter on salvation. But at least we can say that so far we have no evidence of the myth of a light-person whose fall before history makes redemption necessary, nor of a cosmic dualism. The creation of the world by the one God is not under attack. Bultmann, in describing the "early oriental gnosticism" [7] he finds in the source of the prologue of the Fourth Gospel, characterizes it as lacking a theory of the development of evil in a cosmic fall, and as holding that the Logos stands in a unique position between God and the world, although there is no theory about the means by which he is related to the Father. Most important of all is the failure to see in the creation either of the world or of man a tragic event. Although we do not have evidence on all of these points, something rather similar seems to have been the position of the docetist Christians whom Ignatius faced.

The group of those standing to the right, who preach a doctrine influenced by Judaism, is more lightly sketched in the letters. References to them appear in both the Philadelphian and the Magnesian letters, and the arguments that Ignatius brings against them seem to be integrally related to his conception of the Christian gospel; it is as reasonable as in the case of the Docetists to suppose that here we catch a glimpse of his

7. Bultmann, *Das Evangelium des Johannes,* pp. 6–15.

old opponents in the church in Antioch. In the case of the
Judaizers, however, it is not so clear that they are teaching in
Asia Minor. Ignatius writes to the Magnesian church that he has
no knowledge that any of them hold such beliefs, but that he
wants to warn them (*Mag.* 11.1), and he assures the Philadelphians that no one has told him of divisions among them
(*Phld.* 7.2). Perhaps the Judaizers were difficult only in Antioch.

We shall first look at them as they are drawn in the allusions
in the letters, and only later try to identify them. They are not
orthodox Jews, for they do not practice circumcision (*Phld.* 6.1).
The problem was not that they insisted on observing the whole
Torah. They are convinced enough about Christianity to
preach that it has real truths, although in important respects it
is dependent on Judaism. But they continue to prize the old
and refuse to relinquish it wholly. Ignatius charges them with
harking back to "profitless ancient myths" (*Mag.* 8.1), and their
slogan seems to be "Christianity bases its faith on Judaism"
(*Mag.* 10.3). This historical judgment leads them to be open to
Jewish ways of living and therefore in some respects to "practice
Judaism" (ibid.), as Ignatius charges they do, although what
forms the practice takes we presumably know only in small part.
They apparently observed the Sabbath (*Mag.* 9.1), although the
reference to this is not wholly clear. They probably celebrated
distinctive and separate ritual meals (*Phld.* 4.1); the emphasis
on the *one* eucharist clearly suggests the existence of competing
forms. They seem to have held theories about priests, for Ignatius draws a striking contrast between the priests who are
noble and Christ the High Priest who is greater (*Phld.* 9), and
although this is a familiar contrast in Christian preaching it
occurs in a long passage dealing with those who "interpret
Judaism."

With Ignatius they accepted the authority of written documents, the ἀρχεῖα (*Phld.* 8.2). Ignatius says he reminds the
Judaizers that these are writings with authority, "Γέγραπται." It is
difficult not to draw the conclusion that the ἀρχεῖα included at
least the Law and the Prophets.[8] In the passage mentioned

8. The reference to belief ἐν τοῖς ἀρχείοις seems from an early date to
have been understood as meaning the Old Testament. So A; and G and L

above referring to the High Priest, Ignatius goes on to say that Christ is "the Door of the Father through which Abraham and Isaac and Jacob and the prophets pass . . ." (*Phld.* 9.1). The last inevitably suggests the notion that Ignatius had the Law and the Prophets in mind. It is possible that there were other documents among the ἀρχεῖα, but whatever they included, the problem of the relation between them and Christian tradition stands out, for in the same passage in the Philadelphian letter Ignatius concludes his argument by saying that the prophets "preached his coming, but the gospel is the consummation of immortality" (ibid.). They and Ignatius are evidently reading the prophets differently. They see a contradiction between the ἀρχεῖα and the gospel. Ignatius maintains there is none because the prophets bear witness of Christ. The Judaizers reply, as Ignatius quotes them: "That is the question at stake" (*Phld.* 8.2). They and Ignatius accept the prophets, but the Judaizers probably insist that Christian truths must be consistent with the prophets as they interpret them.

In respects not wholly clear their beliefs about Christ or his work seem wrong to Ignatius. He declares once that they do not "speak of Jesus Christ" (*Phld.* 6.1), but we must conclude that that is an unwarranted exaggeration, since in another reference he says, "It is absurd to talk of Jesus Christ and to practice Judaism" (*Mag.* 10.3). One may surmise that to them Christ was primarily a teacher, and perhaps not the only one, for Ignatius seems to be meeting their arguments when he declares that Jesus Christ is "our *only* teacher" and that even the prophets looked forward to him as their teacher (*Mag.* 9.2). Ignatius sees no difficulty in accepting Christ as teacher, but he is emphatic in saying that he is the only one, and that moreover he is more than a teacher. "Our life rose up through him and his death, which some deny" (*Mag.* 9). The sentence is ambiguous, but it seems most likely that the last clause should be taken as modifying the whole preceding clause, for then it would fit in

substitute respectively ἀρχαίοις, veteribus. See Lightfoot, for a discussion of the text. He holds the contrast to be between the Old Testament and the new writings. Schlier, p. 109, n. 2, suggests that the books referred to are books of revelation.

with an obscure reference in the earlier paragraph in which the problem of grace is raised (8.1,2) and Ignatius has gone out of his way to stress the coming of grace through Christ. We may conclude that the Judaizers accepted Christ as teacher but denied that he brought grace, and therefore that through him "our life" could spring up. As we shall see later, life and grace are for Ignatius closely allied concepts. They seem, then, to have been willing to follow Christ as a teacher, perhaps one among others, but they were hesitant about emphasizing the death and resurrection (*Phld.* 8.2., cf. 9.2 and probably *Mag.* 11).

Interpreters of Ignatius differ as to whether the false teachers comprise one or two groups.[9] The decisive point in my judgment is that the groups hold contradictory views about the scriptures and about Christ. As we have seen above, the Judaizers emphasize the law and the prophets and seem to consider Christ primarily a teacher. The Docetists, on the other hand, deny the authority of the Jewish writings and emphasize above all the grace-bringing eternal Christ. Both have difficulty with the passion and resurrection, but we conclude that it was for diametrically opposite reasons. On such an understanding it is difficult to see how there could possibly be only one group. The passage which is most important for those who believe that only one heresy faced Ignatius occurs in *Mag.* 11, where Ignatius urges the church "not to fall under the spell of false teaching, but to be fully convinced of the birth and passion and resurrection . . ." From there he goes on into what sounds like a typical antidocetic passage, and to find antidocetism in a passage directed otherwise against the Judaizers has seemed understandably to prove that there is only one group. If, however, we are right in holding that the Judaizing Christians consider Christ primarily a teacher,[10] then both parts of the quotation can quite well refer to them, since the birth and passion and resurrection, which for Ignatius are the crucial points of the event of Christ's life, mean little or nothing to them. The passage then ceases to be antidocetist, and certainly nothing else

9. Above, p. 52 n.

10. In *Phld.* 8.2 he also refers to the coming, the passion, and the resurrection in a passage that seems quite certainly to refer to the Judaizers.

in the Magnesian letter seems to be directed against the Docetists. The conclusion that his opponents are a single group of Jewish gnostics is difficult to maintain in view of the essential differences pointed out above.

Our description of this party of the "right" has so far been based on Ignatius' letters. When, however, we ask whether the group can be identified, it is clear that to a startling degree they bear the marks of Essene Judaism. In A.D. 68 [11] the headquarters at Qumran was destroyed, and it is not at all difficult to suppose that during the subsequent years of turmoil in Palestine some of the members fled north to Antioch, where the Jewish community was well established. They may even have penetrated into Asia Minor.[12] If they found at Antioch the rabbinical tradition of the Pharisees, which they found inadequate, as well as varieties of Hellenistic Jewish thinking, it would not be surprising if at least some among them found themselves attracted to the Christian churches, especially since certain of these were made up of men from a Jewish background.

The people that Ignatius faces in the group to the right represent what we might suppose would be the characteristics of an Essene practice and belief that had partly accommodated itself to Christianity. They resisted the observance of the Lord's Day; Sabbath-keeping is strong in the *Damascus Document* and *Jubilees,* and emphasis on a reformed Jewish calendar was one of the most jealously held beliefs.[13] They apparently observed

11. R. de Vaux, "Fouilles au Khirbet Qumran," *RB, 61* (1954), 233. M. Burrows, *More Light on the Dead Sea Scrolls* (New York, 1958), p. 21.

12. Rev. 2:9, 3:9 indicate difficulty in Smyrna and Philadelphia with "those who say they are Jews and are not." This might be an Essene-Christian group, though the author gives no basis for identification.

13. For references to the pseudepigrapha, I follow throughout the chapter and line references in R. H. Charles, *The Apocrypha and Pseudepigrapha of the Old Testament,* Oxford University Press, 1913. I am also indebted to him for the translations which I quote. CDC 13.1–11, 13–27; 14.6. See also *Jub.* 50.6–13; 1.14; 6.23, 29–30, 32 ff. CDC 5.1 f. implies conscious divergence from most Jews on the correct days to observe sabbaths and feasts. DSD 1.14 f. A. Dupont-Sommer, *The Jewish Sect of Qumran* (London, 1954), pp. 107 ff., discusses the importance of the calendar. Burrows, *More Light on the Dead Sea Scrolls,* pp. 373–78, summarizes the

a meal that Ignatius considered an invalid eucharist, and the *Manual of Discipline* tells us that common meals of bread and wine [14] were part of the observance of the Essene group. The presence of priests [15] among them as leaders of their groups was important, and Ignatius finds it necessary to point out that although the priests are good, the High Priest is greater still, and it is through him that the patriarchs and prophets as well as the apostles have access to the Father. One may doubt that ordinary Pharisaic Judaism would lay such emphasis on priests.

The mention of the patriarchs in this connection might be surprising if we did not recall that they dominate the Book of *Jubilees* which was so important to the Qumram group, and that they are also claimed in the *Damascus Document* to be the forerunners of the Essenes.[16] The importance of prophets is almost too obvious to need mention, and again it would seem to be the mark of a sectarian, rather than Pharisaic, Judaism. The *Habbakuk Commentary* is from beginning to end an interpretation of prophecy, and the Teacher of Righteousness of the Essenes is distinguished by his ability to interpret. To him it is said, "God made known all the mysteries of the words of his servants the prophets." [17] The discovery in the caves of a leaf from a Testimony book, as well as the evidence in the *Damascus Document* that the prophets, like the Pentateuch, served for the Essenes as a basis for halachah, further underscore the importance of prophecy. It is no wonder that Ignatius discusses so carefully the status of prophets.

---

debate about the calendar, and concludes with Mlle. Jaubert and Milik that the sect's calendar was that of *Jubilees*.

14. *DSD* 6.5 describes the blessing of bread and wine. It is difficult to know whether this is more than a regular meal made sacred because only initiates can partake. Josephus, *Bell.* 2.130–32, suggests this interpretation. But only after two years probation may a member receive the drink (*DSD* 6.20 f.), although he is not separated from some parts of the "Purity" (6.16 f.). In any event Essene-Christians might continue "invalid meetings" (*Mag.* 4.1).

15. *DSD* 1.21; 2.2, 11, 20; 5.9; 6.5, 8; 8.1; *CDC* 6.1–3.

16. *CDC* 4.2 f.

17. *Hab. Com.* 2.10 (trans. M. Burrows, *The Dead Sea Scrolls*, New York, 1955, p. 368). See Charles, intro., *Apocrypha and Pseudepigrapha*, 2, 790 f.

Most significant of all is Ignatius' emphasis on Christ as "our only teacher" (*Mag.* 9.1). Although every group maintaining a separate and self-conscious existence has its teachers and leaders, there is surely an implication that some teacher of special eminence has influence. Since this doctrine was important in Essene groups, as it was not in Pharisaic Judaism, it is tempting to recognize behind Ignatius' rebuttal their claim that the Teacher of Righteousness has a position beside Christ.

The only characteristic of the group of the "right," as Ignatius describes them, which does not fit our knowledge of the Essenes is the fact that they do not practice circumcision (*Phld.* 6.1). What he faced, however, was no longer pure Essenism but the practice of a group that had gone through at least enough adjustment to have considered themselves Christian. The abandonment of circumcision might have gone along with this accommodation, especially since it took place in Antioch where circumcision had been from Paul's time a crucial point in the church. Perhaps Paul really did win his case. An additional factor may have been that neither in the *Manual of Discipline* nor in the *Damascus Document* do we find a specific reference to literal circumcision. Since we know both in incomplete form, we may surmise that the section urging circumcision has been lost. Since it was a practice so well established, and they were admonished "not to transgress in any one of all the words of God in their periods . . . not to turn aside from his true statutes . . ." [18] it may be argued that circumcision was simply taken for granted. But if indeed clear reference to it was lacking, Essenes might be vulnerable to the preaching of Christians who no longer practiced it, who could point out that even if it stood in the Torah it was lacking from the later writings, which did not fail to emphasize similar concrete observances. In any case, the absence of circumcision is no more difficult to explain if these are Essene-Christians whom Ignatius faces than if they are Christians from some other Jewish background. And in striking respects what we know of them independently fits what Ignatius tells us.

Later we shall discuss both Ignatius' agreements with and his

18. E.g. *DSD* 1.13–15 (trans. Burrows, p. 371).

differences from them, but perhaps there has been enough said here to establish a presumptive identification. Any "identification" can be made only with full awareness of all the debate aroused by the Qumran documents.[19] However, if the term Essene is used in a general sense, it describes just such a Jewish sectarian group as that represented in Ignatius' letters, although of course we cannot know in detail what their background was. Whether they had been celibate or marrying Essenes, whether they had come from the Qumran area or from cells that lived elsewhere, perhaps in the towns, or which of the books found in the Qumran library they valued [20]—on all these matters and on many others we are ignorant. Nevertheless, what we know of the Judaizing group in Antioch accords in important respects with a Judaism of an Essene character and certainly better with it than with a Pharisaic form of Judaism.

Ignatius himself is clearly the leader of a centrist party, which was maintaining a balance between the two extremes he believed were menacing the church. His full theology as we presume it to be will be presented in the following chapters, but here we shall consider the temper of his party. As one might expect, it relies, on the whole, on a strategy of inclusiveness. At least part of the time it is definitely irenic. "Every tongue believing in God was gathered together in Christianity" (*Mag.* 10.3), and there is given a "hope of repentance" (*Eph.* 10) for all the world. Ignatius declares that the saints and believers may be drawn from either the Jews or the heathen (*Smyr.* 1.2), and he holds that men are "believers" by their own deliberate choice (*Mag.* 5.2). Once he uses a phrase which has sometimes been interpreted as implying the docetist view of men divided

19. See the beginning of the Bibliography, below, for the editions of the Essene material used constantly.

20. Apocalyptic writings seem to dominate in the fragments identified, and judging from the known longer apocalypses and pseudepigraphs variety of view in *detail*, even within a general theological and eschatological unity of interest, would be inevitable in the community. See F. M. Cross, *The Ancient Library of Qumran and Modern Biblical Studies* (New York, 1958), pp. 147 f., for a statement of the "common tradition." But see Burrows, *More Light on the Scrolls*, esp. chaps. 25–27, for indications of variety of view, not only in interpretation today but, no doubt, originally.

into predestined groups, when he praises the Trallian church for having a mind "unblameable and steadfast in patience not by habit but by nature" (*Tral.* 1.1). It is more likely, however, that he has in mind something like St. Paul's distinction between works and faith rather than that between *sarkikoi* and *pneumatikoi*, although his words lay him open to the charge of being gnostic. But in choosing, they accept the established truth, not some eccentric interpretation of it.

This kind of universalism certainly does not mean that Ignatius accepts all doctrines as true, however welcome men from different backgrounds might be as members of the church. On the one hand, Christianity is the new leaven, and the completion of Judaism. In fact, without it Judaism really lacks meaning (*Mag.* 10.2). On the other hand, he has no patience with a docetic christology, and whoever teaches it is not even to be listened to. They are "beasts in human form" (*Smyr.* 4.1) or again, "mad dogs, biting stealthily" (*Eph.* 7), and danger from them is so great that they must be shunned. He is sharply critical, in spite of his invitation to all men to return to the church.

If, then, in the house churches one could find at least the three groups we have described, it would follow that the influences at work within them would be varied, exerted either directly by leaders of strong conviction or through writings. Although leaders must remain unknown, writings may be tracked down; and if we are to understand the situation in early second-century Antioch, it is important to know as clearly as may be which New Testament [21] books were well known and what others were highly esteemed. It is obvious that the Old Testament books would be available, although few can be identified in the letters,[22] and certainly not all of them were

21. For the most useful tables setting forth the parallels between the Ignatian letters and the New Testament see the work of W. R. Inge in *The New Testament in the Apostolic Fathers* (Oxford, 1905), edited by a Committee of the Oxford Society of Historical Theology, and von der Goltz, *Ignatius von Antiochien*, pp. 178–206.

22. *Eph.* 5.3, cf. Prov. 3:34; *Eph.* 15.1, cf. Ps. 33:9; *Mag.* 12, cf. in the Septuagint Prov. 18:17; *Smyr.* 1.2, cf. Is. 5:26.

necessarily read. Scrolls were bulky, and perhaps hard to come by for any single small church. But, as we have argued above, the word ἀρχεῖα (*Phld.* 8) must designate the Jewish books of greatest authority, though it may include others also.

In addition to the Prophets and the Law, the Antioch church depended on some of the writings from the earlier generations of Christians. Ignatius himself knew best I Corinthians and the gospel of Matthew, which was the favorite if not the only gospel used. These two of the New Testament books provide the largest number of direct quotations in the letters. Because his references to I Corinthians are relatively clear and numerous, they make us aware of his freedom in paraphrasing and in using a quotation in changed context. This very freedom shows why, when we are on less secure ground, it is so difficult to know whether he is dependent on a written source. An examination of two or three examples will show up the problem plainly enough. I Cor. 6:9 f. reads, "Be not deceived: neither fornicators . . . nor adulterers . . . shall inherit the kingdom of God." Ignatius writes, "Be not deceived, my brothers; they who corrupt households shall not inherit the kingdom of God" (*Eph.* 16.1). Even though the Corinthian passage is not precisely quoted, it is difficult to doubt that he had it in mind. Gal. 5:19 f. contains similar words, but it is less close. In *Eph.* 18.1 Ignatius writes, "My spirit is a humble offering to the cross, which is a stumbling-block to unbelievers but to us salvation and life eternal. Where is the wise? Where is the disputer? Where is the boasting of those who are called intellectuals?" I Cor. 1:18, 20, 23 reads, "For the word of the cross is to them that perish foolishness, but unto us who are saved it is the power of God . . . Where is the wise? . . . where is the disputer of this world? . . . but we preach Christ crucified, unto Jews a stumbling-block . . ." It cannot be doubted that he is recalling I Corinthians, but he uses it freely. There are other reminiscences, but these examples will show that he knew the letter and will at the same time illustrate his method of referring to a source.

Which other Pauline letters he knew is less certain. The dependence of *Smyr.* 1.1 and *Eph.* 19.3 on N.T. Rom. 1:3 and 6:4

respectively is possible, as is that of *Phld.* 8.2, on Philippians
2:3, but none of the parallels is very convincing. The similar
phrases are too easily explained as common oral property to
constitute proof of literary dependence. We know from Ignatius himself that he was acquainted with more than one
letter, for he writes to the Ephesian church (12.2) that the
apostle Paul mentioned [23] them "in every letter." Although the
remark must be recognized as polite exaggeration, it shows that
Ignatius' knowledge of Paul rests on more than I Corinthians,
although we cannot say on which letters.

The gospel of Matthew is also unquestionably familiar to
him, and may well have come into existence in Antioch in
earlier years. He declares that Christ was baptized by John "in
order that all righteousness might be fulfilled by him" (*Smyr.*
1.1 = Matt. 3:15). This is the only quotation bearing directly on
the life of Christ. The others, like most of Ignatius' borrowings
from the New Testament, are of the nature of proverbs or short
exhortations: "The tree is known by its fruits" (*Eph.* 14.2 =
Matt. 12:33); "he that receiveth, let him receive" (*Smyr.* 6.1 =
Matt. 19:12); "bear the ills of all" (*Poly.* 1.3 = Matt. 8:17); "be
wise as the serpent and harmless as the dove" (*Poly.* 2.2 = Matt.
10:16). Several other references that are not quotations probably imply the use of the gospel of Matthew, as we shall see in
Chapter 4. One or more of the quoted bits might have been
borrowed from the oral tradition of preaching, but it is extremely unlikely that all of them can be so explained, and it
must be considered as nearly certain as anything in this early
period can be that Ignatius knew Matthew well, although we
cannot be as certain that he had the gospel in exactly its present
form. We can assume that *at least* the tradition contained in it

23. References to the Ephesian church occur in I Cor. 15:32, 16:8, and in
I and II Tim., though evidence in the letters for his knowledge of others
than I Cor. is very slender. It is very doubtful whether he knew N.T. Eph.,
and certainly we cannot know whether he considered it to be by Paul. Inge,
New Testament in the Apostolic Fathers, pp. 67 ff., believes his knowledge
"almost certain." With von der Goltz, pp. 103–5, and Schlier, p. 6, I
would hold that literary dependence is not the explanation of the resemblances.

is familiar to him—enough so that he remembered even the words.

Both Ignatius' familiarity with the gospel and the situation revealed in the letters make it reasonable to suppose that it was in Antioch [24] in earlier years that the gospel came into existence, influenced in part by the need to demonstrate to Jews and to Essene-Christians that the teachings of Jesus, grouped as we find them in the Sermon on the Mount, constituted a new Law which took the place of the Torah, and perhaps also of the regulations of the *Manual of Discipline*.

There does not seem to be any evidence that Ignatius knew the gospel of Mark, and wholly insufficient evidence to show that he knew Luke. In *Smyr.* 1.2 he mentions Pontius Pilate and Herod the Tetrarch in dating the crucifixion, and this combination appears in Luke 3:1; since, however, Matthew refers to both, and in any case what is involved is a simple historical fact readily carried in oral tradition, there is little reason to use it to prove Ignatius' knowledge of Luke. It has been suggested that the extremely antidocetic passage on the resurrection appearance of Jesus (*Smyr.* 3.1) may be a paraphrase of the Lukan story of Christ's eating with the disciples (24:39 ff.) rather than a reference to the *Teaching of Peter,* which Origen believed it to be. Unless this is true, which seems doubtful, there is no evidence that Ignatius knew Luke, and Matthew remains the dominant gospel and probably the only one of the synoptics [25] used in Antioch in Ignatius' time.

Ignatius' use of Matthew and I Corinthians demonstrates why it is difficult to apply normal criteria of literary dependence; and when the resemblances between possible parallels are still less sure, it is hazardous to try to draw conclusions. In consider-

24. So, e.g., B. H. Streeter, *The Four Gospels* (New York, 1925), p. 504. K. W. Clark, "The Gentile Bias in Matthew," *JBL, 66* (1947), 171 f., believes it was written by a Gentile Christian in Syria. Inge, *New Testament in the Apostolic Fathers,* p. 79, believed that "indications on the whole favour the hypothesis that he used our Greek Matthew in something like its present shape."

25. So also von der Goltz, p. 138. If one holds that Matthew was probably written in Antioch, his source, Mark, either never became familiar to the church there or else was quickly displaced by Matthew.

ing Ignatius' relation to the Fourth Gospel and the *Odes of Solomon* we are on that kind of treacherous ground. It is our belief that he probably knew them both, but the conclusion is at best tentative.

There are only two passages in the letters which are close enough to the Greek of the Fourth Gospel to be seriously considered as quotations. *Phld.* 7.1 says that the spirit "knows whence it comes and whither it goes"; John 3:8 reads, "The wind (πνεῦμα) bloweth where it will, and thou hearest the voice thereof, but knowest not whence it cometh and whither it goeth: so is everyone that is born of the spirit." The phrase is the same, but the contexts are different; in the gospel the wind is analogous to the spirit-filled life to which Nicodemus is called, though since the Greek word may mean either wind or spirit the reference is probably deliberately ambiguous; in the letter the word unquestionably means "spirit," for it is contrasted with flesh. If we had only these passages, we should be more secure about the judgment that Ignatius knew the gospel. It is the very fact that there are so many partial echoes of the phrase that raises doubt. In John 8:14 Jesus says: "for I know whence I came and whither I go; but ye know not whence I came or whither I go." Suggestions of the idea stand in John 7:27 f., 9:29, 12:35, 13:3, and 14:5, and in I John 2:11. The variety of expressions makes it at least probable that we have here a commonplace of teaching in Johannine circles; [26] and if so, dependence upon a written source is not very certain.

The second example is, if a quotation, a less exact one, since in *Mag.* 7.1 the declaration that the Lord "did nothing without the Father" is made in the third person, and in John 8:28 it is in the first person. The idea is the same and the same Greek words are used. This may be interpreted as an idea that would naturally occur in any circles which were developing a logos theology, but it is also close enough so that it can be held to show direct knowledge of the Fourth Gospel. The difficulty in

26. G. P. Wetter argues that this is a gnostic phrase used by the evangelist. "Eine gnostische Formel im 4. Evangelium," *ZNTW*, *18* (1917–18), 49–63. It is not clear to me that its gnostic use precedes the writing of the Fourth Gospel.

both these examples is that only a short phrase is used, and
there are fewer points of connection than in the quotations
cited from I Corinthians. Furthermore, if they are quotations
they are remarkably general.

The negative side of the question must also be considered. An
argument from silence is always dangerous, but this is not
precisely such an argument. If Ignatius knew the Fourth Gospel
and made use of concepts so similar to it, why did he not quote
more from it? It is the fundamental nature of the similarities
discussed below that makes the paucity of what may be considered direct quotation so difficult to understand. If he knew
the passage from the prologue, καὶ ὁ λόγος σὰρξ ἐγένετο, why did
he not quote it? Why did he not refer to the Thomas incident
after the resurrection instead of relying upon the unknown
gospel? Both passages would have been excellent ammunition
against his archenemies the Docetists. More significantly still,
how does it happen that among the relatively numerous references to events in the life of Christ *not one* comes from the
Fourth Gospel? [27]

It is an elusive and crucial problem.[28] The most reasonable
hypothesis seems to be that Ignatius knew the outlines of the
gospel as it was being written—that is to say, primarily, that he
knew its author and belonged with him to circles using similar
concepts. It is therefore probable that in the course of writing it

27. Christ was anointed on the head (so Matt. 26:7) rather than on the
feet (John 12:3).

28. Scholars divide on the question. To name only a few, Inge, *New
Testament in the Apostolic Fathers*, p. 83, considers Ignatius' use of the
Fourth Gospel "highly probable, but [it] falls some way short of certainty";
von der Goltz, p. 143, concludes that there is "völliger litterarischer Unab-
hängigkeit, aber starker geistiger Verwandtschaft"; R. M. Grant, "The
Origin of the Fourth Gospel," *JBL, 69* (1950), 321, is doubtful, having
maintained a strong negative position in "The Fourth Gospel and the
Church," *HTR, 35* (1942), 98. Schlier, p. 177, denies literary connection.
C. Maurer, *Ignatius von Antiochien und das Johannesevangelium* (Zürich,
1949), devotes a monograph to proving that Ignatius knew and misunder-
stood the Fourth Gospel. I find it difficult to deny knowledge of the gospel,
but think that it is in any case not the explanation of the likenesses. For
a nearly similar position see W. von Loewenich, *Das Johannes-Verständnis
im zweiten Jahrhundert* (Giessen, 1932), pp. 37 f.

the Evangelist and his disciples lived in or near Antioch,[29] although the gospel may have been completed, as tradition holds, in Ephesus.

We turn now to books other than those in the New Testament which may well have been part of the background of Antiochene thinking. The obvious ones to consider are the *Odes of Solomon* and those connected with the Essene tradition.

We cannot show that Ignatius was directly acquainted with any of the Essene books, for there are no quotations. There is no reason to believe that he knew even the *Manual of Discipline,* although it is of course impossible to show that he did not. We do not know that he read Hebrew, and there is no evidence that the *Manual* was translated. *Jubilees* and *I Enoch* existed in Greek versions, though how early is uncertain. Even though the *Testaments of the Twelve Patriarchs* has not been found at Qumran, the similarity of its thought to that of *I Enoch* and to a lesser extent that of *Jubilees* suggests a connection, and justifies its use as background material for Ignatius.[30]

29. Streeter, *Four Gospels,* pp. 454 f., holds that it was known by Ignatius, but was as yet without authority. C. F. Burney, *The Aramaic Origin of the Fourth Gospel* (Oxford, 1922), pp. 129 f. holds that it was written near Antioch; so P. N. Harrison, pp. 263 f. Schlier, p. 176, n. 1, would place its writing somewhere in Syria close to the Palestinian border, in order to be available to Mandaean influence. R. M. Grant, "Odes of Solomon and the Church of Antioch," *JBL, 63* (1944), 377, believes that the Fourth Gospel was not written in Antioch, but that the evangelist "was influenced by the spiritual atmosphere of the city." For recent statements affirming the traditional Ephesian provenance of the gospel see B. W. Bacon, *Gospel of the Hellenists* (New York, 1933), p. 118, and C. H. Dodd, *Fourth Gospel,* p. 5, n. 1.

30. J. T. Milik, "Le Testament de Lévi en Araméen," *RB, 62* (1955), 400 ff., publishes an Aramaic fragment of the *Testament of Levi,* and concludes that it does not lie directly behind our Greek *Testaments of the Twelve Patriarchs.* He considers the latter a writing by a Jewish-Christian, "utilisant largement les ouvrages juifs proprement dits" (p. 406), and inspired by them to write testaments for the rest of the patriarchs. A fragment from a *Testament of Naphtali* in Hebrew has also been found. The strong similarity between the Greek *Testaments of the Twelve* and *I Enoch* suggests that the writer, if Milik's thesis be true, knew *I Enoch.* Burrows, *More Light on the Scrolls,* p. 254, holds that the *Testaments* grew up on the "same religious soil" as that which produced the *Manual of Dis-*

All that would suggest his knowledge of the writings is his emphasis on choosing between death and life (*Mag.* 5.1), and his list of the unfortunates whom it is the duty of the Christian to help (*Smyr.* 6.2, cf. *Test. Jos.* 1.5 ff.). But both are commonplaces of teaching [31] and do not prove literary dependence, especially in the second instance, where only a few of the words of the series match. It is conceivable that he may have known some of the Essene writings, since he shared so much with them, but there is no evidence for it. Precisely because the ideas were generally influential, it is the less possible to assume direct knowledge of any particular source.

The evidence for Ignatius' knowledge of the *Odes of Solomon* is hard to evaluate, since the letters are in Greek and we have the *Odes* in Syriac, which according to Harris was the original language.[32] Nevertheless the most probable conclusion is that he knew at least some of the *Odes*. The case for his knowledge rests chiefly upon similarities between Ode 38 and *Tral.* 6.2, and between Ode 11 and *Rom.* 7.2.

Ode 38 describes the work of the "Deceiver and the Error," who are either false teachers or the Evil One personified. Unlike Psalm D of the *Psalms of Thanksgiving*, which it recalls, it is extremely difficult to believe that the Ode refers to a definite historical situation: [33]

> All the drugs of Error and the plagues of death
>   which are considered to be sweet (beverage) . . .

> This is the Deceiver and the Error . . .

---

cipline. We are justified in using the *Testaments* to illustrate the religious background of Ignatius' thought.

31. *Smyr.* 6.2; Matt. 25:31 ff.; *Test. Jos.* 1.5–7; Job 29:12–16, 31:16–22. This is a favorite form of ethical teaching.

32. R. Harris and A. Mingana, *The Odes and Psalms of Solomon*, John Rylands Library (Manchester, 1920), 2, 170. Throughout the following chapters quotations from the *Odes* will be from their translation.

33. The seven spirits of Deceit and of Error (*Test. Reub.* 2 and 3), and comparable activities of Beliar or Satan in the other pseudepigrapha are related to the kind of thought represented in the Ode rather than the reference to the Man of Lies (*CDC* 9.39), which probably carries historical reference.

And they invite many to the Banquet
And give them to drink of the wine of their
    intoxication . . .

And then they leave them;
And so these go about like madmen and corrupt. . . .

[8, 10, 12, 14a]

Harris and Mingana [34] also translate verse 8 "All the drugs of Error and the plagues of death which they think to be honey-wine . . ." They justify this interpretation on the similarity between the Syriac words for "wine sweetened with honey" and "sweetness" (which stands in the manuscript), and on the fact that Ephrem later translates the same word "honey-wine." Ignatius in *Tral.* 6.2 writes of the false teachers who "mix Jesus Christ with their own views to gain confidence, as though they offered a deadly poison with honey wine, which the unknowing one takes gladly, in wretched pleasure, which is his death."

Psalm D of the *Psalms of Thanksgiving* [35] has a comparable passage, which uses the figure of those suborned at a feast:

And they [lying preachers] have withheld the drink
    of knowledge from the thirsty;
And for their thirst they give them vinegar to
    drink
In order to gaze upon their error (or staggering),
That they may act insanely at their festivals.

Here the similarities to Ode 38 are more apparent than real. There is no mixing of truth and error, no direct deceit.

In spite of the fact that reference to poison in wine is not unusual,[36] the connections between *Tral.* 6.2 and the Ode are numerous enough to make it likely that Ignatius knew the

34. Harris and Mingana, 2, 41 f.

35. Translation of W. H. Brownlee, "Biblical Interpretation among the Sectaries of the Dead Sea Scrolls," *BA, 14* (1951), 59; cf. A. Dupont-Sommer, *Dead Sea Scrolls,* p. 74.

36. Cf. the examples cited in Bauer, *Die Briefe,* pp. 235 f.; also R. M. Grant, "Odes of Solomon and the Church of Antioch," *JBL, 63* (1944), 370, n. 22.

latter. Both have in mind evil teachers, the figure of error as
sweet wine which masks poison, dealing death or madness in
spite of the pleasure with which the deceived one drinks. Even
if the emendation by Harris of the word "honey-wine" is not
allowed there is still the deliberate deception through mixing
of poison and wine. There can be no final proof of direct knowledge but a strong presumption of it.

A perhaps stronger parallel can be seen between Ode 11 and
Rom. 7.2. The Ode reads:

> And speaking waters drew near my lips
> From the fountain of the Lord plenteously.
>
> And I drank and was inebriated
> With the living water that doth not die;
> And my inebriation was not one without knowledge
>
> But I forsook vanity
> And I turned to the Most High my God,
> And I was enriched by his bounty.   [6–9]

Ignatius writes to the Roman church, "My passionate desire
has been crucified, and there is in me no fire of yearning for
material things, but water living and speaking in me and saying to me from within, 'Come to the Father.' " Harris points
out the association of the *living* and *speaking* water in the two
passages, but fails to mention the connection with the Father
which is prominent in Romans and plainly in the context of
the Ode. In the Ignatian passage the speaking waters cry,
"Come to the Father," and in the Ode the speaker "turned to
the Most High," apparently as a consequence of drinking the
living and speaking water. For them both there is a play on
words in affirming that the Father is the source of both Life and
the Word. This is a far closer parallel than that in John 4:14
which Lightfoot suggests: "Whosoever drinketh of the water
that I shall give him shall never thirst; but the water that I
shall give him shall become in him a well of water springing
up unto eternal life." It seems probable that Ignatius knew
this Ode.

The notion of water as conveying life, or as being the symbol of the life which is God is so frequent in the writings cherished by the Essenes that one wonders whether the Ignatian passage is grounded on them instead of on Ode 11. It is a figure that goes back at least to the familiar passage in Jer. 2:13 where God laments that they have forsaken him, the "fountain of living waters," and to Zech. 14:7 f., where the description of the day of the Lord that has only darkness closes with the beautiful promise that "at evening time there shall be light . . . and living waters shall go out from Jerusalem." Again in the *Damascus Document* the backsliders are accused of leaving the "spring of living waters" (9.28B), which might mean the Covenant, or the Commandments, or God himself. A similar indeterminate use occurs in *I Enoch* 96.6, and less clearly in 22.2, 9(Gg). But nowhere does one find the connection of living and speaking water, and it is not easy to suppose that the association is accidental.

A third passage that may indicate literary dependence on the *Odes* is in *Eph.* 19.3, which says "Ignorance was purged away, the old kingdom was destroyed, for God appeared as man to bring in the newness of eternal life." Ode 7.21 reads, "For ignorance hath been destroyed, because the knowledge of the Lord hath arrived." Both refer to similar results of the incarnation, but the parallels do not seem as strong as those discussed above.

If there is direct connection, which seems the most probable explanation, then it is easier to argue that Ignatius knew the *Odes* [37] than the converse. A hymn book is more readily quoted than are letters such as those of Ignatius. It is not possible to prove that Ignatius knew all the odes we have, but that he knew some is extremely likely, and, as we shall see below, the similarities of thought when he is *not* quoting are striking.

What we have attempted was necessary, but it is unsatisfactory at best, for the results are meager. The conclusions can

---

37. That the *Odes* arose in Syria is generally held; precisely where is debated. Harris and Mingana, 2, 67 f., argue for the "district of Antioch." Grant, "Odes of Solomon and the Church of Antioch," pp. 372–77, argues for Edessa. Both believe it probable that Ignatius knew them.

be summed up quickly: we cannot show that Ignatius knew books of the Essenes or Docetists, proof for his knowledge of I Corinthians and Matthew is good, and the evidence is tentatively on the positive side for his knowledge of the *Odes* and the Fourth Gospel. The letters show, however, that he did not consider either of the last two authorities for the church. It is not surprising that we do not have more, and more accurate, quotations, when we remember that he was writing under very difficult circumstances, as a prisoner. He undoubtedly knew other books than those he quoted. Literary dependence is not everything, however. Beyond this stands the actually more important question of what has been called the spiritual kinship of Ignatius, the Fourth Gospel, and the *Odes,* to which must now be added the writings of the Essenes.

In this matter the Ignatian letters are important because they establish a small but highly significant fact. Because they and they alone of these related writings have a place reference, we are assured that in Antioch, late in the first or early in the second century, groups representing all these interests existed. Here is at least one definite place where the conversation between these different groups could and did go on. If Ignatius knew the *Odes* and the Fourth Gospel, then they were in some sort of form before the last years of his life, though it is not necessary to move them back very far, and they may well have been written during his lifetime.

Precisely the reason why it is so difficult to explain Ignatius' relationship to the Fourth Gospel is that there does not seem to have been a relationship of dependence, but rather of the development of both within the same thought milieu. If the Fourth Gospel were a "quite primitive product from the very early church," as Goodenough [38] has conjectured, it is difficult to understand why Ignatius would not have used it more, as he did St. Paul, even if he disagreed with it in some respects. He agreed with it too profoundly to have used it as slightly as he did. Albright's [39] suggestion that it was carried by

38. E. R. Goodenough, "John a Primitive Gospel," *JBL, 64* (1945), 145.
39. W. F. Albright, "Recent Discoveries in Palestine and the Gospel of St. John," in W. D. Davies and D. Daube, eds., *Background of the New Testament and Its Eschatology* (Cambridge, 1956), pp. 154–56.

oral transmission for a decade or two after A.D. 70 fits the evidence from the Ignatian letters. It is easier to understand the facts presented if the Fourth Gospel was written down toward the end of the century rather than earlier, and Ignatius' evidence for the presence of Essene-Christians in Antioch explains the influence of a sectarian Judaism influenced by Iranian concepts which must be assumed in the background from which the Fourth Gospel emerged.[40] Even if the gospel was completed in Ephesus, it is probable that it was substantially written on Syrian soil. The conjecture that the *Odes* developed in the neighborhood of Antioch would rest on similar arguments. Whether the churches within the city were all Greek-speaking [41] is problematical, and there may have been a greater variety in the population than some have been willing to grant. The conservatism of religious groups with respect to language is a not uncommon phenomenon even today. Almost certainly in the outlying towns in the territory belonging to the city there would have been Syriac-speaking churches. The writing of these books within Ignatius' lifetime would help to explain the fact that they had no particular authority for him, and their extraordinary resemblance to one another in style and idea makes such a date probable.

The extent and form of that likeness is arresting. In later chapters we shall have occasion to observe the evidences of the common background of some of the important concepts, but here we shall note the striking similarities in figures of speech and what might be called temperament.

In Ignatius, the *Odes,* and the Fourth Gospel there is unmistakable resemblance to the rich imagery of the Essene psalms and the earlier pseudepigraphs, although none is simply

40. L. Mowry, "The Dead Sea Scrolls and the Gospel of John," *BA, 17* (1954), 82 ff., discusses the dualism in both. K. G. Kuhn, "Die Sektenschrift und die iranische Religion," *Zeitschrift für Theologie und Kirche, 49* (1952), 304 ff., contrasts the ethical dualism both in the *Gathas* and the *Manual* with the metaphysical dualism of gnosis. See also Albright, "Recent Discoveries," pp. 168 f.

41. R. M. Grant, "Odes of Solomon and the Church of Antioch," p. 373. That the "cultural atmosphere was Greek" certainly would not rule out the possibility that some of the modest house churches were Syriac-speaking.

derivative. There is a delight in sensuous imagery, such as one finds in full flower in the Song of Solomon. The evil odor of the teaching of the Prince of this world (*Eph.* 17) and the pleasant odor of the Lord (Ode 11.15) might be contrasted with each other, and perhaps the Fourth Evangelist suggests this figure when he dwells on the sweet odor of the ointment that filled the house (12:3). The sweet odor of the righteous and of the elect appear in *Test. Sim.* 6.2 and *I Enoch* 25.6; and particularly in the Enoch writings there is evident pleasure in the miraculous fragrance of the tree beside the throne of God— probably the tree of life (24.5)—and of the tree of knowledge in the Garden of Righteousness (32.3).

For all of them the fruitful earth is a recurrent theme, enjoyed partly for its own beauty and partly because it is the bounty of God. The Odist exults that he "became like the land which blossoms and rejoices in its fruits" (11.12), and he speaks of "the beautiful planting of his right hand" (38.20) in the widely used convention that on the right is all strength and virtue. Similarly, Ignatius implies that the church is the planting of the Lord (*Tral.* 11.1, *Phld.* 3.1), and the Evangelist develops the close relationship of Christ and "his own" in the elaborate allegory of the vine and its branches (15:1 ff.) cared for by God, the husbandman. In this vein is Ignatius' symbol of the branches of the cross (*Tral.* 11.2), which bear incorruptible fruit—the figure of the tree of life. Fruit in all three is usually, as it were, visible and not allegorized. The Odist writes, "Thy fruits are full-grown and perfect" (1.5). All these and many comparable figures appear in the Essene writings. The Council of the Community after the "anguish of the refining furnace" will be seen to be "an eternal planting" [42] (*DSD* 8.5, 11.8). The figure itself goes back to the late Isaiah passages [43] that we now see had so much influence on the Essenes and the rising Christian community, but the particular delight in all these metaphors is widely characteristic.

It is not only the senses of smell and sight that provide figures of speech, for the Odist and Ignatius are fond of dwelling on

42. Brownlee's trans.
43. Is. 60:21, 61:3.

what is available to the ear. Thus we find references to the harp, which may suggest the bishop, "attuned to the commandments as a harp to its strings" (*Phld.* 1.2), or the Holy Spirit (Ode 14.8, cf. 6.1 f.), and of course it may simply be an instrument of praise as in Ode 26.3 and the *Manual of Discipline* 10.9. Again they all rejoice in singing, whether of the Spirit (Ode 24.1 f.) or in the church group (*Eph.* 4.1,2, Ode 7.17) or simply the praise of an individual worshiper (*DSD* 10.9). Similarly the silence-speech metaphor is extended to the worshiping congregation (Ode 8.4, *Rom.* 2.1).

In a somewhat different vein another favorite figure is that of the crown. More than once the Odist speaks of Truth or of the Lord as a living crown or garland (1.1–4, 5.12, 9.8, 17.1, 20.7) and Ignatius calls the bishop and the council a "spiritual crown" (*Mag.* 13.1). The fountain of the Lord appears in the *Odes* (11.6, 26.13, 30) and in *I Enoch*.[44] These are only examples of a wealth of images used in common, which could scarcely come from a single source but which represent a style or perhaps a common temperament. Based ultimately on the Old Testament, they are used with a characteristic exuberance in the pseudepigraphic and the Essene writings; they continue to express feeling for nature and the sensuous, until in some cases, as in the Odist's figure of milking the breasts of the Father,[45] they pass the bound of what is acceptable to modern taste. Ignatius uses them more soberly, but his taste and enthusiastic temperament are to some degree expressed in them.

Many of the figures occur in gnostic texts, and Reitzenstein, Schlier,[46] and others consider them of gnostic origin. That they represent a type of oriental thought no one would deny, but it is simpler to hold that they came to Ignatius through the influence of the Essene and pseudepigraphic writings rather than through the Mandaeans or a pre-Valentinian gnosis. It is far

44. *I Enoch* 96.6, fountain of life; 22.9, the "bright spring of water" for the righteous.

45. 8.16, 19.2 f.

46. The *religionsgeschichtliche* parallels to Ignatian figures and the conclusions drawn are most fully assembled in Schlier, e.g. planting, pp. 48–54; singing, etc., pp. 144 ff.; the cross, pp. 102 ff., etc.

more likely that somewhat later gnostics pressed them into conventional and sometimes mythical patterns than that they always carried those meanings.

In spite of the evidence of a common background, the letters make us aware that Ignatius presided over a church that was anything but tranquil. Disagreements were deep, and the preaching of the contradictory points of view was vigorous. In a situation of that kind a concern for stabilizing forms was inevitable. And there are not many possibilities: a creed, writings that can be appealed to as having absolute authority, the power of persons respected by virtue of their position, or the fellowship of a group united in devotion and worship. In the course of time the later church made use of all, but for Ignatius none of them lay ready at hand, for the church had only begun to be threatened by tragic schism, and the importance of a degree of uniformity was only beginning to be apparent. There is no evidence that Ignatius knew a creed, though many of the beliefs of the later Roman symbol appear scattered through his letters. It has sometimes been suggested that one or more of the rhythmical antidocetic statements, as in *Eph.* 7 or *Poly.* 3.2, was in fact a creed in Antioch. That seems very doubtful. They are expansions of a single point of doctrine, and in no sense statements of grouped doctrines, nor is there evidence that they had status as authoritative confessions. It is possible that one or another of the passages is a quotation of a single item from a creed, but they are sufficiently unbiblical to make this unlikely, since most of the earlier creeds used biblical phrases. If they are quoted at all, it is more likely that their sources are hymns or canticles that were used liturgically. The very obvious and bitter strife among Christians in Antioch is further evidence that the church had no creed to which agreement was given— at least none which touched the points under discussion, and Ignatius has no recourse to the authority of such a symbol.

We have seen above that there were no writings that could serve as a universally recognized authority. The books taken over from Judaism did not clarify the points on which discussion raged. One party ignored them entirely—the other two disagreed profoundly about their import. Christian writings were used, but their status is not clear. Once, indeed, Ignatius seems to appeal to a written gospel as having authority equal to the Jewish writings, but he passes on to the content of the gospel. He declares that "it is right . . . to pay attention to the prophets and especially to the gospel, in which the passion has been made clear to us . . ." (*Smyr.* 7). Here the writings of the prophets and the written gospel seem to be placed together. But Ignatius closes the sentence by saying that in the gospel "the resurrection has been completed." At that moment his mind has turned back toward the more characteristic idea of the gospel as the proclamation of the passion and resurrection and from the word of preaching to the events proclaimed. All one can say in the face of the evidence is that it is possible he was already using the word *euanggelion* to mean a written gospel, although it is not the primary meaning of the word for him. There is no evidence that any Christian writing carried convincing authority, since the appeal is still to the facts available in the great central tradition.

It is the last two of the possible seats of authority that Ignatius develops, for his policy in Antioch seems on the one hand to have been to emphasize institutional unity, symbolized by a united ministry, and on the other to develop unity in a shared experience of worship. By these two means he had apparently hoped to stabilize the church, threatened as it was by divergent theologies. Ignatius is confident that if the laity will stay by the bishop and presbyters and deacons, unity will be assured. As we shall see in Chapter 7, his doctrine of the church is based on the *theory* of such unity, but it is difficult to imagine that he could have held it in the teeth of widespread defections among the clergy. Perhaps some of the small church groups had a less formally recognized leadership and were therefore open to the preaching of traveling prophets.[47] Ignatius, as bishop, evidently approved of an ordained local clergy, since they were more readily controllable.

Ignatius has been described as concerned chiefly to buttress

47. The traveling prophets of the *Didache* would fit well into this picture.

the position of the bishop, and there is some ground for this
opinion of him. He writes, for instance, "where the bishop is
there let the church be" (*Smyr.* 8.2), and "look upon the
bishop as the Lord" (*Eph.* 6.1). One finds the idea also put in
reverse: "as many as belong to God and Jesus Christ—these are
with the bishop" (*Phld.* 3.2, cf. *Smyr.* 9.1). These are cate-
gorical statements which express a determination that the position of the bishop must be recognized. But the whole picture is
changed when one places beside those sentences another passage, "Give heed to the deacons as to Jesus Christ, just as the
bishop is patterned after the Father, and the presbyters the
council of God and the college of Apostles. Without them the
'church' could not be so named" (*Tral.* 3.1, cf. *Tral.* 7.2). It
seems clear that however important the bishop may have been
as the head of the church, Ignatius was staking his hopes for
unity on the clergy as a whole. His usage throughout the letters
shows that. There are eight references [48] to the bishops, presbyters, and deacons taken together as the seat of unity in the
church, and four to the bishop and presbyters as the chief
authority.[49] Once there is a general reference to the "bishop
and those who rank above you" (*Mag.* 6.2). The bishop is undoubtedly head, but the significant point seems to be the authority of the total clerical group.

It is not surprising, then, to discover that practice in the
Antioch church was more democratic than the first three
sentences quoted above about the bishop would suggest. There
were different groups that acted for the church, in addition to
whatever bishops did singly. Thus Polycarp (7.2) must call together a "godly council" in order to elect a delegate to send to
Antioch.[50] It is possible, of course, that this is a situation unique
in the Asia Minor church,[51] but it is strongly reminiscent of the

48. *Mag.* 13.1; *Tral.* 3, 7.2; *Phld.* Ins. 4, 7.1; *Smyr.* 8.1; *Poly.* 6.1.

49. *Eph.* 2.2, 20; *Mag.* 7.1; *Tral.* 2.

50. H. de Genouillac, *L'Église chrétienne*, p. 45, points out that the
assembly or κοινόν is composed of delegates (σύνεδροι) elected (χειροτονεῖν)
by the ἐκκλησία or popular assembly. There is then experience in the civic
life for the kind of group action described.

51. He makes the same reference to election (χειροτονῆσαι) in *Phld.* 10.1
and *Smyr.* 11.2.

church group that Acts tells us gathered together in Antioch when Barnabas and Saul were chosen to go on a preaching mission (Acts 13:1 ff.), and it may well reflect the practice of the Essenes (e.g. *DSD* 6.16). The custom must have been followed in Antioch, for Ignatius seems to take this quite for granted as the step preliminary to dispatching the delegate, and one may wonder whether he would have known of such a Smyrnaean or Philadelphian custom.

Similarly there is mention of the "council of the bishop" (*Phld.* 8.1), which may be the same body named above, before whom the repentant members who had been led astray by false doctrine, and perhaps by other sins, must present themselves. Apparently the practice was for this council to act for the congregation according to the command in Matt. 18:17. It is possible that the council was made up of the church as a whole, but references to the council of presbyters make it tempting to surmise that the presbyters sitting jointly acted so, for they are spoken of collectively in three important passages. They are described as the "council of God" (*Tral.* 3.1).[52] They are also, of course, occasionally mentioned individually, but Ignatius in these three passages considers them the ruling body of the church. He even speaks of them once as "the law of Jesus Christ" (*Mag.* 2.1).

Each of the two lower grades of ministers is subordinate to the one above. Thus it is appropriate that the presbyters should refresh the bishop (*Tral.* 12.2), and should respect and "yield to him" (*Mag.* 3.1). And deacons are subject to both the bishop and the presbyters (*Mag.* 2.1). But it is not this subordination alone that is important, but the unity that it guarantees among them, as the chapter on the doctrine of the church will make clearer.

Each grade has its own functions to perform in the church, though we are told less about this than we could wish. The bishop is the symbol of unity, and was effective in specific ways. He acts to call a council, and presides over it (*Mag.* 6.1, *Poly.* 7.2). He recognizes marriages (*Poly.* 5.2), authorizes baptisms

52. Probably *Tral.* 7.1 is a shorthand reference to the college of presbyters.

(*Smyr.* 8.2), and is at least the authority behind the eucharist, since he appoints those who can celebrate it (*Smyr.* 8.1). The need for the restriction would be wholly evident if we are right in recognizing that the Essene-Christians may well have brought over from their past their own common meal of bread and wine, which had different meanings from those of the Christian eucharist (*Mag.* 4). Still more importantly, the Essene experiments in the organization of a voluntary religious group as well as the precedent suggested by the government of the city may even as late as Ignatius' time have influenced the position of the bishop. It was the historical situation that made evident the need for such a leader and largely shaped his function, but perhaps the position of the chief "overseer" or "censor" of the Essenes, since he was in authority over smaller groups of the Many,[53] suggested to Ignatius the pattern for the bishop, head over many churches. The evidence, thus, for the development of the "monarchical" bishop, at least in Antioch, seems to be early rather than late.

The functions of the presbyters are taken so wholly for granted that Ignatius never defines them, and we know little about them except that in some important sense presbyters acted together for the ruling of the church. We should not know very much about deacons, either, except that Ignatius writes a bit more extensively of them in the letter to the Trallian church, where perhaps a local problem had arisen with respect to deacons. He urges that deacons are to be respected as Jesus Christ himself (*Tral.* 3.1) and recognized as servants of the church of God and the mysteries of Jesus Christ (*Tral.* 2.2).

53. It is interesting that τὸ πλῆθος is Ignatius' word for the laity (*Mag.* 6.1; *Tral.* 1.1, 8.2; *Smyr.* 8.2) as it is also esp. in *I Clem.* Cf. also Acts 15:12, 30. This sounds like the terminology of the Essenes—see *DSD* 6 and 7 passim and *CDC* 16.1, 18.1. Burrows, *More Light on the Scrolls*, pp. 359 f., holds that the word elsewhere translated "the many" means "masters," and if so it would not be equivalent to Ignatius' word, which clearly suggests the lay group. Since the discovery of the Qumran documents, the presumed relationship of bishop and superintendent is much discussed. See esp. B. Reicke, "The Constitution of the Primitive Church," in K. Stendahl, ed., *The Scrolls and the New Testament* (New York, 1957), pp. 150, 154 ff.

Emphatically they are not to be thought of as merely serving meat and drink. Ignatius seems to suggest that their function was somehow connected with the celebration of the eucharist, if indeed it is that which is in his mind when he speaks of the "mysteries."

But Ignatius did not rely simply on the authority of the clergy, important as that was as a kind of safeguard against the factiousness in the church. He believed deeply that a shared life of worship was important, and that this was the real basis for unity. The full meaning of this unity is so important that we shall consider it at length in Chapters 7 and 9. Here we are concerned to understand not the theory but what we can about the life in the church as it was experienced by the ordinary Christian. Private houses probably still serve as the normal meeting places for the congregation (*Eph.* 5.2, 20), of which he speaks directly more than once. He placed great faith in the effect of these meetings, and he urges Polycarp to have more of them (*Poly.* 4.2). He was interested, too, as we have seen above, in breaking down the impersonality and coldness that threatened the church as it grew larger; he tells Polycarp to know people by name (ibid.). It is this that makes one wonder whether the house churches by now were beginning to meet together. He enjoins the Magnesians to "come together as to one temple of God, as to one altar" (*Mag.* 7.2) for common prayer and for rejoicing in the salvation brought by Christ (ibid.). There we must suppose was the preaching, sometimes "in the Spirit" with a loud voice, as Ignatius spoke to the church in Philadelphia (*Phld.* 7.1), sometimes of a more pedestrian and moralistic sort in which homely and persistent problems had to be considered like the love of a husband for his wife (*Poly.* 5.1). It was preaching before a congregation which he hoped would have a common life, people who would "work with one another, struggle together, meet together, suffer together, lie down together, rise up together as God's stewards and assessors and servants" (*Poly.* 6.1). It is clear from this that the Christians—at least of any given small church—formed a group bound together by many ties into a common life perhaps in the degree to which they felt themselves different from their non-Christian neighbors. They shared memories of baptisms (*Poly.* 6.2) and perhaps of the trying occasions when repentant members had to appear before the council of the bishop to confess (*Phld.* 8.1) and to be readmitted to full participation in the congregation in a ceremony which we may suppose to have been influenced by the readmission ceremony of the Essenes (*DSD* 7.21). Above all, they shared memories of formal and joyous occasions of worship, of choirs singing (*Eph.* 4.2, *Rom.* 2.2), of festal processions or perhaps pilgrimages (*Eph.* 9.2), carrying with them sacred objects. Although these references stand as figures of speech not literal descriptions of events, we may suppose that Ignatius uses them because he believes them common memories and therefore persuasive.

The eucharist was the most important shared experience (*Mag.* 7, *Phld.* 4), and to that Ignatius reverts again and again. The most interesting things he has to say belong, however, to doctrine about it rather than description, and we shall consider them below. It is possible that in Antioch the old custom had persisted of holding an *agape* or communal meal before at least some of the eucharists. He says to the Smyrnaeans, "It is not allowable either to baptize or to celebrate an *agape* (ἀγάπην ποιεῖν) without the bishop" (*Smyr.* 8.2). This may represent custom only in Smyrna and not Antioch, for it is a very *ad hoc* remark. In any case the connection of the *agape* with baptism suggests strongly that Ignatius is thinking of sacraments, and that the eucharist is the climax of the communal meal.

Baptism in a missionary situation was doubtless more central than it came to be later. By it the churches marked the entrance of new converts into their body. The emphasis Ignatius places on the anointing of Christ (*Eph.* 17.1)—since by it the Lord breathed immortality on the church—suggests how greatly it was revered, and, as we shall try to show below, the anointing implies that chrism was a part of the baptismal service.

We have seen, then, that the letters reveal a situation in which the bishop is important, or Ignatius hoped he might become more important, but in which the greatest hope for unity in the face of the conflicts in the church is placed on the clergy as a whole, and on the maintenance of a healthy and vigorous fellowship in the congregations. The Antioch church was anything but a model of quiet and peace at the time Ignatius wrote. It had just passed through a crisis, and some insight into the nature of the opposing groups can be gained from the letters. The Christian group was not isolationist, holding itself rigidly apart from nontraditional ideas, but those ideas were persuasive to Christians themselves in the church where speculation was rife and sometimes pushed to dangerous conclusions.

It is a dramatic situation that is suggested, fascinating because of its boldness and vigor but tantalizing because the interpretation we have developed has had to be made from gossamer. As we go on to a consideration of Ignatius' central Christian convictions, we shall be on somewhat firmer ground, but the material of this chapter, tentative as many of its conclusions must be, makes clear that these matters were not dry theology. What was at stake was of central importance, and Christianity in Antioch was vigorous in proportion to its tempestuousness.

PART TWO

Theology

4. The Incarnate Lord

SINCE the docetic christology was so lively an issue in Antioch, and beginning to be a problem in the Asia Minor churches, it is not surprising that thought about the incarnate Lord dominates Ignatius' mind. In a systematic presentation of theology the incarnation would not stand first, but in Ignatius' thought it does. In swift phrases he declares that it is the very heart of Christianity; if there is something new in the gospel it is this preaching about the Lord who is God-become-man. Belief in the incarnate Lord is the ground of Christian piety and the source of whatever unity the churches achieve, as well as the indispensable core of the Christian view of the world. The incarnation has implications both for the practical life of the Christian and for his understanding. And these two facets of the faith are for him not accidentally associated; right thinking about this truth issues in fullness of living. As Ignatius sees it, it is when the churches are fully conscious of being dependent on the incarnation of the Lord that their fellowship has vitality, and by contrast it is precisely because the teachers of strange doctrine no longer have certainty on this point that they are perishing.

Behind the rich variety of phrases in which Ignatius affirms the centrality of the Lord there are two basic interests. One is the conviction that in the life of Christ a real and true incarnation took place: he was in fullness and actuality God entered into human life on the scene of history. And in the second place Ignatius is concerned to develop the consequences of this event which was so crucial for the world. The incarnation was revolutionary both in itself and in the effects that flowed from it.

Ignatius' teaching about Jesus Christ starts, then, with the affirmation that real incarnation means that he is *God in Man* (*Eph.* 7.2). The fact, rather than subtleties about its nature, possesses him, and neither aspect overpowers the other. On the

one hand he has no hesitation in applying the word God to
Jesus Christ. He uses it so naturally throughout the letters that
it is obviously a point about which he has no doubt. He accepted the idea and the word wholeheartedly, as the earliest
Christians had not. On the other hand Ignatius affirms stoutly,
and with every indication of meeting opposition, that Christ is
man. Actually his total theology, as distinct from his polemic
against the Docetists, springs from the paradox that Christ is
both God and Man:

> There is one Physician, both of flesh and of spirit, born
> and yet existing unborn,[1] God in man,[2] true life in death,
> both of Mary and of God, first suffering and then above
> suffering, Jesus Christ our Lord.   [*Eph.* 7.2]

No one set of categories is adequate for affirming the truth about
him. In another passage Ignatius declares him to be Son of God,
and Son of Man, but the intent is the same (*Eph.* 20.2). Life and
death, deity and humanity seem mutually exclusive orders of
being, yet Christ participated in them all. He belongs to more
than one order, for he is "truly of the line of David according
to the flesh, but Son of God by the divine will and power"
(*Smyr.* 1.1). He manifests himself in ways that to the uninitiated
seem completely contradictory, for he is the "Invisible who
became visible for our sake . . . the one beyond suffering who
suffered . . ." (*Poly.* 3.2).

That it is precisely the paradoxical god-manhood that Ignatius wishes to emphasize becomes clearer as one recognizes that
neither side of the paradox is emphasized at the expense of the
other. Comparison of passages makes it clear that Ignatius pours

1. The phrase γεννητὸς καὶ ἀγέννητος has a difficult textual history. It is
supported by G and probably underlies Theodoret's reading. See the *ex-
cursus* of Lightfoot, *Apostolic Fathers*, 2, 90–94. In the context Ignatius is
clearly suggesting another contrast between the historical life and the divine life which was ἐν ἀρχή. To say that Christ was ἀγέννητος does not mean
that he was uncreated.

2. 'Εν ἀνθρώπῳ θεός is justified by patristic references from Athanasius on.
GL read ἐν σαρκὶ γενόμενος θεός and Zahn, Bauer, Hilgenfeld, and Funk accept them; Lightfoot assigns priority to the patristic evidence. See the
latter, *ad loc.* Both readings affirm incarnation.

forth his affirmations without respect to order. In the passage from *Eph.* 7 quoted above the historical characteristic usually leads in the parallels. The statement that he was *first* suffering and *then* beyond suffering might naturally be understood to emphasize the order in time of the experiences. One could even conclude from such a statement that Ignatius held that Christ became God only at the resurrection. But in the rhythmical passage in the letter to Polycarp (3.2), the qualities are reversed in order, so that characteristics which belong to him as deity—he is invisible, impalpable, impassible—precede those belonging to him as man. It is clear that in neither case is the order significant, for it is the unity of deity and humanity that Ignatius is concerned to affirm. The unity is so unshakable that it makes no difference whether it is approached from the human or from the divine side. Jesus Christ is God in Man.

This is proclaiming in dramatic terms the reality of the incarnation. It is not explaining in a doctrinal sense how it could be, nor does Ignatius anywhere in the letters raise the question why it is so important. But clearly he holds that had Christ been God only, there would have been no incarnation; had he been man only, he would not have differed either in power or nature from other men. Were he God only he would have lacked that representative character which made it possible for men to participate in his experience of suffering and so also in the experience of resurrection. Were he only man, he could not have been the revelation of God and the source of life for the churches. It is because the churches believed that he was *both* God and man that they could have hope in him. Ignatius never develops in this sort of argument his ideas on the incarnation, but we must suppose that such apperceptions lie behind the rhythmical passages which declare the incarnation, and may well have been expressed in his preaching.

Since the very idea of incarnation is paradoxical, it is peculiarly difficult to discuss it satisfactorily. Inevitably some parts of Ignatius' thinking about it belong more closely to the divine existence of Christ, and other parts develop the meaning of the human life. It is necessary to separate them for purposes of examination, even at the risk of weakening our recognition

that in Ignatius' mind they could no more be separated than
the obverse and the reverse of a coin. But the consideration of
the human life as a divine event, the revelation of the Father,
and the central act in the redemption of the world, will be post-
poned to the next two chapters, while here we concern ourselves with Ignatius' beliefs about the life in its human setting.

As we saw in the last chapter, the Docetists viewed the life
of Jesus Christ as differing from ordinary humanity in being
spiritual and not incarnate (although still "real"). To Ignatius
such an interpretation suggests *unreality,* and against it he insists on the importance of historical facts. The word "historical"
is foreign to him, but the central meaning conveyed by it is not.
The historical event to which the church bears witness is utterly
real; it happened. He knows no other way of saying this than
by insisting on its reality, its truth. He underlines the time of
the persecution and the crucifixion (*Mag.* 11.1, *Smyr.* 1.2, *Tral.*
9.1) in three of the letters. It is not too much to say that he
dates them. He makes it clear that there were witnesses to the
crucifixion (*Tral.* 9.1). There is a concreteness of detail about
this which is striking. The fundamental character of the emphasis on history appears both in the frankly antidocetic passages
in which the reality of the incarnation is affirmed and in the
many scattered references to the events of the life of Christ. Both
will be worth examining in some detail.

We saw in the last chapter that both Ignatius and presumably the church knew the gospel of Matthew, and so knew at
least the tradition contained in it. But access to facts is not the
same thing as interest or emphasis. A list of passages demonstrates the extent of Ignatius' interest in the historical life, and
underlines the events that seem most important to him:

1. Genealogy. He was of the seed, or of the family: of David— *Eph.* 18.2,
20.2; *Tral.* 9.1; *Rom.* 7.3; *Smyr.* 1.1; of Mary— *Eph.* 7.2, 18.2; *Tral.* 9.1
(of the family of David and of Mary); [of God—*Eph.* 7.2; and the Holy
Spirit, *Eph.* 18.2]

2. Birth
   a. Born of the Virgin: *Smyr.* 1.1, *Eph.* 19.1. The virginity of Mary and
   the birth are two of the three mysteries— *Eph.* 19.1
   b. Development of a star story: *Eph.* 19.1

3. Baptism
  a. By John: *Smyr.* 1.1
  b. Purpose: (1) that all righteousness might be fulfilled— *Smyr.* 1.1
       (2) to cleanse water— *Eph.* 18.2

4. Anointed on the head. Purpose: that he might breathe immortality on the church— *Eph.* 17.1

5. Persecuted under Pontius Pilate: *Tral.* 9.1

6. Suffered and died on the cross
  a. In the procuratorship of Pontius Pilate: *Mag.* 11.1, *Smyr.* 1.2; and in the reign of Herod the Tetrarch, *Smyr.* 1.2
  b. References to his death, passion, and suffering: *Mag.* 5.2; *Tral.* Ins.; *Phld.* 3.3, 8.2; *Smyr.* 1.2, 12.2
  c. The cross the effective means of resurrection for men: *Eph.* 9.1
  d. Suffered for our sins: *Smyr.* 7.1.; for our sake, *Tral.* 2.1, *Rom.* 6.1; that we might attain salvation, *Smyr.* 2.1
  e. His passion our resurrection: *Smyr.* 5.3
  f. The cross (or the resurrection?) an ensign to attract all nations: *Smyr.* 1.2, cf. *Tral.* 11.2.

7. Rose from the dead
  a. General references to the resurrection: *Eph.* 20.1; *Mag.* 11.1; *Phld.* 8.2, 9.2; *Smyr.* 12.2
  b. Truly raised by the Father: *Tral.* 9.2; truly raised himself, *Smyr.* 2.1, cf. Gal. 1:1
  c. On the Lord's day: *Mag.* 9.1
  d. Resurrection (or cross?—see above) an ensign to attract the nations: *Smyr.* 1.2
  e. His resurrection appearances were in the flesh: *Smyr.* 3.2,3, 7.1
  f. Experienced as incarnate by Peter and others; ate and drank: *Smyr.* 3.2,3

8. Raised the prophets: *Mag.* 9.2

9. Apostles subject to him: *Mag.* 13.2

10. Teacher, Lawgiver, Physician
  a. Teacher: *Eph.* 15.1; *Mag.* 9.1,2, 10.1; His word equivalent to an act— *Eph.* 15.1
  b. Gave ordinances (δόγμα): *Mag.* 13.1. Commandments (ἐντολή)— *Eph.* 9.2, *Mag.* 4.1, *Rom.* Ins., *Phld.* 1.2. Law— (νόμος) *Mag.* 2.1
  c. Physician: *Eph.* 7.2

There are a few other possible echoes of the Matthean or general preaching tradition about the historical figure of Jesus Christ that can be cited very briefly. There is perhaps a sug-

gestion of the parable of the evil one who sowed tares among
the wheat (Matt. 13:24–30, 36–43) when Ignatius praises the
Ephesian church because they did not suffer those who have
evil doctrine to sow it among them—although this would not
be an uncommon metaphor (*Eph.* 9.1). In a list of the needy
for whom the teachers of strange opinions have no care there
is a haunting reminiscence of the hungry and thirsty, and the
prisoners in the parable of the last judgment who accuse the
man who was above common charity (*Smyr.* 6.2; Matt. 25:31–
46). The οἰκοδεσπότης who finally sends his own son to take care
of the vineyard seems to be in the mind of Ignatius when he
writes that "Everyone whom the master of the house sends to
be in charge of his household we ought to receive as him who
sent him. Therefore it is clear that we must look on the bishop
as the Lord himself" (*Eph.* 6.1, Matt. 21:33 ff.). There is no
certainty that these parables in the Matthean form were influ-
encing Ignatius as he wrote, but it seems probable, although it
is also true that he might have known them independently of
a written gospel.[3]

However, it is not his possession of the tradition but the use
that he makes of it that is most interesting. As we have seen
above, polemic against the Docetists is prominent. Ignatius goes
out of his way to assert in defiant terms—certainly in terms
offensive to the Docetists—that the Lord was "clothed in flesh,"
a σαρκοφόρον (*Smyr.* 5.2). To doubt this is, he says, to deny the
whole gospel:

> Be hard of hearing, therefore, whenever anyone speaks to
> you ignoring Jesus Christ, born of the line of David, and of
> Mary, and truly born, who ate and drank, truly suffered
> under Pontius Pilate, was truly crucified and died as the
> denizens of heaven, earth, and the underworld saw; who
> was also truly raised from the dead . . .   [*Tral.* 9.1–2]

Elsewhere Ignatius adds that he was "truly nailed in the flesh,
under Pontius Pilate and Herod the Tetrarch" (*Smyr.* 1.2, cf.

3. Cf. *Test. Jos.* 1.5–7 for general likeness to Matt. 25:31–46.

1.1). Schlier maintains [4] that references to the historical crucifixion play no great role; but this is difficult to grant, for they
make up in vividness what they may lack in number. These
points which Ignatius emphasizes are chosen to underline in the
most vigorous way the veritable humanity of the Lord. He was
of the royal line; his mother was known; and he was "truly"
born [5] of her, being like all men so much a creature of flesh
that he was dependent on food and drink. His death, likewise,
emphasized his vulnerable human nature, for his body was
"truly nailed to the cross" (*Smyr.* 1.2), and the time of his crucifixion could be dated. These are the most striking of the direct
affirmations of the real humanity of Jesus Christ, but throughout the letters the same points are made in other ways, frequently by general references to the flesh and blood of Christ
(e.g. *Smyr.* 1.1, 6.1). To prove his point, Ignatius not only uses
the tradition that we know in Matthew but quotes approvingly
from an unknown gospel source, possibly the *Teaching of
Peter:* [6]

> As for me, I know and believe that even after the resur-
> rection he was in the flesh. And when he came to them who
> were with Peter he said to them, "Take hold, feel of me
> and see that I am not a bodiless spirit." [7] And at once they
> touched him and believed, being joined to (κραθέντες) his
> flesh and spirit . . . And after the resurrection he ate and
> drank with them as one in the flesh . . .   [*Smyr.* 3.2]

It is possible that we have here a statement of Ignatius' memory
of the oral tradition. But although he may have embroidered
the tradition with imaginative touches, it is other than what

4. Schlier, *Relig. Untersuch.*, pp. 67 f.

5. This probably implies that the Docetists taught that the birth was
only in appearance. See, e.g., *Ascension of Isaiah* 11.8 ff.

6. Origen, *De principiis*, praef. 8, thought it came from the *Teaching
of Peter.* Jerome assigns it to the *Gospel to the Hebrews.*

7. See the article on δαίμων by Foerster in G. Kittel, ed., *Theologisches
Wörterbuch zum Neuen Testament.* Here the meaning is not the more
usual spirit that possesses, or a demon, but an insubstantial being. Matt.
11:18 and Luke 7:33 use the word similarly of the charge against John
the Baptist. Luke in a post-resurrection passage (24:39) uses πνεῦμα.

can be found in Matthew, or for that matter any of the canonical gospels. Whatever the source of his reference, he uses it to emphasize the veritable life, death, and fleshly resurrection of the Lord.

Ignatius was interested not in reminding the churches of the separate facts they already knew, which were accessible in the preaching, but in using the facts to show that the life had been lived in a full sense on the scene of history. Prominent though the antidocetic theme is, it is not the only one. Ignatius is eager to relate the historical life to the events of the past and future. Thus he emphasizes the notion that the life of the Lord fulfilled the teaching of the prophets.[8] This is no doubt partly traditional Christian preaching and partly polemic against the Essene-Christians for whom the prophets were final authorities, but it is connected with other aspects of his thought, and it is one way of declaring that the incarnation occurred in a human context. And he looks on into the future in connecting the events of the life of the Lord with the church.

The grounding of traditional events in the life of Christ on texts in the Old Testament was an important part of the Christian *kerygma* from the earliest days, and it would be remarkable if some evidence of that concern had not appeared in the Ignatian letters. We find in the first place the idea that "the beloved prophets announced him" (*Phld.* 9.2). This is a general statement that Christ fulfilled prophecy. One of the relatively few concrete examples of fulfillment is probably to be seen in the passages referring to the Davidic descent, which *could* be considered antidocetic but are much more likely to have been part of the familiar stock of preaching that emphasized reliance on the Old Testament. In one passage the prophetic and the antidocetic join in an assertion that Christ was "born of the line of David and of Mary" (*Tral.* 9.1). Probably the descrip-

8. See C. H. Dodd, *Apostolic Preaching*, 2d ed. New York, 1944. It is significant that Matthew emphasizes the theme of the fulfillment of prophecy more than does Mark or Luke. Like Ignatius, Matthew presents Jesus as foretold by prophets but superior to Judaism. Cf. K. W. Clark, "The Gentile Bias in Matthew," *JBL, 66* (1947), 166 ff.

tion of the cross as an "ensign for the nations" (*Smyr.* 1.2) [9] should also be understood as a prophetic witness.

But in other respects his statements about the prophets are not to affirm that prophecy has been fulfilled. For the prophets are described as themselves living by anticipation according to the Lord (*Mag.* 8.2). What was important was not primarily that to them was entrusted revelation of his life but that their lives were oriented to, and received meaning from, this crucial event still in the future. They were his disciples in the Spirit (*Mag.* 9.2). Through his grace [10] they were able to endure persecution, in order to "convince the unpersuaded" (*Mag.* 8.2). They "expected him as their teacher; and he whom they rightly waited for, at his coming raised them from the dead" (*Mag.* 9.2). They are even said by Ignatius to have preached the gospel (*Phld.* 5.2), although this is hyperbole and he later contrasts the prophetic announcement of Christ with the gospel itself (*Phld.* 9.2). Lake [11] believes that Ignatius probably has Christian prophets in mind; but since the reference later in the same letter (*Phld.* 9.2) is almost surely to the Hebrew prophets, it seems better to assume that here, too, he intends to refer to them. What is chiefly important about the prophets, then, is that by anticipation they lived by the grace of Christ. It is an idea not unlike Paul's interpretation of Abraham as living by faith.

Not only was the incarnate life of the Lord the completion of past events that were related to him in complex ways, but it was instrumental in preparing the future, for Ignatius declares that the Lord acted to endow the church. He never directly says that Christ founded the church, although he assumes it, and in this respect agrees with the gospel of Matthew. But what interests Ignatius, as contrasted with Matthew—or at least what he comments on—are not only the specific commands of of the Lord, but his sacramental acts. Twice he interprets acts of Christ's life as performed in order to empower the church.

9. Cf. Is. 5:26; 11:10, 12; 18:3; 49:22; 62:10.
10. Cf. *Barn.* 5.6, which is similar.
11. In a note *ad loc. Phld.* 5.1.

Thus, although once he says that Christ was baptized in order that all righteousness might be fulfilled (*Smyr.* 1.1), which is a quotation from Matthew, the other reference to the baptism is of a very different sort. Christ, says Ignatius, accepted baptism that by experiencing it himself he might purify—and, one must understand, make efficacious—the means of baptism: "He was born, and was baptized, that by experiencing it he might purify the water" (*Eph.* 18.2). Interpreters differ on whether baptism as a rite in the church is connected with the passion of the Lord or with his acceptance of baptism for himself,[12] and certainly both meanings are possible. But according to either interpretation the act of Christ "purifies water," and hence has a central sacramental significance for the church.

Similarly, in the unique exegesis which Ignatius offers for the anointing he expresses his conviction that like baptism it empowers the church. He says that the Lord received the ointment on his head in order that he might "breathe incorruption on the church" (*Eph.* 17.1), and here, as we shall see later, it seems likely that Ignatius has in mind the oil chrism connected with baptism in the later Syrian church.[13] We may infer from this passage that the custom goes back to Ignatius' time. There is no comparable reference to the establishment of the eucharist, and a discussion of the theology bound up with it follows in Chapter 7, but it is difficult not to believe that Ignatius held a similar view about it. He thought of the Lord as preparing for the church of the future by giving it sacramental power. He initiated the sacraments and endowed them.

Neither of these interpretations of the sacramental acts stands in Matthew, nor elsewhere in the gospel tradition as we know it, but they display a concern for sacraments that is characteristic of the Fourth Gospel and has great significance for Ignatius. They form a link between the events of the human life

12. The passage is ambiguous; . . . ἐβαπτίσθη ἵνα τῷ πάθει τὸ ὕδωρ καθαρίσῃ. Whether τῷ πάθει refers to the Passion (see Lightfoot, Lelong, Bauer, etc.), which is its usual meaning in the letters, or to the experiencing of baptism (so Lake *ad loc.*), which in the context seems more probable, in either case the event is of importance for the church.

13. Cf. below, pp. 206 f.

of the Lord and the power of the continuing church. The institution of the church becomes the means of handing on to its worshipers the divine life, and in this way present history is redeemed. The event of the incarnation thus fulfills the prophecy of past history and at least in part redeems it as well as the future; so that, as Ignatius sees it, the coming of Christ is no event on another plane—an event primarily cosmic in its elements, as the Docetists would have it—but warp and woof of life in this world. He offers no theory of the relation between the incarnation and the more obviously "secular" events of life; he was too fully possessed by the Hebrew-Christian view to raise the question. But he holds stubbornly to the idea that at least some historical events are to be taken seriously as the work of God.[14] The incarnation is real, and of transcendent importance, and unique. Above all, it took place on the human scene and penetrated deeply into it.

It may be asked whether we have not been overstating the significance of Ignatius' emphasis on the true humanity as implying a particularly vivid sense of the reality of history. After all, it may be said, Paul also emphasized the relation of the Lord to the acts of God reported in the Old Testament, and he came close to stating as unequivocal a doctrine of the incarnation as Ignatius did. He declares that Christ was "born of the seed of David according to the flesh" and was "declared to be the Son of God with power . . . by the resurrection from the dead" (N.T. Rom. 1:3 f.). And the letter to the Philippians goes farther. "Existing in the form of God . . . he emptied himself . . . being made in the likeness of man; and being found in fashion as a man he humbled himself, becoming obedient even unto death . . ." (Phil. 2:6–8). In other words, he was man, and at the same time uniquely related to God in

14. Those who interpret Ignatius as strongly gnostic deny any *Heilsgeschichte* in him. Schlier, *Relig. Untersuch.*, p. 64, holds that even the prophets spread gnosis. Bartsch, *GG*, pp. 42 ff., on the basis of the contrast between priests and High Priest in *Phld.* 9.1, holds that Ignatius has destroyed the continuity necessary for *Heilsgeschichte*, and that the unity between the prophets and Jesus Christ ultimately is derived from the notion of the unity of God and is a proof that Ignatius has not understood the tradition of the community (p. 43).

such a way that the category of humanity is not adequate to carry all that is true about him, even if Paul does not, like Ignatius, apply to Christ the words θεός and ὁ θεός. But in the situation Paul faced what needed clarification in the churches was that Christ was more than man. Thus he emphasizes in these passages that Christ was *the son of God with power* and deliberately abased himself in becoming man. In neither case is the simple fact of the incarnation the point at issue. One can say that the real humanity was everywhere taken for granted, which is of course true; but it is precisely for this reason that Paul does not become fully aware of the need to place limits on the mythological-theological interpretation of Christ.

The Johannine writings and the *Odes of Solomon,* on the other hand, emerge from a situation very similar to that suggested in the Ignatian letters. In all we find an emphasis on the incarnation, but Ignatius shows a sharper awareness than the others of the danger of docetic thought. The *Odes* are most lacking in awareness, for—clearly Christian as they are—their christology is naively docetic and could be read with satisfaction by those who despised matter. A quotation from Ode 7 will show their characteristic ambiguity of expression:

He became like me that I might receive Him.
In similitude was He reckoned like me, that I might put
    Him on . . .
Like my nature He became, that I might learn Him
And like my form, that I might not turn back from Him.
[4, 6]

To be "like" man in form and nature does not necessarily mean the same thing as becoming flesh, although the writer may have had in mind a full incarnation.

The Fourth Gospel does not fall into the docetic error, but in spite of the fact that it sets out to relate the story of the life of Christ it does not challenge the Docetists. It lacks the birth story, the temptation, the agony in the garden, the transfiguration (perhaps because the divine glory is always apparent), and the agony on the cross. The cry of thirst is explained as a fulfillment of prophecy. The Christ moves serenely through his earthly life, having upon him all the marks of the divine: perfect knowledge of the future, command over the material world, the ultimate power to turn back death itself. With the marks of divinity in the Gospel, Ignatius would have no difficulty. But the parallel marks of humanity are lacking. Even the prologue does not state the fact of the incarnation as sharply as Ignatius does. To be sure "the Word was with God, and the Word was God [or was divine in nature] . . . and the Word became flesh" (John 1:1,14). But although the incarnation is the climax of the prologue, it is only by bringing together the first and much later verses that the full force of the paradox is felt. The Ignatian letters are, of course, in no way comparable to the superb creation of the Gospel, but it is nevertheless true that Ignatius was more acutely aware of the need to emphasize historical events against the Docetists' challenge than was the Fourth Evangelist.[15]

To say this is not to affirm special genius on Ignatius' part in his preaching that Christ was both man and more than man. The Fourth Gospel and the first Johannine epistle were trying to say just that, as was Paul years earlier. But Ignatius, facing the situation in the church in Antioch, stood at the precise moment when a clear-cut doctrine of the paradoxical nature of the incarnation was the most effective way of affirming the facts of God's actions in history, and also was able by good fortune or insight to achieve a sound balance between emphasis on the divine ground and the human expression. He was faced by some who denied or ignored history, and by others who foreshortened history by resisting the genuinely new that could enter it. His docetic opponents held no less vigorously than he the belief that in the life of Jesus divine forces were at work. But their hold on the real humanity was not merely precarious—it was lacking altogether; and as a result they neither could nor wished to relate the Christian church to the previous acts of God in his long self-revelation to the Hebrew people. Ignatius' Essene-

15. Bultmann, *Theology*, 2, 8 ff., discusses the lack of the *heilsgeschichtliche* perspective in John.

Christian opponents, on the other hand, appear to have fore-shortened history by interpreting Jesus Christ in a rather limited sense as teacher. They found it hard to accept the crucial relevance of the death and resurrection, perhaps because they were unwilling to ask the questions about cosmic meaning that might put in jeopardy the secure gains of the scriptures. And considering the uncertain ground on which the Docetists moved, one cannot wholly blame them. The position that emerged owed much to both. Although it cannot, of course, be maintained that Ignatius developed his theology by the simple kind of rationalistic argument we have suggested above, something like these notions must have moved him.

As we said above, there is an inevitable difficulty in examining so paradoxical a notion as incarnation, for rational analysis of its parts tends to dissolve their relationship. An additional problem of method arises from the fact that some events of the incarnate life are more important than others. Logically one might expect at this point a full discussion of the meaning of the truly crucial events of the incarnate life, the crucifixion and resurrection. But they, as part of the three mysteries that effected salvation, are more appropriately considered when we examine the whole complex of ideas by which Ignatius affirms the nature of the saving work of Christ. Here we have been concerned with Ignatius' emphasis on the fact of the "real" and "true" life of the Lord.

Before we leave his interpretation of the life of the Lord we must examine the general descriptive terms he uses. These do not point directly to particular events but are rather reflective comments on the life as a whole. They are something less than titles, and other than names. Those which might have been influenced by either the Matthean or the oral tradition are Teacher, Physician, Lawgiver, Son of Man (once only), and of course Kyrios (passim) and Christos. Others which belong with these but which do not stem from the gospel tradition are New Man and Perfect Man. Of these, the more traditional words are least controversial, because they raise fewer problems of connotation.

Three times Ignatius calls Jesus Teacher [16] (*Mag.* 9.1, 2; *Eph.* 15.1), but the idea has greater significance for him than the number of direct references would imply. His remarks are highly allusive, and it is difficult to be sure that one comprehends everything they suggest, although they start on a modest plane. Jesus Christ is in the first instance "our only Teacher," and for the same reason the Teacher of the prophets (*Mag.* 9.1, 2). This title, as we maintained in Chapter 3, is probably used initially to press the claims of Christ as against the Teacher of Righteousness of the Essene-Christians, but we may surmise that it perhaps also emphasizes the historical and ethical work of Christ in contrast to the cosmic role which the Docetists favored. Ignatius quite clearly holds that specific teachings are important. He places high value on truly possessing "the word of Jesus" (*Eph.* 15.2), and here one can only understand the concrete spoken word carried in the tradition, for the passage contrasts it with silence. It seems to mean what it meant for Paul. In some sense the historical Teacher in Galilee and Judaea is present to his mind.

But this is only the beginning of his thought. Christ, he says, is a teacher unlike most, since there is no contrast at all between his profession and his actions. "Teaching is good if one practises what he preaches" (ibid.), and this correspondence between profession and action is supremely true of the One Teacher. He has an absolute clarity and a complete lack of any hypocrisy. But it is not only the integrity of the teacher that distinguishes him, but his unique power. "He spoke and it came to pass"; [17] at these words to the minds of both the writer and the hearers of the letter must have occurred the image of the mighty acts of creation: "And God said . . . and it was so." It is precisely because the words of Jesus are in a sense mighty acts that they must be seen in the largest perspective. He who has a word of Jesus for his possession can also "hear his silence,"

16. Cf. the article by Rengstorf on διδάσκειν, διδάσκαλος in Kittel's *Theologisches Wörterbuch*. The religious importance of the notion of the teacher is widespread. Cf. the discussion of the Teacher of Righteousness, above, pp. 59, 63.

17. Ps. 33:9.

or his reserve: "Even what he has done in silence is worthy of the Father" (*Eph.* 15). His teaching, then, is communicated both by word and by act; in this sense the death and resurrection of the Lord become parts of his teaching. It is in their suffering that Ignatius hopes the Christians may be found the disciples of their master.

We are justified in discerning in these pregnant phrases an emphasis on the many-sided uniqueness of Jesus in his role as teacher, but there is still another implication in this passage in the letter to the Ephesian church. The *silence* of the Lord, and its comprehensibility to the one who truly possesses his word, suggests a kind of protest against too literal a dependence on the words, important as they are.[18] Christ is to be understood by his followers not merely in the important but restricted sense of knowing his spoken teachings, but by comprehending the eternal significance of his life. It is an idea only half explicated, but it is surely what Ignatius implies as he passes quickly from one idea to another. We see here an interest closely akin to the mood of the Fourth Gospel. Even though Ignatius must almost surely have heard men talk who had known the Lord in his historical life, and even though he knew well the gospel of Matthew, the Teacher who spoke the words of the Sermon on the Mount is less in his mind than the one whose words are indeed mighty acts significant in both history and eternity. The teaching has this deeper implication because it is the act of the incarnate Lord.

Ignatius never directly calls Christ Lawgiver, although references to that function are more numerous than references to him as Teacher. They are numerous enough so that the omission of the direct title can only be considered an accident. Perhaps the reason for the omission is that no single word is employed by Ignatius to express the giving of authoritative commandments; ἐντολή occurs six times in the letters,[19] but νόμος [20]

18. Lightfoot, *Apostolic Fathers, ad loc.,* sees in this a reference to the modesty and reticence of Jesus, to the "Messianic secret," and so on. Surely it does not mean this; such an interpretation belongs to the historical bias of liberalism.

19. *Eph.* 9.2, *Mag.* 4.1, *Tral.* 13.2, *Rom.* Ins., *Phld.* 1.2, *Smyr.* 8.1.

20. *Mag.* 2.1.

and δόγμα,[21] occurring once each, seem to be used as equivalents. In two of the passages it is not said explicitly that it is Jesus Christ who gives the commandments, but it is made so clear in the others that we may probably take it for granted that the unqualified references assume that he is either the author or the guarantor of the authority of the commandments. Our problem is to discover what content these words had for Ignatius. There is no slightest suggestion that the Ten Commandments are in his mind, though in two passages something quite as definite seems to be suggested. Once he urges the holding of meetings "valid according to the commandment" (*Mag.* 4.1). We can no longer identify this particular commandment, although it is possible that reference is made to the "command" of Matt. 18:17: "And if he refuse to hear them tell it unto the church." A formal meeting is certainly suggested. Although we may consider this clearly a development of early church practice and not a word of Jesus, Ignatius would not have so considered it. Perhaps even if he had, this recognition would not have bothered him, since he speaks (*Mag.* 13.1) of the "ordinances of the Lord and the apostles." All require submission, and the problem is not one of judging between competing authorities, for the subordinate authorities themselves submit to the final one.

In one passage we infer that Ignatius thought of Jesus Christ as giving the two commandments as we find them stated in Matthew.[22] Immediately after a direct reference to the "commandments of Jesus Christ" (*Eph.* 9.2), he goes on to say that he is glad that they "love nothing according to the standards of men but God alone." [23] This is certainly reminiscent of the "first" commandment and the first part of the Shema. But since Ignatius is quite careless as to whether he speaks of the "commandment" or the "commandments," one cannot be sure whether he thought in clear-cut terms of Jesus' summary of the Law as two commandments, or in general terms of the "law of Jesus Christ" (*Mag.* 2.1), as one of the ultimate bases of au-

21. *Mag.* 13.1.
22. Matt. 22:34–40.
23. Here following Lightfoot's emendation, based on g as against GL.

thority. He seems to think of it as fundamental and definite, and one may suppose that in being Lawgiver as well as Teacher Christ is superior to the Teacher of Righteousness. The church is to be "subject to the bishop as to the grace of God and to the presbytery as to the law of Jesus Christ." His authority guarantees that of the ministry functioning for the church.

It is interesting to observe certain agreements between the gospel and Ignatius' thought. They represent a similar emphasis on Jesus Christ as the ultimate completion of the message of Judaism. "You have heard that it was said to them of old time . . . but I say unto you . . ." "Think not that I came to destroy the law or the prophets; I came not to destroy but to fulfil" (Matt. 5:21 f., 5:17). It is in Matthew that the two commandments are uniquely described as the "whole law and the prophets" (22:34–40), whereas in Mark that phrase is lacking and in Luke the two commandments are not spoken by Jesus himself.[24] Matthew and the Ignatian letters supplement each other in suggesting aspects of Antiochene theology, at least of the middle party.

It is reasonable to suppose that the gospel came into existence in Antioch in earlier years, influenced by some of the same circumstances that faced Ignatius and the need to demonstrate to Jews and to Essene-Christians that the teachings of Jesus, grouped as we find them in the Sermon on the Mount, constituted a new law which took the place of Torah. The gospel does not presuppose Essene-Christian influences alone, and Pharisaic-Christians might also have defined the issues, but the writer of the gospel was convinced that the claims of Christianity, although in certain ways similar were superior to the beliefs of Judaism. In the gospel of Matthew the Essene-Christian or more widely Jewish party had perhaps won on a central matter: Jesus' teachings are in an important sense of the same kind as that which they displaced. They are "commandments," "law."

But lest we be misled by the idea of an ultimate authority and consider it a straightjacket for the early church, it is important to observe that for Ignatius this is not its effect. It oper-

24. Cf. Mark 12:28 ff., Luke 10:25.

ates in a church still open to the spirit. The commandments of
Jesus Christ are to be celebrated as grounds for thanksgiving
and gratitude. They are strengthening, not repressive. In a vivid
description he speaks of the members of the churches as taking
part in a sacred procession, "bearing God and the shrine, Christ
and the holy things, being arrayed from head to foot in the
commandments of Jesus Christ" (*Eph.* 9.2). This suggests a
scene of joy and ecstasy. Again, he speaks of the bishop as "in
accord with the commandments as a harp is with its strings"
(*Phld.* 1.2). The figure does not come through with complete
success, but it connotes inner harmony and sureness of performance. And again he rejoices with the Roman church because they are "united in flesh and spirit with every one of
his commandments" (*Rom.* Ins.). This, too, suggests that their
lives are permeated by the spirit of the commandments, which
in this case becomes almost a synonym for the spirit of the
Lord himself.[25] And since Ignatius held that Jesus Christ was
a teacher whose acts and preaching were in no way at variance
with each other, to be "united in the commandments" would
mean to be dominated by his spirit. As the author of the commandments, in other words, Christ is thought of not merely as
the one who gave specific and concrete direction, moral and
institutional, to his followers, but much more truly as the center
of life, and hence the authority, for his church.

Once Jesus is spoken of as the Physician [26] (*Eph.* 7.2), a term
which recalls the healing activity and which is quite specifically
used to describe him in the synoptics (Matt. 9:12). In the letters
it stands both as the introductory term in the lyrical description
—which is antidocetic in its motive but much more than that
in its effect—and as the closing phrase in a bitter reminiscence
of the false teachers:

> For some make a practice of carrying about
> the Name with evil craftiness . . . you must

25. A similar view is expressed in Johannine circles; see esp. I John
1:3, 3:24.

26. Cf. the article on ιατρός by Oepke, in Kittel, *Theologisches Wörterbuch,* for the agreement of both nonbiblical and biblical usage that healing
arises from a divine potency.

> turn from them as wild animals, for they
> are mad dogs, biting stealthily, and you
> must guard against them, for they are hard
> to cure. There is one Physician, who is
> both flesh and spirit . . .

In the context of the passage Jesus the Physician is the only one
who can treat the churches, attacked—as by mad dogs—by the
teachers of false doctrine; so that the reference of the figure is a
very different one from that used in the gospels, where the pa-
tients are sinners in need of repentance. There seems to stand
behind this passage both the general gospel tradition of Jesus
as healer and the idea in the *Odes of Solomon* 28, where the unpersuaded Jews are described as mad dogs: [27]

> And they came round me like mad dogs;
> Who ignorantly attack their masters.
>
> For their thought is corrupt
> And their understanding perverted.   [13, 14]

As we have observed in Chapter 3, Rendel Harris argues for
the dependence of the Odist on the 22d Psalm, pointing out
that Ignatius would seem to have known Ode 28 itself, since
for him too they are mad dogs—a touch lacking from the
psalm. The notion of Christ as Physician, like the thought of
him as Teacher and as Lawgiver, is unquestionably related to
the gospel tradition, but it also has special meaning in correct-
ing the Docetists, whom Ignatius has in mind in the passage
quoted.

The other titles deriving from the earlier tradition, such
as Son of Man and Lord, do not appear in the Ignatian letters
with any peculiarity of meaning. Son of Man occurs once,
paired with Son of God (*Eph.* 20.2), and there it clearly points
to the humanity. Once Jesus is spoken of as ὁ χριστός (*Eph.* 18.2);
but since it occurs three or four sentences after the mention of
the anointing, it may well be merely the completion of that
idea. The most frequent title, "Jesus Christ," is to all intents
and purposes a proper name, as it has been from the time of

27. Harris and Mingana, *Odes, 2,* 48 f. discuss the passage.

Paul on. Like him, Ignatius sometimes reverses it and speaks of Christ Jesus, but there is no shift in meaning. And as we have said above, the title Lord is used to indicate the many-sided relation of Christ to his church. The single use (*Phld.* 9.1) of High Priest might suggest a reminiscence of Hebrews, or the *Odes*, but is more likely to have been directed toward the Essene-Christians, as we have seen above.

Two more references remain to be considered, the New Man (*Eph.* 20.1) and the Perfect Man (*Smyr.* 4.2). The question could be asked whether these two are indeed titles, and so should be capitalized, or whether they describe functions. There is some evidence to suggest that it is possible Ignatius is using gnostic titles, but as we shall see below, this is not a conclusion that can be drawn with any certainty, and on these titles even a reasonable degree of certainty is beyond reach. To say this is not to prejudge the question of his use of other terms with gnostic meaning, but merely to hold that in this case the presence of a phrase does not of itself guarantee any particular meaning.

In the Naassene document both appear, used by the Naassenes among many other terms to describe the Urmensch. The difficulties of dating a greatly worked-over text are well known, but there does not seem to have been any period when the message of the document was not the identity of a number of the redeemers celebrated in the sects at the eastern end of the Mediterranean. At some period, later than the original pagan document, a Christian editor made a final redaction, pointing out that it was Christ who perfectly fitted all the formulae. Even if for the sake of argument one accepts an early date, it is still difficult to see any connection between the Document and Ignatius' thought. Reitzenstein's identification [28] of the oldest pre-Christian stratum is in general satisfactory. Wilamowitz-Möllendorf [29] dates this pagan document in the time of Hadrian, which would put it somewhat later than the letters, but not

28. Reitzenstein and Schaeder, *Studien,* pp. 161–73. References are given below to the figure of the Anthropos in this text, although its occurrence in Hippolytus' *Refutation* is placed first.

29. *Hermes,* 37 (1902), 329. The original Attis hymn may have existed some centuries before the Naassenes used it.

necessarily much later, and it is not antecedently improbable that its terms were the property of the sect before they were incorporated in this particular document. Bousset [30] and Reitzenstein agree that the central strand is the hymn to Attis, which would presuppose Syrian origin.

In this oldest stratum one finds various descriptions of the redeemer: ὁ μέγας, καὶ κάλλιστος, καὶ τέλειος ἄνθρωπος [v.2(2)], ὁ μέγας ἄνθρωπος ἄνωθεν [ibid.], ἄνωθεν κεχαρακτηρισμένος τέλειος ἄνθρωπος [v.3(21)], ὁ ἔσω ἄνθρωπος [v.2(14)], and so on. There is "Perfect Man," clearly used, along with others, as a title. It refers however, to a representative cosmic figure, masculo-feminine, who is presented with strongly phallic symbolism in some of the syncretized mysteries.[31] He is "from above" and is closely related to the Unportrayable One. In similar fashion the phrase "new man" occurs once [32] in the Naassene document, but in a section which Reitzenstein considers part of the work of the Christian-gnostic editor and therefore later. If this is a correct analysis, the latter term might not have existed in the circles known to Ignatius.

The differences between this figure and the Christ whom Ignatius preaches are profound. Both are related to the ultimate unknown Power and both are representative Man, but in general character they are worlds apart. That there is any direct influence of the Naassene document on Ignatius, or that he knew it, seems unlikely. The differences in nature are too deep,

30. W. Bousset, *Hauptprobleme der Gnosis* (Göttingen, 1907), p. 186, in agreement with R. Reitzenstein, *Poimandres* (Leipzig, 1904), p. 99, and later, *Studien*, p. 106.

31. C. H. Kraeling, *Anthropos and Son of Man* (New York, 1927), p. 53, maintains convincingly that in the original Naassene writing the Anthropos is not manifested as a savior. Schlier, *Relig. Untersuch.*, pp. 172–74, believes that for the Naassenes this is a clear example of the redeemed redeemer, and that Ignatius similarly holds that through death he will become Christ.

32. Hippolytus, *Ref.* 5.2; see Reitzenstein's text, sec. 6 (n. 10). It occurs in conjunction with a reference to Paul's phrase, a "new creature" (II Cor. 5:17, Gal. 6:15), but the Naassene-Christian goes on to say that the new man will be hermaphroditic.

the similarities too easily explained otherwise. Ignatius may possibly have known in some other context the sort of speculation discussed here, and seen some of its terms as suggestive. He certainly did not appropriate it as the later Christian-gnostic editor did.

The reference to Christ as New Man (*Eph.* 20.1) comes in the context of the difficult chapter 19, where he is declared to be "God appearing as man to bring in the newness of eternal life." Since his incarnation inaugurates the new dispensation in which God's power becomes newly operative, it would be wholly appropriate, even without using a technical term, to speak of him as the new man. On the other hand, it is quite possible that here an echo of gnostic terminology appears.[33] The new man, as redeemer, implements the divine purpose. Because both connotations of the word are possible, we cannot be sure of its provenance.

Although a reference to the Perfect Man also occurs only once, its context is such that the probability of its being a gnostic technical name seems slighter. Ignatius uses it as he thinks of his own martyrdom, and he cries out, "the Perfect Man himself gives me strength" (*Smyr.* 4.2). In connection with that stands another reference to martyrdom when he declares that by it he will "become a man" (*Rom.* 6.2). The only inference to be drawn from this use of man in an absolute sense is that it is manhood in its fullness or perfection that he will achieve, and this is a quite normal use of τέλειος. We must examine the term somewhat more at length in connection with Ignatius' teaching about both the general saving work of Christ and martyrdom in particular. Here we may say that so far there is no evidence either way on the matter of its gnostic provenance.

The vivid sense of the present Christ does not blot out from Ignatius' mind the memory of the historical Christ, and in particular his very real and moving suffering. This has peculiar ap-

33. Schlier, p. 88, n. 2, connects Ignatius' usage with the light redeemer who by collecting his members is reconstituted. For a discussion of this view in general see below, Chap. 6.

peal for him because his own martyrdom lies just ahead. But his memory is moved by more than the thought of the suffering. He urges the Ephesian Christians (*Eph.* 10.2,3) to act toward those with whom they differ as "imitators of the Lord." And it is "gentleness," "steadfastness," "humility," that make up the picture. "Let us try earnestly to be imitators of the Lord, and see who may be the more wronged, be the more scorned, the more despised." This seems to be something short of martyrdom, and to reflect the summary of the historical life that moved Ignatius.

We have maintained in this chapter that in order to counter the views of the Docetists, Ignatius chose to underline what we can only describe as "history." There is a real danger in applying a modern conception to a man who had no word for it, and many of the connotations the word has for us would be, we must suppose, baffling to Ignatius and his contemporaries. But in other respects we believe he would have found it useful. When he says that the birth, the suffering, the crucifixion "truly" happened, he is trying to affirm the fact that they occurred on the ordinary scene of human life—are what we would call historical events. If we had any reason for believing he knew a creed, we might admit that reference to the crucifixion under Pontius Pilate is a creedal phrase; but when he goes on to add "and in the reign of Herod the Tetrarch" we must conclude that he does this to offer more evidence of the inescapable reality of the fact.

The relation of Christ to the Hebrew prophets is another example of the same general concern. Ignatius believes that Christ fulfilled their prophecies. But this very generally held notion does not interest him so much as the idea that they lived by anticipation by his grace. Christ gave meaning to past events as well as to the future—because the incarnation was of this world. His life is related to the significant core of the history of the Hebrew people in their involvement with God.

But if we should be understood as affirming by this use of "history" that only events in this world are important for Ignatius or that they are basically like other human events, it would be a serious misunderstanding. Even the truly crucial event of the incarnate life of the Lord, his death, is a "mystery." God is acting in time, as man, but it is nevertheless the divine one who acts. And for this reason history alone is not a category that could explain the incarnation, which can be stated only as a paradox.

5. The Divine Event: Revelation

THE INTENSITY with which Ignatius preached the incarnation arises not only from his convictions that Essene-Christians and Docetists were in different respects mistaken, but also from his desire to confirm the faith of a great middle group. Polemical and theological interests were intermingled. Because it was true incarnation, neither the conception of the Lord as a mere Teacher nor as the one whose life was spiritual, not carnal, could be countenanced. But the very idea of incarnation posed problems with a new insistence: fresh ways had to be found of understanding the relation between Christ and the Father, and the nature of the work of Christ. Ignatius stood near the beginning of the search that the church took more than two centuries to complete, but the affirmations he makes about the Father and Christ and their relation to one another show that some of the questions were in his mind which troubled his successors. Why should God become man? What *is* God in his nature? These are deceptively simple but not naive questions that must have been voiced by his contemporaries.

It would be a mistake to suggest that Ignatius approached the tasks of Christian theology in a logical and rationalistic way, but that he had some awareness of the force of these questions we shall see by observing two opposite but complementary tendencies in his thought. On the one hand the independent activity of God, thought of in the early tradition as Father, is clearly reduced. It cannot be said to have disappeared, but it is apparent that it is less central. On the other hand Ignatius introduces and makes explicit the notion of the *reserve* of deity. As we read the letters for examples of these trends, we shall see how profoundly they affected the theology.

At first sight the doctrine of Ignatius about the Father appears to be conventional, if one means that it agrees with earlier Christian thinking. The inscriptions of the letters offer the best example of this side of Ignatius' thought. In all of them the greetings are almost self-consciously in the name of the Father and of Jesus Christ. This is no doubt in part an imitation of Paul's usage, but Ignatius goes almost beyond Paul in proclaiming the power and the glory of God. The letter to the Romans is inscribed to "the church that has received mercy in the munificence of the Most High Father and Jesus Christ his only Son, beloved and enlightened through the will of him that willed everything that exists." The Ephesian letter opens on the same note. It is addressed to "her endowed with greatness in the fullness of God the Father, the church ordained before time to live forever in glory enduring and unchanging, united and chosen in a true passion by the will of the Father and Jesus Christ our God . . ." In this passage Ignatius seems to think of the Father as both the divine source and the ultimate end. The Father's goodness is not directly proclaimed, but since what Jesus Christ had done is "worthy of the Father" (*Eph.* 15.1), the goodness is clearly implied; the Father is the standard by which even the Son is judged. The churches are "beloved of God the Father of Jesus Christ" (*Tral.* Ins.), and it is the "Father in the Highest and Jesus Christ his only Son" (*Rom.* Ins.) whose will is the sustaining force. The letters give a sense of his timelessness and eternal existence and power. All of this is wholly to be expected in Christian thinking.

But it is startling how few references there are to the Father alone. It is as the ground of Jesus Christ, who manifested and expressed him, that the Father most frequently appears. So closely are the two linked that the independent activity of the Father has largely disappeared. Jesus Christ has become the means by which the action of the Father is effected. Ignatius says that men are like two kinds of coins, one of the world, and one of God, and the faithful "bear the stamp of God the Father through Jesus Christ" (*Mag.* 5.2). Again, the Father is "faithful in Jesus Christ to answer prayer in full measure" (*Tral.* 13.3). The Magnesian church is described as "blessed by the grace of God the Father in Christ Jesus" (Ins.). Twice (*Eph.* 4.2, *Rom.* 2.2) he urges the churches to sing to the Father *in* or *through* Jesus Christ. The Father is not active in his own power or might upon the church, but Jesus Christ is the agent of that power.

There are exceptions to this kind of thought, but they are not many. Twice (*Mag.* 3.1, *Smyr.* 13.1) there is reference to "the power of the Father," but one of them is apparently prompted by Ignatius' concern to see the Father and the bishop typologically related, and the other is a conventionalized farewell. Once Ignatius expresses the pious wish that the Father of Jesus Christ may refresh Crocus, the delegate from Ephesus (*Eph.* 2.1), and the Trallian church is described as "beloved by God the Father of Jesus Christ" (Ins.). Independent activity is expressed by the statement that the Father has raised Jesus Christ from the dead, but it is difficult to see how this notion could be avoided—although Ignatius does say once that Jesus Christ raised himself (*Smyr.* 2.1, cf. 7.1; *Tral.* 9.2). It would be still more worthy of remark if there were no examples of this sort, for it is wholly characteristic of the earlier Christian writing. What is remarkable is that this kind of language is for Ignatius atypical.

The significance of the fact that it is through Jesus Christ that the activity of the Father is normally channeled becomes clearer when we remember that throughout Paul's epistles [1] and the synoptic gospels run the thought of God the Father as active, compassionate, and intent on the salvation of men.

Ignatius is passing over into a new kind of thinking, and he is forced to use a nonscriptural term to suggest the nature and the activity of God. For although nowhere does he say dogmatically, "God is unknown," it is clear that precisely that is in his mind. God is "Silence," [2] *Sigé*, and his is the hidden realm unknown to all except those to whom he discloses it. The reserve of deity is beyond human ken. This is a notion that would

---

1. The Father will save men (Rom. 8:15; II Cor. 1:21; Col. 1:12); men are dependent upon the Father (I Cor. 8:6; I Thess. 4:8); His compassion (II Cor. 1:4, 6:16; Rom. 2:4); etc.

2. GL reads λόγος ἀΐδιος οὐκ ἀπὸ σιγῆς (*Mag.* 8.2). Zahn, Lightfoot, and most modern scholars follow A and a quotation by Severus and omit ἀΐδιος. See Lightfoot, *Apostolic Fathers, ad Mag.* 8. Lightfoot, however, considers that σιγή refers to the "period before the Incarnation," so that the incarnation is the procession of the word from silence in time.

no doubt not have been denied by the writers of the Old Testament and early Christianity, but it is significant that it never comes to clear expression. There has been no need to make it explicit save as the great poems of the wisdom literature approach it in declaring that man fails to comprehend the mighty acts of God. And this still falls far short of being a comment on the nature of God:

Who is this that darkeneth counsel
By words without knowledge?
Gird up now thy loins like a man;
For I will demand of thee, and declare thou unto me.
Where wast thou when I laid the foundations of the earth?
Declare, if thou has understanding.
Who determined the measures thereof, if thou knowest?
Or who stretched the line upon it?   [Job 38:2–5]

The *Habakkuk Commentary* and the *Manual of Discipline* return often to the idea of "mysteries" of God, but in most cases these either refer, in accordance with the notions of Wisdom writing, to meditation on the mysteries of creation or, more characteristically, dwell on the mysteries of the end of time partly, but only partly, revealed to the prophets and to the Teacher of Righteousness: [3]

For from the fountain of His Knowledge He has opened my
    light,
And mine eye has beheld the wonders He has done,
And my heart is illumined with the Mystery to come.[4]
                                        [*DSD* 11.3]

Once there is a comment on the "mysteries of His understanding" in allowing wrong-doing to exist (*DSD* 4.18), and once a more general reference to the "marvellous mysteries in Eternal Being" (*DSD* 11.5). The former passage is a statement of the

3. *Hab. Com.* 7.5, 14; *DSD* 9.18.
4. Brownlee's translation in *Dead Sea Manual of Discipline, BASOR* (1951). In Appendix H he discusses the justification for using the future tense. Dupont-Sommer translates the verb in the same way in *Jewish Sect of Qumran,* p. 143.

age-old problem of theodicy, but the latter states a view which
is only a step or two before the thoughts expressed by Ignatius
and others.

The recognition can hardly be avoided that the idea of incarnation practically demands some greater insistence, like
that of Ignatius, on the incomprehensibility of God. If it were
not affirmed explicitly, there would be the possibility that the
fullness of God was exhausted in the incarnation, and a serious
problem would result for the reverent imagination. A further
result would be to drain the incarnation itself of meaning, for
the eternal would tend to be reduced to the historical factor and
so no longer be divine. Deity must always remain, inexhaustible
and mysterious, beyond any historical involvement.

Unfortunately for the historian, Ignatius did not develop this
idea, although it is plainly implied. Only in one famous passage
(*Mag.* 8.2) does he directly connect the word Silence with God.
Because it is so used only once, we must start by observing what
connotations the idea of silence has for him when it is not applied to deity, in order to judge whether its use is an important
or a trivial matter.

In the first place Ignatius would have shared with most of his
contemporaries the idea that the world of visible and tangible
things is not all of reality and that behind it there is a real
but hidden world. And for him as for all Christians it is essentially connected with God. "The priests are worthy of
course, but better is the High Priest to whom is entrusted
the holy of holies; for to him alone are entrusted the *hidden*
things of God . . ." [5] (*Phld.* 9.1). Similarly, the "invisible
things" belong to that hidden realm, and they are the content
of revelation. "As for the invisible things, pray that they may
be manifested to you; that you be left behind in nothing, but
may abound in every spiritual gift" (*Poly.* 2.2). All that is hidden is not divine, for knowledge of the angelic forces and rulers
does not make a man a disciple (*Tral.* 5.2), and the demonic
powers are also in part mysterious; nevertheless, the hidden

5. Cf. I Cor. 4:5; II Cor. 4:2, where the phrase appears with a deroga-
tory meaning. For an idea more like Ignatius' thought, Paul uses τὰ τοῦ
θεοῦ (I Cor. 2:6–16).

divine things are real and fundamental. This is a view of the cosmos that would be shared by most men of the times, and it will be discussed in detail later.

More than mystery is implied, for it is divine power that works in the revelation described in *Eph.* 19. From the silence of God welled up three mysterious events,[6] according to the divine plan. These were mysteries to the world, wrought "in the stillness [7] of God." This phrase seems clearly to suggest the reserve of the being of God, the unexplored stillness which is behind all revelation—the hidden, from which crucial events emerge clear-cut and unmistakable. What has been prepared in the counsels of God, partly known, partly unrevealed, is eternal and unexhausted.

Not only do we meet the idea of the "stillness of God," the world of "invisible things," but—more suggestive because more individual—are the connotations of silence when Ignatius considers its human expression, or as it illuminates the acts of Christ. The most important passage must be quoted, even though in the last chapter parts of it were discussed when we examined the notion of Christ as Teacher.

> It is better to be silent and be a Christian than to talk about it and not be one. Teaching is good if one practises what he preaches. For there is one teacher who spoke and it was done, and even what he has done in silence is worthy of the Father. Whoever truly possesses the word of Jesus can also hear his silence, that he may be perfect, that through his speaking he may act and through his silence be known. [*Eph.* 15.1-2]

The passage opens with the contrast between appearance and reality, or between hypocrisy and integrity, in the ethical life. But it does not go on with the exhortation to live as Christians; instead the center of thought becomes the meaning of the "silence" of the Lord. And this silence is not, as some would have it, the passive side of Jesus' life: "His retirement in child-

6. Cf. N.T. Rom. 16:25, I Cor. 2:7.

7. Here ἡσυχία. Ignatius' four words relating to silence—σιγή, σιγᾶν, σιωᾶν, ἡσυχία—seem to be used without difference of meaning.

hood and youth, his refusal to allow His miracles or His kingship to be published, His withdrawal for the purpose of prayer,
His silence before His accusers, and the like . . ."⁸ This
sounds like the analysis of the modern student of the historic
Jesus, not in the least like the interest Ignatius had in him.
For the silence is something active and positive. What Jesus has
wrought by his silence is good in the eyes of the Father. The
Christian can "hear" it only after he has mastered the speech
of the Lord.⁹ Then and only then can he pass on to the hearing
of silence, the apprehension of the inapprehensible. This is
nothing less than the knowledge of the meaning of his life,
perhaps even of his inmost being.

This ultimate knowledge carries with it perfection. It means
clarity and unity of inner being and outward living in the man
to whom that knowledge comes, "that through his speaking he
may act and through his silence be known." That man becomes
perfect as his Teacher is perfect. Unless this is language other
than that of ordinary ethical exhortation, it is difficult to understand how a recognition of the power of Jesus Christ when he
remained silent could have taken so great a hold on the im-
aginations of men that knowledge of that silence should tran-
scend in power and value the understanding of the force of his
words. Unless the idea of silence points not to the historical
silences of the Lord but to the very core of his being, it is hard
to see what Ignatius means.

Twice he refers to the silence of bishops.¹⁰ He writes to the
Ephesian church that in the short time that he had had with
their bishop there had come about an understanding that was
"not after the fashion of men, but on the spiritual plane" (*Eph.*

8. Lightfoot, *Apostolic Fathers, ad loc.*
9. Bartsch, *GG*, pp. 55 ff., 66–71, holds that προελθεῖν in *Mag.* 8.2 coupled
with the subordination of Word to Silence in *Eph.* 15.2 points to the notion of Christ not as revealer but as cult god, adored in the silence of
worship. But this is possible only by playing down the implications of
revelation of the Word-Silence paradox. See below, pp. 135 f.
10. H. Chadwick, "The Silence of Bishops in Ignatius," *HTR, 43* (1950),
170 ff., recognizes the analogy of the silence of the bishops and the fact
that God is Silence, but seems to me to press too far the notion that the
earthly church is the counterpart of the heavenly. See below, pp. 197 f.

5.1). It is of this man that he says one paragraph later, "And the more any man is aware that the bishop is silent, the more let him stand in awe of him. For everyone whom the Master of the household sends to be in charge of his household we ought to receive as him who sent him" (*Eph.* 6.1). Again he writes of the Philadelphian bishop, "And I was astounded at his reasonableness, for even silent he is able to accomplish more than those who speak idle words" (*Phld.* 1.1). This is a natural silence of which he writes. However strange it may seem that two out of the six communities to which Ignatius wrote should have found it a problem that their bishops were reserved or inarticulate men, it nevertheless was so. But Ignatius' insistence on the power and awe-inspiring quality of that silence seems to be connected with his conviction that in silence the real person resides. It is almost as though Ignatius used the silence of the bishop as an analogy of the divine silence from which Christ came forth.

It may be said that for Ignatius "silence" seems to mean roughly what in more philosophical circles would be expressed by the metaphysical term οὐσία. He never uses οὐσία, and it would clearly be foreign to his thought, for his terms come from myth not metaphysics. But silence is its equivalent. It means the real which cannot be further defined: existence *sui generis,* whether of man or God. Silence is mysterious, undifferentiated, unexplained. It is opposed to activity, expression, the explicit.

When, therefore, we find Ignatius speaking of God as Silence, we conclude that he is not using a conception of only peripheral importance. If in human silence the real meaning of the person lies, to a greater degree it must be so with God: "There is one God who revealed himself through Jesus Christ his Son, who is his Word proceeding from Silence, who in every way was pleasing to him that sent him" (*Mag.* 8.2). This is direct testimony of the God who acted to manifest himself to the world—the Silence that is broken by the Revealing Word. Silence is not an attribute of God; it is God himself.

In Ignatius' idea that God is Silence [11] and in the last analysis

11. Parallel conceptions appear in later gnosis, especially Valentinian thought, where, however, Silence is not quite the equivalent of the being of God himself but is an accompanying aion. See Irenaeus, *Adv. haer.*

the Unknown [12] we find a part of the explanation of the fact
that as Father he is represented as acting only through the
Son, though as we have seen he is the ground of the Son's being.
The name that is deep in the Christian tradition is a natural expression for Ignatius: God is Father. But since Ignatius also
thinks of him as Silence, the compassionate activity of the
Father is curtailed; he must work through the Son. This is at
least in part because Ignatius tries to express by Silence the
transcendent aspect of the Godhead. He is the Source whence
all life comes, the Reality to which all go at the last. But he is
transcendent in nature, and therefore unknown. However,
to think of God as Silence is not for Ignatius to declare that he is
finally inaccessible, for the Father "revealed" himself in the Son,
the Word came forth from Silence. Revelation is presented as
the deliberate act of God, the ultimate act of divine condescension.

1.1.1, 2.12.2; *Excerp. ex Theod.* 29. *Evangelium Veritatis,* in the Jung
Codex, ed. M. Malinine, H.-C. Puech, and G. Quispel (Zurich, Rascher,
1956), p. 37, lines 10 ff., speaks of "the Mind which pronounces the unique
Word in silent Grace," but this still seems to be a metaphor about the divine
activity, not a title for the Father. (In some of the quotations from the *Even-
gelium Veritatis* I have taken the liberty of changing the English translation
slightly, by relying on the German translation of the Coptic, in the interest
of a more idiomatic English reading.) The *Qolasta,* chap. 5 in the edition of
M. Lidzbarski, *Mandäische Liturgien* (Berlin, 1920), p. 9, says that over the
Mandaean firmament lay "Silence, Stillness, and Brilliance." It associates
light and silence with the heaven where Mana dwells (as in *Qol.* 8), but this is
something less than equating Mana and Silence. A late Mithras service
uses σιγή as Ignatius does, σιγή, σιγή, σιγή, σύμβολον θεοῦ ζῶντος ἀφθάρτου.
A. Dieterich, *Eine Mithras-liturgie* (Leipzig, 1903), p. 6, lines 21 f. *Corp.
Herm.* 1.30, ἡ σιωπή μου ἐγκύμων τοῦ ἀγαθοῦ (according to Dodd, *Fourth Gospel,* p. 12, n. 2 dated *ca.* A.D. 125–130) is close in date and idea, but obviously not identical. For a discussion of the idea of God as Silence see
G. Mensching, *Das heilige Schweigen* (Giessen 1926), pp. 149–53; *GG,* pp.
53–61; Schlier, *Relig. Untersuch.,* pp. 27, 38 f.

12. There is comparable thought in the pagan form of the Naassene
document. See *Naassenerpredigt* 8, Reitzenstein, *Studien,* p. 164—ὁ ἄρρητος,
ἀνεξεικόνιστος, ἀνεννόητος, ἄμορφος. For a discussion of Naassene teaching see
Jonas, *Gnosis, I,* 348–51. Saturnilos of Antioch preached the Unknown
God. Hippolytus, *Ref.* 7.16. E. Norden, *Agnostos Theos* (Leipzig, 1913),
pp. 24 f., summarizes the Stoic view.

The Logos in this passage is clearly the revealer, a role by no means always played by him in the contemporary thought-world. In the writings of Philo, image follows image describing him; but although it is impossible to discover a clear-cut and unvarying conception, one can say that revelation, though present, is subordinate, and the total picture is very different from that of the imperfectly described Logos of Ignatius' thought. The Philonic Logos is the most ancient "power" that stands between the Self-Existent and his world, implementing the purposes of God for creating and sustaining the universe [*Opif.* (vi)24] and giving wisdom. As the Intelligible World he serves as the model of the visible world and therefore as its "creator," in the same way that he is the "limit" [*Quis rerum* (xlii)205], or the orderer, and the "bond" or "prop" of the universe [*Plant.* (ii)8, 9]. But as the ground of the ideas individuated in the world, and of the powers of the Self-Existent One (*Som.* i (xi) 62) [13] he is the means by which God makes his will known, the means by which wisdom or thought becomes available to men. This is revelation of a sort, but it is different from revelation in Ignatius' thought, because for Philo whatever is comprehensible and rational in one sense is mediated by the Logos. All knowledge is available in this way, not simply "hidden things" or the nature of Silence itself. Knowledge of the Logos is as far as ordinary men can go in their search for God (*Conf.* (xx)97). The "friends of God," like Moses and Abraham, seem to go on to immediate knowledge, and here perhaps the Logos is by-passed [*Mig.* (xiv)76], although on this matter Philo seems not quite to have made up his mind. On the one hand God disclosed himself to Abraham "so far as the beholder's power of sight allowed" [*Abr.* (xvi)79 f.], although the passage might encourage the reader to believe that the powers of sight were very great. However, elsewhere it is said that even Abraham saw only "the manifestation of the Ruling power" [*Mut.* (iii)15]. In any ordinary case the Divine Logos is the ground of reason and

13. See E. R. Goodenough, *By Light Light* (New Haven, 1935), pp. 24 ff., for a discussion of the powers. But cf. E. Bréhier, *Les Idées philosophiques et religieuses de Philon d'Alexandrie* (2d ed. Paris, 1925), pp. 101–7.

meaning for men, and for Philo the hypostasis was not complete.[14]

For the Stoics, Logos was indwelling Reason, giving rational meaning and coherence to what would otherwise be irrational and formless stuff, and the very notion of revelation would be a contradiction. But for Ignatius that is its primary meaning, though it does not exhaust his ideas.

That Ignatius meant by Logos the Spoken Word,[15] not indwelling Reason, can be gathered from the contrast of silence and speech in a human setting. In the letter appealing to the Romans not to try to get him acquitted he says: "For otherwise I shall have no such fitting moment for attaining to God, nor will you have a better deed ascribed to you—if only you will be silent. For if you are silent about me, I am a word of God; but if you love my mortal self, once more I shall be only a meaningless cry" (*Rom.* 2).[16] This is a natural silence, that of refraining from appeal. But he is convinced that out of their silence he will go forth a "word"—a meaningful declaration of God to the world. By martyrdom his life will acquire revelatory power; short of that consummation he is only a sound. In a far more complete sense Jesus Christ as the Logos is a meaningful declaration of what in the Father is otherwise unfathomable.

The fact that for Ignatius the connotations of the term "Logos" are those which contrast it with speech shows he is not using it in a philosophical sense. He is not grappling with the problem of how God could be connected with that which is so apparently antithetic to him as the material creation. He has, so far as we can see in the letters, no developed doctrine of the Logos. Only one supremely important fact stands out, expressed as a dramatic truth: that the Logos makes plain what is unexpressed in Silence but truly there. This is possible because Speech and Silence are simply two sides of the same coin; what

14. Dodd, *Fourth Gospel,* pp. 69 ff.; cf. Goodenough, p. 37.

15. For the *religionsgeschichtliche* parallels see Bultmann, *Das Evangelium des Johannes,* p. 44, n. 1. Schlier, pp. 36 ff., discusses the relation of this usage to that of the Fourth Gospel and links with it Mandaean gnosis.

16. Reading φωνή with LΣS$_m$ instead of τρέχων. See Lightfoot, *ad loc.*

is said in words is what is intended before thought reaches expression. Christ is, in an allied figure of speech, "The Mouth which cannot lie by which the Father has spoken truly" (*Rom.* 8.2).

We have placed so much weight on the meaning of the *Sigé*-Logos paradox that it seems necessary to explore the justification for this interpretation and to say more precisely what seems to be implied. We must ask whether it is, in fact, reasonable to consider *Sigé* as more than a figure of speech. Many scholars treat it as only a figure; for example, as we have seen, Lightfoot believes that silence refers to the time before the incarnation.[17] But such an interpretation fails to catch the importance of meaning which the word carries for Ignatius. It is more than metaphor in the same way that Logos is more than metaphor. For him Logos is not the divine reason—and Ode 12 uses the concept in the same way—but the Utterance: in it the divine speaks out to the world. *Sigé*, linked as it is with Logos, is surely mythological.

This distinction demands clarification of the much-used word "myth." Myth, as we are using it, is a statement of truth cast in dramatic form to suggest the dynamic interrelations of the divine, the world, and man. With Lohmeyer[18] we hold that no one of the three can be ignored, as Bultmann[19] seems to do in his treatment. It is by nature connotative and allusive and therefore never precise. It is to be distinguished from metaphor, however, by the fact that it deals with fundamental and enduring relationships of the divine. In the book of Job, for example, metaphor is brilliantly employed to illuminate the

17. Lightfoot, *Mag.* 8 *ad loc.*

18. "The Right Interpretation of the Mythological," in *Kerygma and Myth,* ed. H. W. Bartsch (London, 1953), pp. 127 f., and throughout his essay. Cf. A. N. Wilder, "Mythology and the New Testament," *JBL, 69* (1950), 113–27. For discussion of the psychological and epistemological aspects of myth see Jonas, *Gnosis,* 2, introductory chapter.

19. In "New Testament and Mythology" (in Bartsch, *Kerygma and Myth,* p. 10) Bultmann defines mythology as "the use of imagery to express the otherworldly in terms of this world and the divine in terms of human life," but this is interpreted in existential terms which emphasize human experience.

plight of man, and is also used to describe or accuse God, as
when Job cries out, "Mine adversary sharpeneth his eyes upon
me" (16:9) or complains, "Am I a sea or a sea-monster, that
thou settest a watch over me?" (7:12). These are obviously
metaphors, suggestive of aspects of the revelation of God to Job,
but in no sense believed to be centrally or universally true, and
for that reason not to be described as myth.

Bultmann [20] maintains that the appearance of isolated mythological motifs is explained by the fact that something akin to a
process of demythologizing was going on in the New Testament
period and the years adjacent to it. It is this that explains why—
with the Mandaean myth, as he believes, available—early Christian writers do not make use of the full myth but seem to strip
it, taking from it elements consonant with their emerging beliefs about the salvation wrought by Christ. He assumes their
knowledge of it, and their discarding of those parts of it which
do not serve their purposes.

It is not clear to me that the Mandaean myth was in existence
so early, although the general notion of divine redeemers certainly existed in Syria and the processes of syncretism were constantly developing new forms. The very unprecise nature of
myth suggests rather that the creative imagination was constantly at work on it, developing and changing it, just as in
certain Christian groups the imagination made use of pseudo-
historical materials to produce apocryphal gospels. Ignatius
himself is without doubt thinking mythologically, perhaps using
materials at hand in his environment, but using them crea-
tively. The Silence-Logos paradox is a mythopoetic statement
of the revelation of God to the world. Here is myth in its most
pregnant form, reserved, suggestive, very different from late
Valentinianism, in which the fecund imagination has run riot
and has created the "tale." This latter is an excellent example
of the expanded form, that has all but lost its power to evoke
religious devotion and is conceived of as literal description.

20. In describing the gnosis in the source of the prologue of the Fourth
Gospel (*Joh. Ev.,* pp. 14 f.) he says that the failure to see the origin of
evil as an *Urfall* means that the mythology is *zurückgedrängt* and *reduziert.*
This certainly suggests *Entmythologisierung.*

One may even go on to say that in thinking mythologically Ignatius is using a method hardly to be avoided when one dares to speak of deity. Myth, when it degenerates into the expanded form, with every detail hammered out, has lost its religious power, but when it is "reserved," still emphasizing the nature or the activity of God, it has power to speak arrestingly to men, and it is particularly appropriate to the Semitic ideas of God as personal and active. Even Aristotle's idea of God as *Telos* makes use of mythological language; for although God is not active in himself, he is that to which all tend, and there is in this sense a dynamic relationship. Mythological thinking is not in itself sufficient as the expression of religious belief, for myth suggests and does not explain, and theology is essential. But without the mythopoetic affirmation at the core of religion it seems doubtful that theology would ever be called into being, since there would then be no potent symbol pointing to the divine, which must be interpreted to the understanding. Something of this sort seems to be admitted in the reticences of negative theology, which by its nature recognizes the virtues of mythological affirmation but is held back by the rational faculty from taking the plunge. It lacks the courage of the poet to affirm what he sees of reality, but its cautions are an important reminder of the limitations of myth.

Ignatius expressed his convictions in what we have been calling "reserved" myth, for his interests lay in suggesting the nature of deity and the divine events, not in dull details about *how* the Logos "proceeded" from Silence. It is enough to say that the hidden God discloses himself; Silent, he utters the revealing Word. Ignatius is expressing an idea fairly widely disseminated, though the explicit use of the word "Silence" cannot elsewhere be found in early thinking. But Menander taught a doctrine of the Unknown God in Antioch,[21] and the Fourth Gospel implies a similar notion. The late Valentinians who seized on the word itself and made much of it caused it to come under suspicion, but for them the heart of the matter is the process by which, stage by stage, the divine was changed

21. Irenaeus, *Adv. haer.*, 1.23.5. Justin connects him with Antioch: *I Apol.* 26.

into the undivine, and then that which was of the divine world
returned to its place. For Ignatius *Sigé* remained allusive, but
it was necessary for any theology that took seriously the doctrine
of the incarnation. Silence is never exhausted by the Word; the
deus absconditus remains. But Silence is still personal god, not
in a philosophical sense quite the ground of being, since true to
the earlier tradition Ignatius' notion continues to be influenced
by the idea of the activity of the Father.

We find then in Ignatius' letters a rich doctrine about God
and his activity, even though like almost every other aspect of
his thought it is *suggested,* not developed in systematic form.
We have been attending primarily to one factor in it, the idea
that there is a real reserve of deity, which nevertheless is manifested in the incarnation.

Another facet of his thought is seen in the insistent affirmation that there is only one God, Father and Son, *Sigé* and Logos,
characterized throughout by unity, and that therefore Christ is
God.

The lengths to which Ignatius goes in expressing the unity
of the Father and the Son can best be seen in his use of the word
θεός both with and without the definite article.[22] Its application
to Christ is something new in Christian usage, which did not
occur until nearly or quite the time at which Ignatius wrote.
Because there has been dispute whether Ignatius does, in fact,
accord to Jesus Christ the full title of deity, ὁ θεός, we shall examine his use of both θεός and ὁ θεός as they are applied to Christ
and to the Father.

The most striking fact that emerges is that Ignatius only
once used ὁ θεός of God the Father. He urges the Ephesians to
"live in harmony with the mind of God (τῇ γνώμῃ τοῦ θεοῦ)," and
goes on, for "Jesus Christ also, our inseparable life, is the mind
of the Father" (*Eph.* 3.2; possibly also *Rom.* 2.2). Here the
phrases "the mind of God" and "the mind of the Father" are
equated, and ὁ θεός is used of the Father. But it is the single in-

22. For Jewish and early Christian usage see the article on θεός by
Stauffer in Kittel's *Theologisches Wörterbuch, 3,* 91. Josephus used θεός
and ὁ θεός indiscriminately, but favored the latter.

stance of what in Paul's writings and the Old Testament is the characteristic usage. Furthermore, Ignatius frequently speaks of the Father simply as θεός. In most of the instances this is not surprising, in view of the idioms that Ignatius is using. θεὸς πατήρ occurs regularly in the inscriptions, as it does in the Pauline formula of greeting. But in several cases θεός occurs when we should certainly expect ὁ θεός. One instance seems to make a clear distinction between Jesus Christ and the Father when Ignatius says that Polybius visited him in Smyrna "by the will of God (θεοῦ) and of Jesus Christ" (*Tral.* 1.1). Here θεός can mean only God the Father. Another example is the phrase in *Eph.* 7.2: . . . καὶ ἐκ Μαρίας, καὶ ἐκ θεοῦ. Surely one might expect to find τοῦ θεοῦ here.

In eight passages Ignatius applies ὁ θεός to Jesus Christ. In five of these references [23] the phrase used is "our God," ὁ θεὸς ἡμῶν. In *Rom.* 6.3 the context shows that ὁ θεός applies to Jesus Christ; Ignatius writes of "the passion of my God (τοῦ πάθους τοῦ θεοῦ μου)," and the "bread of God (τοῦ ἄρτου τοῦ θεοῦ)" of *Eph.* 5.2 is similar. In *Smyr.* 1.1 Christ is "the god who has endowed you with wisdom ('Ιησοῦν Χριστὸν τὸν θεὸν τὸν . . .)." In most of these passages there is a qualifying adjective or phrase.

More frequently it is θεός that is applied to Christ. In *Poly.* 8.3 Ignatius uses the phrase "in our God Jesus Christ (ἐν θεῷ ἡμῶν)," and in *Eph.* 15.3, "we should be his temples, and he our God in us (ἐν ἡμῖν θεὸς ἡμῶν)." In other cases, when θεός is used of Jesus Christ the reference must be gathered from the context. Such examples occur when he speaks of Christians as being "imitators of God (μιμηταὶ θεοῦ)" (*Tral.* 1.2, *Eph.* 1.1), or having been "rekindled by the blood of God (ἐν αἵματι θεοῦ)" (*Eph.* 1.1); or in *Eph.* 7.2 where Jesus Christ is described as "God in man (ἐν ἀνθρώπῳ θεός)."

There are three references, with disputed textual support, in which Christ appears as ὁ θεός without any qualifying word, or which link Christ and θεός to form a single name, similar to the usage θεὸς πατήρ. In *Smyr.* 6.1, according to two Syriac fragments that differ from each other, the text should probably read ". . . if they do not believe in the blood of Christ the

23. *Eph.* Ins., 18.2; *Rom.* Ins. *bis*, 3.3.

God." Lightfoot brackets the last words, but with GLACB they
should probably be entirely omitted on textual grounds. *Tral.*
7.1 [24] reads, with GLC and against A, ". . . if you are inseparable from God Jesus Christ (ἀχωρίστοις θεοῦ Ἰησοῦ Χριστοῦ)." It
probably should be accepted, since on the whole the Armenian
version has a slight tendency to avoid the absolute use of the
word. *Smyr.* 10.1 is the third of the disputed passages, and this
reads, with GL, ὡς διακόνους Χριστοῦ θεοῦ,[25] which is most awkward
but a form not wholly unlike θεὸς πατήρ. The textual witness is
too confused, however, to bear much weight.

⋅It seems probable that Ignatius did call Jesus Christ "God"
in an absolute sense, and not, as Lightfoot [26] maintained, only
when he spoke of him as the God of the Christians, or "our
God," or in some other way qualified the word. Christ seems
to have been for him so fully God that there was no point at
which he hesitated to accord him the divine name. However,
the significance of the question is completely changed when
we remember that even the Father is only once in the letters
called ὁ θεός. The significant fact is that Ignatius does not make
the usual distinctions between the use with the particle and
the use without it. The important truth is that Jesus Christ
and the Father are equally recognized as God, whatever the
terminology may be.

The cases that are most numerous of all speak of "God,"
using either θεός or ὁ θεός and making no attempt to make clear
whether Jesus Christ or the Father is meant. One can take at
random from the letters sentences like those which use ὁ θεός:
". . . let us learn to live in a Christian way. For whoever is
called by a name other than this, does not belong to God
(τοῦ θεοῦ)" (*Mag.* 10.1). Another example is the following
sentence: "A head cannot be born without members, since God

24. The Erzherzog Rainier Papyrus K9416–9421 offers another evidence
for the inclusion of the word θεός as against Lightfoot's decision not to include it. See Wessely, *Neue Materialien*, p. 42. Funk, Hilgenfeld, Zahn, and
Bauer all accept the reading.

25. According to G (L); g witnesses to the disputed words but reverses
their order. A and B omit χριστοῦ.

26. Lightfoot, *Apostolic Fathers*, 2, 26, 29 f., and *ad Tral.* 7.1, etc.

(τοῦ θεοῦ) offers union . . ." (*Tral.* 11.2). θεός unqualified stands
in still more places: ". . . for they are not those who serve
meats and drinks but servants of the church of God (ἐκκλησίας
θεοῦ)" (*Tral.* 2.2), and similarly throughout the letters.

It would be interesting to determine whether this usage is
simply second nature to Ignatius because it was unself-
consciously accepted in the church or whether there is in it an
element of urgency or emphasis that betrays the awareness of
contrasting views. It is a difficult question precisely because the
use of θεός and words compounded with it are so common and
occur both in passages that seem to express passionate pleading
and in others that are less obviously controversial. An answer,
interesting as the question is, can only be speculative. We may
surmise that such a thought would not have been easy for the
Essene-Christians. In one passage in the Magnesian letter, where
Ignatius apparently has them in mind, he writes: "Everyone
hasten to come together as to one temple of God, to one altar,
to one Jesus Christ, who came forth from the one Father,
abiding in the one, and returning to the one" (*Mag.* 7.2). Here
the emphasis is achieved not by the word θεός but by insistence
on the unity of Christ and the Father, and something about the
"strange teachings and ancient myths" seems to have denied
this unity. The teaching that there is *one* God (*Mag.* 8.2) is
here a way of emphasizing the deity of Jesus Christ which may
well have been one of the points at issue in the church if we
are right in our conclusion that the Essene-Christians were uneasy about the passion and resurrection.

The case of the Docetists is different. Some gnostics, at least,
might hesitate to use the word God in an absolute sense of the
redeemer, but many Christian gnostics would not find this hard
to affirm, and we may suppose that at this point they and Ignatius would have seen eye to eye. But even for them it would
be new. As late as the New Testament letter to the Ephesians
the word "God" was not used of Jesus Christ in spite of the
high christology of the letter, and even in the Fourth Gospel
the unity of the Father and the Son is not commonly affirmed
by the use of θεός. One may suspect that perhaps Ignatius and
the Docetist-Christians were at one in holding that the deity of

Christ was an important matter because by it Christ was differentiated from other redeemer figures.

It is no accident, then, that we find the Father and Jesus
Christ linked in so many ways in Ignatius' thought. The Father
manifests himself in the Son; the Silence is expressed in the
Logos. And the revelation is true because both the Father and
Jesus Christ are God—not merely because they play a divine
role in relation to the churches but by their very nature.

The less frequent descriptive titles that link Christ with
the Father show the same thing; revelation is possible because
Son and Father are united. Christ is the High Priest who alone
knows the secret things of God (*Phld.* 9.1). Here the intent is
to show identity of understanding between the Father and the
Son, but the figure is not wholly successful. He is the Door of
the Father (ibid.) through which all must enter. That unity is
in Ignatius' mind (even if this figure, too, is faulty) is shown by
the next sentence: "All these things come together into the
unity of God." Jesus Christ is the "Mouth [27] . . . by which
the Father has spoken truly" (*Rom.* 8.2). Here is a variation of
the idea of the Speech which expressed the Silence. He is the
Mind, the Purpose (*Eph.* 3.2) or the Will of God.[28] Finally,
Christ is the knowledge of God (*Eph.* 17). It is the only time
that Ignatius uses the word "gnosis," and in view of its later
significant meaning, that it appears only once is interesting. The
idea conveyed is important to him, although other terms are
used for it. Obviously there is no lack of terms to show dramatically how closely the Father and the Son are linked, and
how truly central is the revealing function of the Son. What
is revealed is not knowledge *about* the Father but revelation
of God by God.

27. Cf. Ode 12.11, "For the mouth of the Most High spake to them; /
And the interpretation of Himself had its course by Him."

28. Ignatius does not think of the Son-Logos as the indwelling Reason
and "mind" seems a better translation for passages indicating unity or
will as indicating the active nature of Christ. Schlier, *Relig. Untersuch.*,
p. 40, n. 2, comments on the difficulty but favors *Wille.* Lebreton, *Trinité,*
2, 325, uses *pensée, l'esprit, sens.*

Contrary to the position we have been developing, Bartsch
in his *Gnostisches Gut und Gemeindetradition bei Ignatius*
maintains that revelation, far from being an important conception for Ignatius, is almost peripheral, save as he has uncritically taken over aspects of earlier Christian thought. Bartsch
believes that Ignatius has been drawn into the circle of gnostic
thought primarily by the fascination of the idea of the unity of
God, and that revelation is all but excluded. No one would
deny that unity is a conception of extraordinary importance in
the letters, and Chapter 9 will explore at length the teaching
about it, but this is not to say that the notion of unity exists in
the clear-cut gnostic sense that Bartsch discovers, nor that it
stands out in the starkly dominant way he describes.

Ignatius certainly believes that any unity which emerges in
the churches will in the last analysis rest on the divine unity,
but, as we have shown above, it is the very ground of revelation.
Bartsch argues that in the long passage in the Magnesian letter
(6–8), which we read as proclaiming revelation, what is really
central is the unity, and revelation is lacking. He sees the word
Logos as unimportant because it is only once used directly of
Christ, and he holds that in any case it is neither an hypostasis [29]
nor a title, but is rather a figure of speech. This rests on what
seem to be unacceptable interpretations of two passages. In the
first instance he presses the significance of Ignatius' words for
Christ's manifestation.[30] One is the word "sending ($\pi \acute{\epsilon} \mu \epsilon \iota \nu$)"
(*Mag.* 8.2), a Johannine term; the other is "procession ($\pi \rho o \epsilon \lambda \theta \epsilon \hat{\iota} \nu$)"
(*Mag.* 7.2, 8.2), which Bartsch believes implies the "pure"
gnostic view of the unbroken unity of Christ with the Father
in the pleroma. Even if it could be shown that $\pi \rho o \epsilon \lambda \theta \epsilon \hat{\iota} \nu$ was a
technical gnostic term in the time of Ignatius, which seems
doubtful, the fact that the two words stand together in the
passage makes it more reasonable to explain the usage as a
matter of style than as an attempt to state a newly acquired
gnostic insight. Bartsch finds further evidence in the description
of Christ as the "unlying Mouth" (*Rom.* 8.2), which he be-

29. *GG,* pp. 63 ff.
30. Ibid., pp. 67 ff.

lieves suggests that "Christ" is thought of as an emanation standing between God and the Logos,[31] and that therefore he never left the Father but remained within the pleroma conceived in a Valentinian sense. But this ingenious interpretation is tenable only if one overlooks the emphasis on the "manifestation" and Ignatus' lack of distinction between Son, Christ, and Logos. In the single long passage it is said that Jesus Christ was "made manifest at the end of time" (*Mag.* 6.1), that he "came forth from the one Father, abiding with the one, and returning to the one" (*Mag.* 7.2), and finally that "Jesus Christ his son is his Word proceeding from Silence" (*Mag.* 8.2). Granted that this is confessional rather than systematic writing, it nevertheless seems unjustified either to remove any of these declarations or to force on them, on a priori grounds, distinctions between Christ and Logos. Unity is of course central; but for Ignatius the unity is in no way a barrier to revelation but its condition, and the presence of both notions argue against his holding any clear gnostic notion of unity.

We would further suggest that even the central notion of unity is impinged upon by other aspects of Ignatius' beliefs about God, so that it does not stand in the position of unassailable eminence that Bartsch sees. "Unity" is not always distinguished sharply from "uniqueness," but discussions about God seem in the contemporary thought world to have involved both. It is difficult to read Ignatius in any other way (cf. *Mag.* 7.2), and the quotation from the *Hermetica* that Bartsch quotes as nearest to Ignatius affirms that there is one greatest God, and that it is "impossible that place or number or measure should be maintained without a creator" (*Herm.* 5.4). This is not very different from the declaration of Psalm E [32] from the Dead Sea collection: ". . . and there is naught apart from Thee, and no power exists beside Thee." Even the cry of N.T. Eph. 4:5 f. that there is "one Lord, one faith, one baptism, one God and Father of all who is over all, and through all, and in all" emphasizes the uniqueness of the ultimate God as the basis for unity. The two seem to be indissolubly connected. Furthermore, God is

31. Ibid., pp. 70 f.
32. Translation of Dupont-Sommer, *Dead Sea Scrolls,* p. 77.

marked by more than unity. He is the Silence who reveals himself in the Word, the source of the eternal life that characterizes the new dispensation (*Eph.* 19.3). Neither of the latter affirmations seems dependent on the first. In this respect, too, Bartsch' ingenious and finespun construction seems oversubtle as an interpretation of the letters.

We turn now to ask in what respects if at all Ignatius anticipates later theological positions, although we cannot force on men of one period what was not clarified until later. For instance, by the end of the century there was lively interest in the matter of subordinationism, certainly not present in the minds of the men of the early second century, and it would be interesting to inquire whether in describing the relation between the Father and the Son Ignatius emphasized either at the expense of the other. The amazing fact seems to be that his belief in the unequivocal unity between them, which is close to the later orthodox position, was maintained without the subtler theological distinctions that later generations worked out.

On the one hand Ignatius believed with Paul and one must suppose with most Christians of his time in Christ's existence before the incarnation. Indeed he was more explicit, for he held that Christ had existed from eternity. He was "with the Father before all ages and was made manifest at the end of time" (*Mag.* 6.1). He is described as the "Timeless one, the Invisible who for our sakes became visible, the One beyond suffering who for our sakes suffered . . ." (*Poly.* 3.2). The eternal existence could not be declared more unequivocally. There is here no hint of adoptionism.

But although Ignatius affirms the pre-existence of Jesus Christ with characteristic vigor, there is no evidence that he used words with technical precision in describing the relation of Christ to God the Father. Ignatius says he is "the only Son" of the Father (*Rom.* Ins.), but he does not go on to develop any doctrine about the sonship. He does not, for instance, seem to restrict the name Logos to the pre-existent Christ and the name Son to the incarnate Christ, for the two are equated:

". . . There is one God, who revealed himself through Jesus
Christ his Son, who is his Word proceeding from Silence, who
in every way was pleasing to him who sent him" (*Mag.* 8.2).
Whether as Son or as Logos Jesus Christ is the revealer. Some
scholars have held that the name "Son" is never used of the
pre-existent Christ, but such a theory suggests a clarity of distinction that is very difficult to discover in the passage above.
It is also difficult to see how on that basis one can interpret the
phrase describing Jesus Christ as "Son of Man and Son of God"
(*Eph.* 20.2) where the humanity and the divinity are paradoxically opposed to each other and "Son" applies to both.

Even if Ignatius does not distinguish sharply between the
pre-existent and the incarnate Lord, it would not be surprising
if he held that, as incarnate, Christ is in some sense subordinate
to God the Father, since eternity and history are not inter-
changeable categories, and this expectation is borne out in the
letters. In two passages the Father appears as the norm by
which Christ is tested. Ignatius urges the Philadelphian church
to be "imitators of Jesus Christ as he himself also was of his
Father" (*Phld.* 7.2). And he declared that what Christ has done
in silence is "worthy of the Father" (*Eph.* 15). In both the
passages the Father is the perfection of goodness by which even
the Son is judged. Although this indicates a measure of subordination, it is clear from the contexts of both quotations
that Ignatius is considering the historical life, not the eternal
existence. Another instance belongs here in what is its most
probable form, although unfortunately the versions differ. In
Mag. 13.2 Jesus Christ is described as subject to the Father
"according to the flesh." If GL be followed, κατὰ σάρκα should
be read, and again it is the historical Jesus who submits to the
Father. All these instances clearly refer to the subordination of
the incarnate life and tell us nothing of Ignatius' thinking
about the relation of the pre-existent Christ to the Father.

There are two passages that at first sight go farther, seeming
to suggest that even in eternity the Son was subordinate. In
one of them Christ is described as "of the line of David according to the flesh, the Son of God by the will and power of God"
(*Smyr.* 1.1). This has frequently been taken to mean something

like adoptionism—subordinating the Son in the extreme degree. This interpretation is reasonable, however, only if the last parts of the two phrases are emphasized, so that the point of the contrast is his status according to the flesh, over against that which is "by the will and power of God." If we had no similar descriptions with which to compare it, this would be a wholly tenable interpretation; but since the paradox immediately suggests the others in which the humanity and the deity are paradoxically distinguished and united, one must suspect that its true meaning is the same as theirs. It brings to mind the description of Christ as "both of the seed of David and of the Holy Spirit" (*Eph.* 18.2) or "both of Mary and of God" (*Eph.* 7). The "will and power of God" seem to indicate the action of the Spirit, or of God, at the incarnation, which explains the virginity of Mary, and not to have anything to do with the subordination of the Son to the Father in eternity. It is, furthermore, an echo of N.T. Rom. 1:3, 4, where the reference to the power and the spirit is explicit.

The last phrase to be considered is the most difficult. It occurs at the end of the crucial passage about revelation. Ignatius writes that the Son, "who is his Word proceeding from Silence . . . in every way was pleasing to him who sent him" (*Mag.* 8.2). It is the last clause that admittedly comes closest of anything in the letters to suggesting that Ignatius held, unreconciled with most of his beliefs, the view that Christ was basically and eternally dependent on the Father. And it may be that the passage should be read in that sense. It would be easier to do so, however, if Ignatius did not seem to be echoing a phrase from the gospel. It recalls the baptism story, and the transfiguration. Ignatius is not quoting: the verbs are different. But the idea is inescapably scriptural, and if so it is difficult to consider this a declaration of the eternal subordination of the Son. However swift the transition, it is a reference to the historical life and is therefore to be grouped with the first of the passages we discussed above, in which the historical Lord is subordinated to the Father.

A somewhat comparable stage of thought occurs in the *Odes of Solomon:*

> The Father of Knowledge
> Is the Word of Knowledge:
>
> He who created wisdom
> Is wiser than His works:
>
> And He who created me when yet I was not
> Knew what I should do when I came into being:
>
> Wherefore He pitied me in His abundant grace
> And granted me to ask from Him and to receive from
>   His sacrifice;
>
> For it is He that is incorrupt;
> The perfection of the worlds and the Father of them.
>
> [7.7–11]

Here the Father and the Word are the same, but the author of the *Odes* is naïvely unaware of any problem connected with subordinationism.

As long as the unity is made clear, Ignatius is satisfied; he never raises metaphysical problems. There is no doctrine of an eternal begetting, nor are the other subtleties of later theologians to be found in his letters. "There is *one* God, who revealed himself . . ." (*Mag.* 8). "I consider you blessed who are so united with him [the bishop] as the church is with Jesus Christ and as Jesus Christ is with the Father" (*Eph.* 5.1). "The Lord did nothing without the Father, being united with him . . ." (*Mag.* 7.1). The words "Father and Son," or "Silence and Word" indicate a distinction that had indeed existed from eternity, but it is a distinction of function rather than any difference in status. The distinction in no way denied the unity, as Ignatius saw it. The meaning of Silence is the Word. The promised redemption that came through the agency of the Son expressed the divine purpose. Ignatius preaches the eternal existence of the godhead, whether as Father or Son, and the final revelation of the hidden Father at the end of time.

If one term must be chosen to indicate the tendency of his thought, Ignatius must be said to be monarchian,[33] though he

33. This point is much discussed; for the view that Ignatius maintains an orthodox balance see von der Goltz, *Ignatius*, p. 22; Rackl, *Christologie*,

is very close to the point later declared to be orthodox. Actually it is misleading to apply the words which only later came to have importance to thinkers unaware of the problems of their successors. His very carelessness of the distinctions is one evidence of his early date. He had no fear of using that word "Silence" which became dangerous after the later gnostics had adopted it as their own.

But although doctrine about the Father and the Son is abundant, if undeveloped, there is a paucity of references to the Spirit, and what there are show neither clarity nor originality. Ignatius believes in the Spirit [34] as in some way an aspect of the deity, but we may surmise that Christ's role as revealer blocked any thought of effective action by the Spirit. He accepts the tradition, perhaps from Matthew, that the incarnate Christ was conceived by Mary, of the Holy Spirit (*Eph.* 18.2), and the emphasis of the passages seems to be on the divine act as a whole. "Our God, Jesus the Christ, was conceived by Mary according to the divine purpose, of the seed of David but also of the Holy Spirit." The κατ' οἰκονομίαν θεοῦ calls attention to the divine grounding of the event, and indicates that Ignatius probably thinks of the Holy Spirit as God, as Christ also is. At least this passage can be linked with that which declares him to be the Son of Mary and Son of God (*Eph.* 7). But it defines nothing. The Spirit also operates among men to introduce them to divine things. It is in this sense that the prophets could be said to be "disciples in the Spirit" as they looked forward to Jesus Christ who would come as their teacher (*Mag.* 9.2). It is not absolutely clear that this refers to the Holy Spirit, but it seems the more likely interpretation. In similar vein Ignatius says that the Spirit, which is "from God" (ἀπὸ θεοῦ) cannot be deceived, and that by it he became aware of things not told him

---

pp. 227–31; Richardson, *Christianity of Ignatius*, pp. 42 ff.; Lebreton, *Trinité*, 2, 305–12. For the position maintained above see also Kroymann, *Tertullian*, pp. ix–xvii, although he considers Ignatius an example of an Asia Minor theology; F. Loofs, "Christologie" in *Realencyclopädie für protestantische Theologie und Kirche*, 3d Aufl., Vol. 4, p. 27.

34. Dodd, *Fourth Gospel*, pp. 213–27, discusses the similar usage of John against the background of the Hermetic tractates and Philo.

by men. "I did not know of this [division] by any human agency, but the Spirit was crying out . . ." (*Phld.* 7.2). Further discussion of the relation of the Spirit to man will be found below, in Chapters 6 and 8.

Ignatius is at one with the Old Testament, and in the tradition of the Essene writings and the gospel of Matthew for the idea of the Spirit of God at work in the world; but as in most Christian thought contemporary with him Christ and the Holy Spirit were not carefully distinguished.[35] In *Eph.* 20.2 he looks specifically to "the Lord" for revelation of the true state of affairs in the Ephesian church. And he says that the Philadelphian bishop and presbyters and deacons were "appointed by the will of Jesus Christ" and "established . . . according to his own will by his Holy Spirit" (*Phld.* Ins.). Elsewhere Jesus Christ is himself described as the "undivided spirit" of those churches that live in godly concord (*Mag.* 15). The belief about the Holy Spirit is evidently quite fluid.

. The trinitarian formula appears three times,[36] but none gives any further information about Ignatius' views of the Spirit, and two of them are textually difficult. All that can be said is that Ignatius held together in a general way the Father, the Son, and the Spirit as we find them grouped in the resurrection command in Matthew, but he had not advanced beyond it. The boldest of the passages indicates more about Ignatius' use of vigorous metaphors than of his beliefs about the Trinity. He says that Christians, like stones made ready to be placed in the temple of God the Father, are "raised to the heights by the instrument of Jesus Christ, which is the cross, and using for a rope the Holy Spirit" (*Eph.* 9.1). It is a reflection of the scene he must have witnessed many times, as the great stones of the temples and basilicas which remain scattered through the Near East were hauled into place.[37] The figure expresses the powerful

35. Paul clearly identifies the Lord and the Spirit in a number of passages. Cf. N.T. Rom. 8:9, II Cor. 3:17 f., Gal. 4:4 ff.

36. The Trinitarian formula is rare in the Apostolic Fathers. Outside of Ignatius it occurs in *I Clem.* 58.2 and *Didache* 7.1, 2, quoting Matt. 28:19.

37. Schlier, pp. 110–24, interprets this symbolically and parallels it with other salvation machines. It seems far more likely to have reflected a conscious memory.

action of the Deity in redemption, but adds nothing to our understanding of his views of distinct functions within the god-head. And that it is figure, not doctrine, is further substantiated by the fact that in another passage the Father, Jesus Christ, and *the apostles,* appear instead of the Father, Jesus Christ, and the Spirit (*Tral.* 3.1). The Father and the Son are usually somewhat differentiated, but not the Spirit.

The two other references to the Trinity occur in one para-graph, and both offer some difficulty. Toward the close of the letter to the Magnesians, Ignatius hopes that they may " 'prosper in all things' . . . in flesh and spirit, in faith and love, in the Son and the Father, and in the Spirit . . ." (*Mag.* 13.1). The reading is peculiar, for the Son and the Father are in the text bracketed together as against the Spirit. It is difficult to know how to estimate this passage. From one point of view its curious form is a witness against belief in a clearly conceived Trinity. The Father and the Son seem to crowd out the Spirit, who is present as an afterthought. From another point of view, how-ever, it is significant that the Spirit is mentioned at all, for it is introduced into a passage made up of series of two—a fre-quent characteristic of style in Ignatius' writing. In that case the addition of the Spirit might mean that the idea of the Trinity had enough reality for Ignatius so that he occasionally introduced it even when by doing so the rhythm was destroyed.

Later on in the same paragraph occurs another reference to the Trinity, but it is not admitted by all the versions. If genu-ine, it shows merely that Ignatius held a belief in the three as unified in some respects, since it is to all that the apostles were subject. "Submit to the bishop and to one another as Jesus Christ did to the Father according to the flesh, and the apostles did to Christ and to the Father [and to the Spirit]." None of these passages adds anything to an understanding of what the Trinity meant to Ignatius, and we are forced to conclude that it was a very undefined belief indeed.

The interests of Ignatius as we see them in the letters lay in revelation and redemption rather than inspiration, in at least the last of which the Holy Spirit might have been important. In those two areas the work of Christ was central, as it was occasionally, as we have seen, even in inspiration. The very

form in which revelation was stated, the *manifestation* of the
hidden God, left very little room for even the subordinate work
of the Holy Spirit, and insofar as it is present at all it is amal-
gamated with the general divine work.

But in spite of the new emphasis on the hidden God who
was revealed in the Son, Ignatius' most important affirmation
is the traditional one that God is at work in his world. Creation
is not for him a problem, and for that reason it is difficult to
hold that his opponents distinguished between the good God
and the Demiurge. For God is the creator and sustainer; he has
"willed all things that exist" (*Rom.* Ins.). In the two passages
where Ignatius emphasizes the *one* God, it is in contexts which
imply a different train of thought from that of opposition to a
true gnostic dualism. In the one case (*Mag.* 7.2) he writes of
the "one Jesus Christ, who came forth from the one Father,"
but this occurs as the climax of a passage urging unity on the
church. And when a paragraph later he declares that the
prophets "were persecuted, being inspired by his grace, to convince the unpersuaded that there is one God, who revealed
himself through Jesus Christ his son . . ." (*Mag.* 8.2), this
seems to be a complex and incompletely explicated notion that
the same God spoke by the prophets and then was manifested
in Jesus Christ. It is directed against the Essene-Christians, who,
as we have suggested, were not skeptical about the old writings,
where the revelation of God was to be found, but were re-
sistant to the notion of Christ as God. Neither of these passages
gives evidence of opposing a doctrine of two gods.

It remains to place Ignatius' view of revelation historically.
It is important to explore this matter, for that an emphasis on
revelation is present at all is surprising in view of the nature of
Judaism and early Christianity. If there is one thing that can
be said of both, it is that the will of the Father has always been
accessible to men as it was revealed to the Jews. The very idea
that the Father could be considered to be Silence is astonishing.

It is central to the thought of the Old Testament that God's
will has been abundantly proclaimed. "Surely the Lord God
will do nothing except he reveal his secret unto his servants the

prophets" (Amos 3:7). Between the Lord and the prophets there is a conversation many centuries long in which the will and the judgment of God are made clear. And beside the prophetic word stood the divine command expressed in the Torah, which according to tradition was known in the Mosaic lawgiving to which the people had responded, "All the words which the Lord hath spoken will we do" (Ex. 24:3).

Later Judaism held the same beliefs, though it expressed them differently. The Wisdom [38] of God was in some measure the active creating will (Prov. 8:27 ff.) rather than the command laid upon men in the Torah, but she also taught men "things either secret or manifest" (*Wisd. Sol.* 7.21), since she was thought of as "an effulgence from everlasting light, and an unspotted mirror of the working of God, and an image of his goodness." "And from generation to generation passing into holy souls she maketh men friends of God and prophets" (*Wisd. Sol.* 7.25 f., 27). Here Wisdom truly reveals the activity of God, though the emphasis is laid on her agency as the normal way in which God works rather than on the previous remoteness of God. Wisdom is the process by which God has always been making his will known.

The problems are set for Philo more by Greek philosophy than by the Old Testament when he deals with the question of the transcendence of God and his revelation. He affirms stoutly that "the God of Real Being is apprehensible by no one." [39] But he holds that the creative and the kingly powers of

38. Bultmann, "Der religionsgeschichtliche Hintergrund der Prologs zum Johannes-Evangelium," in *Eucharisterion,* ed. H. Schmidt, Pt. II (Göttingen, 1923), pp. 6–9, and in *Das Evangelium des Johannes,* p. 8, maintains that wisdom has been influenced by gnostic thought to the extent of showing traces of a descent from God, a rejection and a return, but demythologized. In the passages cited from Proverbs and *Wisdom of Solomon* Wisdom's creative role is far clearer than her role in the revelation of God's will, and it is the latter that would be fundamental to the notion of a rejection and a return.

39. *Post.* (v)16 (trans. Whitaker, Loeb ed., *2,* 337). Cf. *Fug.* (xxix) 164–65. and passim; *Som.* 1 (xi)66; *Virt.* (xxxix)215, and with qualifications in *Abr.* (xvii)80. Moses is a true exception, in *Mos.* 1 (xxviii)158. But he says in *Mut.* (iii)15 that the sentence "the Lord was seen of Abraham," means that the potency of kingship became visible to him.

God mediate the power of the invisible One: "Then they shall behold the place which in fact is the Word, where stands God the never changing . . . For it well befits those who have entered into comradeship with knowledge to desire to see the Existent if they may, but if they cannot, to see at any rate his image, the most holy Word . . ." [40]

Here is the Logos, which appears in so much thinking in the Hellenistic world. He plays, however, a rather different role from that played by the Logos in Ignatius' letters. For Philo the role of revealer, if indeed one can find it at all, is subordinated to that of creator and sustainer: "His nature happy and blessed as it was, forbade that He should touch the limitless matter. Instead He made full use of the incorporeal potencies well denoted by their name of Forms . . ." [41] The Logos is the "creative" or "beneficent" power of God after whom the world was patterned. Philo is addressing himself to the question of how the universal and the particular could be related. He answers that it is the Logos who makes possible the dependence of matter on the immaterial, of the creature on the uncreated. As man is said to be created "in the image of God," in being rational, there is a certain element of revelation present. The Logos is a rational power, the Archetype of man's mind.[42] Man's mind is made to apprehend the rational, hence to view the powers even if he can never know God in himself. But the Torah remains the ordinary way by which the commands of God are known. Only the rare "friends of God" seem to become freed from its guidance, and they not on the initiative of God but after long striving.

In the Essene writings and the pseudepigrapha the thought is a continuation of rather standard wisdom notions, ranging from understanding as the gift of God to man (*I Enoch* 14.2), or God's love of wisdom (*CDC* 2.2), to the half-hypostatized form in which wisdom "turns not away from the presence" (*I Enoch* 84.3) or to the parable of the contrasting fates of the spirits of wisdom and unrighteousness when they went forth to

40. *Conf.* (xx)96–97 (trans. Colson, Loeb ed., *4*, 61 f.).
41. *Spec.* I(IX)329 (trans. Colson, Loeb ed., *7*, 291).
42. *Spec.* III(XXXVI)207.

men, a passage sometimes cited as an example of the fallen Sophia. Wisdom "found no dwelling place" and returned to heaven, but unrighteousness was welcomed by those whom she scarcely sought (*I Enoch* 42.1–3).[43] All this is much like wisdom speculation in Proverbs and *Sirach*. When, however, the declaration is made that "from the God of knowledge exists all that is and will be" (*DSD* 3.15) [44] or to the Most High is given the title "Fountain of knowledge" (*DSD* 10.12), there is a further step in the association of wisdom and knowledge with God himself.

Paul starts from a different point. His Pharisaic training left a heritage of belief that the Torah was truly the revelation of God's will. He was not interested, like Philo, in speculating on the process of creation, but he had to explain to himself how the Law could be truly God's will and at the same time abrogated by Christ. His answer from one point of view is that the Torah is indeed the wisdom of God, but that Christ is both the wisdom and the Power of God. The law pointed out how men should live, but did not empower them to live so. If men associate themselves with Christ, they shall be "made righteous." Grace, which is power, has taken the place of law, which is merely prescriptive (Rom. 5:20). "God was in Christ reconciling the world unto himself" (II Cor. 5:19). The emphasis is laid on the new power available to men in the death and resurrection. Revelation is certainly not ignored, for Christ himself is also the wisdom of God, and by that Paul does not mean the creative power. It is given to men to see the "light of the knowledge of the glory of God in the face of Jesus Christ" (II Cor. 4:6). Here is revelation pure and simple. Just as Christ had superseded the law because he brought grace, so the old function of the revelation of God's will was also done away, and Christ uniquely revealed God. But for all the flash of brilliant insight when he said that Jesus Christ reveals the "light of the knowledge of the glory of God," Paul does not develop the revealing work of Christ. More revelation was needed, he says,

43. In spite of the fact that this occurs in the somewhat later Parables, it belongs in spirit with much earlier wisdom speculation.

44. So Brownlee, *Manual of Discipline*.

because there was a "hardening of the mind," a "veil on the heart" (II Cor. 3). It was necessary because of the weakness of man caught in flesh, not because God was by nature unknown.

Belief in the revelation of the God who was *unknown* appears clearly in the Fourth Gospel.[45] Here is revelation in precisely the same sense we have found in Ignatius' thought, and certain aspects of the idea are put more clearly and forcefully than Ignatius puts them. That the Father is unknown is fundamental: "No man hath seen God at any time; the only begotten . . . of the Father, he hath declared him" (1:18). At the end of the great prayer Christ says, "O righteous Father, the world knew thee not, but I knew thee" (17:25). Again he says, "Not that any man hath seen the Father, save he that is from God, he hath seen the Father" (6:46). The Fourth Gospel never calls God Silence, but the opposite member of the paradox, the Logos, is here, and as in the Ignatian letters means the Utterance. "And ye have not his word abiding in you, for whom he sent, him ye believe not" (5:37 f.). The Son is united with the Father, and hence revelation is genuine. "As the Father taught me, I speak these things. And he that sent me is with me; he hath not left me alone . . ." (8.28 f.). In the plainest of all the "I am" formulas which so deliberately suggest the great theophany of Exodus 3:14, Jesus declares, "He that hath seen me hath seen the Father . . . Believe me that I am in the Father and the Father in me" (14:9 ff.), and finally, "I and the Father are one" (10:30). Here then are all the ideas about revelation that we have seen in Ignatius, all more frequently stated than in the letters.

The Ignatian letters and the Fourth Gospel represent the same kind of thought about the revelation of the unknown Father by the Son, a kind of thought that is approached by

45. Dodd, *Fourth Gospel,* p. 156, in his illuminating discussion of knowledge of God, maintains that in John there is no real doctrine of the Unknown God in the sense that "God is essentially unknown, and unknowable." But it is doubtful whether there ever was such a doctrine; always accessibility of some sort is affirmed. John seems, however, to imply just such a notion of the *reserve* of deity as does Ignatius, and both are concerned to say that revelation of the Unknown is central in the acts of Christ.

Paul but nowhere equaled. Revelation is a central part of the work of the Logos and is conceived of in a way new to Christian thinking, although not new in any absolute sense. The thought of God as Unknown is one way of emphasizing his transcendence; this notion has a strong Greek background and was a major influence on Philo. It is when the Unknown God is declared to be God Manifest that a new step has been taken.

One of the most interesting recent additions to the sources bearing on this problem comes from the discovery of fragments of the *Apocalypse of Abraham* at Qumran.[46] This means that it must be dated before A.D. 70, and even though we cannot be certain that at that time it existed precisely in the form in which we know it today, the notion that the "ineffable Name" of God is borne by the angel Jaoel seems to be integral to the structure of the book. If so, speculation about the Name goes back to the first century of our era, and in Semitic thought Name is closely associated with being.

When we inquire what bearing this has on the problem of the revelation of the Unknown God, we find ourselves on difficult terrain, because apocalypses are far from being philosophical treatises. On the one hand even Abraham cannot see God (16), although he hears the divine voice and has it for a guide through all the mysteries of eternal creation and the purposes of God. On the other hand the angel who leads Abraham to the uttermost heaven has had bestowed upon him, to empower him, the "ineffable Name" of Jaoel (10), which in the great chant of adoration (17) is proclaimed the name of God himself:

> Eternal, mighty, Holy, El,
>   God only—Supreme!
> Thou who art self-originated, incorruptible, spotless
> Uncreate, immaculate, immortal,
>   Self-complete, self-illuminating;
> Without father, without mother, unbegotten,
>   Exalted, fiery One . . .

46. So G. Quispel in *The Jung Codex,* trans. F. L. Cross (London, 1955), p. 71, n. 4. Quispel points out the connection of the Name speculation of the *Apocalypse of Abraham* with that of the *Evangelium Veritatis.*

> Eternal, mighty holy Sabaoth,
> very glorious El, El, El, El Jaoel . . .[47]

The Name is something less than an hypostasis, and it is not connected merely with revelation, since it is given to the Angel that by it he may strengthen Abraham. But the Angel plays the revealing role of the mystagogue, during a part of the *Apocalypse,* until the voice of the Eternal One who is also Jaoel takes over from him. Here surely is speculation about revelation and the Unknown God that comes up to the threshold on which the Fourth Gospel and the Ignatian letters stand. The Name, either through the Angel Jaoel or through the Voice, reveals if not the nature of God himself then his creation and his purposes. The *Apocalypse* goes further than the pseudepigraphs to which we have referred above, because the Revealer is both the angel and the Eternal One.

But if the notion of revelation in the *Apocalypse of Abraham* is less developed than that of the Fourth Gospel and Ignatius, the *Gospel of Truth* [48] from the Chenoboskian library shows us a related conception of revelation that is far more developed. If Quispel is correct, it can be ascribed to Valentinus himself [49] in perhaps A.D. 140. Here the Unknown Father and his revelation appear in far more philosophical form than in the *Apocalypse of Abraham,* and again part of the speculation is about the Name, although that is only one facet of the whole.

In the *Gospel of Truth,* revelation is the dominant interest. The Father is unknown to his creatures, although they are said to be "inside him" (17.5 ff.), and out of their dire need they search blindly for him without knowing what it is they seek. They are aware only of the misty world of unreality created by

47. Trans. G. H. Box, *The Apocalypse of Abraham,* London, 1918.

48. *Evangelium,* ed. Malinine, Puech, and Quispel. References in the text are to page and line in this edition. The place of the *Evangelium* among the other manuscripts discovered can as yet be known only second hand. See J. Doresse, "Trois Livres gnostiques inédits," *Vigiliae Christianae, 2* (1948), 137–60; H.-C. Puech and G. Quispel, "Les Écrits gnostiques du Codex Jung," ibid., *8* (1954), 1–51, and the *Jung Codex* referred to above.

49. *Jung Codex,* pp. 47–50.

Error (17.14 f.), and they live therefore in torment and trauma.
They have partial being—perhaps one should say that they
have potentiality—but they need knowledge of the Father if
they are to have real being. Their "end is the receiving of
knowledge of Him who is hidden" (37.38 f.). That knowledge
is mediated by the Logos, the first one to come forth from the
Father, and in order to be accessible to men the Logos or Son
takes on a "similitude of flesh" (31.1 ff.). His essential function
is not limited by the docetism of that word "similitude," for his
unique role is guaranteed by his relation to the Father. How
important this is is indicated by the variety of expressions used
in the *Gospel*. He is the Logos pronounced by the Mind "in
silent grace" (37.7–12). It is the Will of the Father which "de-
sired" him to come forth (37.17 f.). He is the begotten Son
(38.10). But perhaps the most characteristic usage of the *Gospel*
for affirming the relationship between the two is in the conception of *Name:*

> . . . But (δέ) the Name
> of the Father is the Son. It is He
> who in the beginning gave a name to Him who
> came forth from Him and who was Him-
> self, and whom He begot as a Son.
> He gave Him His Name which
> belonged to Him, —He, the Father, to whom
> belong all things which exist
> around Him. He possesses the Name;
> He has the Son. It is possible
> for them to see Him . . .   [38.6–16]

The Son alone has the Name (39.23, 40.14 f.)—in other words
he alone is essentially related to the Father. Another way of
affirming this is the notion that the Son comes forth to declare
truths about the Father which would otherwise remain unknown: that he is absolute Goodness and gentleness, that he
dwells in "the Place" from which the Son has come, that the
pleroma is glorious (40.29 ff., 41.1–7).

The gnosis that is granted is clearly of two kinds, and about
one of them the *Gospel of Truth* displays an interesting un-

easiness. On the one hand the Son reveals intellectual truths, and here is evidence of the esoteric knowledge that became so important in later Valentinianism. On the other hand because the Son is the very Name of the Father he manifests the Father directly; in other words, in the Name men are confronted with real Being. But just here the uneasiness appears, for the *Gospel* denies that in a final sense the Name can apply to the Father, even though it is his. He remains undefined, illimitable:

> For, indeed, the Unbegotten
> has no name.
> For what Name could one give to Him
> who did not come into existence?
> On the contrary, he who did come into existence
> came into existence with his Name. And
> He is the only one who knows it . . .
> The Name, then, is that of the Father
> just as the Name of the
> Father is the Son. . .   [39.11–26]

By this paradox the *Gospel* maintains the unknowability of the Father, in spite of real revelation of knowledge about him and even immediate knowledge of him. Full understanding of the significance of this relevation can come only when in the next chapter we trace its relation to thought about salvation, but for our purposes here the conception of revelation alone is sufficient.

The *Gospel of Truth* clearly speaks a Christian gnosticism, the elements of which suggest very different sources. In part the Name speculation seems to me to be Jewish. The Name carries power so awesome that it cannot be invoked: "One does not pronounce the Name of the Father" (38.22). This notion suggests something of ancient Jewish reverence for the mysterious Tetragrammaton. The fact that the Name can be bestowed on another suggests the speculations of the *Apocalypse of Abraham*,[50] although this is not to say that the author of the *Gospel* knew it. But the fact that the Name is associated with being, since the Father will eventually grant names to his crea-

50. See Quispel's interesting argument in *Jung Codex,* pp. 64–78.

tures, may well also indicate Greek notions. In the Seventh Letter of Plato *Onoma* and *Logos* and *Eidolon* are necessary factors in the knowledge of real essence (342B), and one may suppose that this kind of thought would have been familiar to Valentinus.[51] But probably more directly important than either as a source is the Fourth Gospel, where the figure of the Unknown Father declared by the Son has its most persuasive statement.

In the emphasis it gives to revelation the *Gospel of Truth* resembles the thought of both the Fourth Gospel and Ignatius, although it has a rationale for revelation that neither of them has: full being of the creatures can be achieved only by divine knowledge. Its gnosis is both message and divine disclosure, and to that degree its beliefs differ from theirs for whom revelation begins and ends in the disclosure of God. The discovery of the *Gospel* gives us an early example of a genuinely moving gnostic document in which men's search for God is ended only by God's initiative in the revelation in Christ. Its concern stands there, rather than in esoteric interest in the details of the pleroma, and it occupies a middle position between the teaching represented by the Fourth Gospel and Ignatius and that of the later Valentinians.

51. This connection was pointed out to me by R. L. Calhoun.

6. The Divine Event: Salvation

REVELATION and the incarnation, important in themselves as they are for Ignatius, are nevertheless seen in true perspective only in relation to the divine redemption. When the Son, in whom the Father manifested himself, became true man, the crucial event began. All that preceded it is being brought to an end, for dramatically new power is operating. Ignatius makes this point at length in the well-known chapter of *Eph.* 19, but in most places in the letters he takes for granted that the men in the churches know the outlines of the redeeming work, and in swift phrases he underlines its most important aspects. It is, above all, a mighty act of God. He speaks of it as the οἰκονομία θεοῦ[1] (*Eph.* 18.2, 20.1)—a description which points to the notion of a divine event. It is the implementation of divine purpose, for it is "made ready by God," or "in the counsels of God" (*Eph.* 19.3). The word is used in a similar sense in N.T. Eph. 1:10 and 3:9. Because the church implements the new dispensation, it is itself described by association as "ordained before time" (*Eph.* Ins.).

The event is thus no merely fortunate contingency but the ultimate expression of the divine goodness directed toward men (*Mag.* 10.1). The passage declaring the "goodness" of Jesus Christ comes as the summing up of the argument that begins in *Mag.* 8, and we must conclude that the "goodness" brings to Ignatius' mind all the preceding ideas of the coming forth of the Word, the revelation of the Father in the Son. The wonder of the event is that it is performed for needy humankind. Repeatedly through the letters the fact of the coming of the Lord and the steps of his historical life are declared to be "for us." Ignatius characteristically declares the divine condescension and mercy by reciting the concrete acts of Christ

1. It is used in just this absolute sense in the N.T. in Eph. 1:10; 3:2, 9; Col. 1:25; I Tim. 1:4. For later uses see Schlier, *Relig. Untersuch.*, pp. 32 f.

performed for men, instead of expressing them abstractly. "Wait for him who is above the critical moment, the one beyond time, the Invisible who became visible *for us,* the one beyond suffering who suffered *for us,* indeed he endured in every way *for us"* (*Poly.* 3). He died *for our sake* (*Tral.* 2.1, *Rom.* 6.1), he rose *for us* (*Rom.* 6.1). And the end of this divine act of mercy is the salvation of men: "He suffered all these things for us that we might be saved" (*Smyr.* 2.1). As one might expect, Ignatius not infrequently falls back on another familiar term and speaks of Christ as "our Saviour." [2] The divine invitation is offered to human beings who without help would be lost.

Ignatius' declaration that "these are the last times" (*Eph.* 11.1) is meant in part to underline his conviction that this is the central event of all existence. The passage is less than clear, however, for it inadvertently reveals that Ignatius stands between two worlds. He continues: "Let us either fear the impending Wrath, or love the Grace already present—one of the two—only let us be found in Christ Jesus unto true life" (ibid.). Here we see that in more than one sense these are the "last times." On the one hand the judgment stands ahead and therefore time runs out; on the other hand these are the last times because in them the crucial "gift of God" (*Eph.* 17) has been made. His readers might hold either view. We shall examine Ignatius' eschatology more fully below, but it will suffice here to see that for him any doctrine about the end is less important than the central fact that God has offered true life. It means the beginning of the destruction of death itself (*Eph.* 19.3).

Ignatius has a vivid sense that the salvation which has come to the world is sorely needed. The world was ripe for this saving act, for men and powers alike are caught in situations from which they cannot emerge without divine help. From a cosmic point of view the world is harassed and tormented by the Evil One. The Prince or Ruler of this world is Ignatius' favorite name for the principle of evil, although Satan (*Eph.* 13) appears once, and the devil four times.[3] But by any name he is seen

2. *Eph.* 1.1, *Mag.* Ins., *Phld.* 9.2, *Smyr.* 7.1.

3. Ruler: *Eph.* 17.1, 19.1; *Mag.* 1.2; *Tral.* 4.2; *Rom.* 7.1; *Phld.* 6.2. Devil: *Eph.* 10.3; *Tral.* 8.1; *Rom.* 5.3; *Smyr.* 9.1.

from the human angle as the Adversary of men. He plots against the faithful (*Phld.* 6.2), trying to turn men from God (*Rom.* 7.1), in part by false teaching (*Eph.* 17.1) which can rob them of eternal life, and in part by insults (*Mag.* 1.2) and evil words. He snares men (*Tral.* 8.1) and punishes them cruelly (*Rom.* 5.3). Only if men "live through all the wanton insolence of the prince of this world and escape" can they attain unto God (*Mag.* 1.2).

The operations of the Prince of this world are not exhausted in his hostility against men. His cosmic role appears in fullest form in *Eph.* 19, but although that is the most dramatic passage it does not stand alone: elsewhere (*Eph.* 13.2) Ignatius speaks of wars "in heaven and on earth," and he believes that the prince's machinations are everywhere operative. Satan is seen in the last analysis as the Enemy of God, since the divine purpose to save men was hidden from him (*Eph.* 19). The "old kingdom" which was to be destroyed was marked by magic and ignorance and wickedness (*Eph.* 19.3), and its basic characteristic was death. It was, *per contra,* the newness of eternal life that opposed him.

It is interesting to inquire into the identity of the Evil One. He is clearly in Ignatius' thought not the Demiurge of later gnosticism. He is not responsible for the creation of the world, for Ignatius holds that "all things that are" were willed by God (*Rom.* Ins.). Since he exists, this is a dualistic view; but since he is not operating in a universe of his own making, it is dualism of a limited sort. Ignatius sometimes uses the word *kosmos*[4] to mean the visible, sensible world (*Rom.* 2.2, 3.1, 4.2, 6.1), but again he means by it the aspect of things that contrasts with the things of God. So he sees men as marked either by "the stamp of this world" or the "stamp of God" (*Mag.* 5.2), and he begs the Romans not to "give to the world one who yearns to belong to God" (*Rom.* 6.2, cf. *Rom.* 7.1). The "world" in this sense may be an impersonal entity, or he may think of it collectively as all non-Christian groups, as when he says that Christianity is "hated by the world" (*Rom.* 3.3), but neither of these uses of the word indicates a belief on his part that the world is alien to God in a metaphysical sense.

4. For Paul's use of the word see Bultmann, *Theology, 1,* 254–59.

The name of the power in control, the Prince of this world (ἄρχων τοῦ αἰῶνος τούτου) indicates as it does in the Fourth Gospel and elsewhere sovereignty over an "age." It is a time-scheme [5] rather than a space-scheme, and it suggests that during "this world," which seems to be the equivalent of the "old kingdom" (*Eph.* 19.3), the Ruler who is the devil is sovereign, but only for a limited period. The incarnation brought to an end his unchallenged power. The evil power is effective and dangerously persuasive during the existence of this aeon, but is not thought of as locked in an indeterminate struggle with God.

Like his contemporaries Ignatius thought of the universe as peopled with spiritual beings of whom the Prince of this world was only one. He claims knowledge of "heavenly things, and the orders of the angels and the associations of principalities, and things seen and unseen" (*Tral.* 5.2) and again of "heavenly powers and the splendor of the angels,[6] and the rulers visible and invisible" (*Smyr.* 6.1). There is no specific scheme suggested here, for the passages suggest without being exhaustive, and unlike Paul [7] Ignatius offers no view of a hierarchy of powers. One would gather that he was less interested than Paul in celestial hierarchies although in one breath he boasts of his knowledge, and in the next deprecates such an interest because it has nothing to do with the practical matter of being a disciple of Jesus Christ (*Tral.* 5.2). One significant point about his belief is that these powers are apparently neutrals in the cosmic warfare between God and the Prince of this world, for he implies that they too can experience salvation "if they believe in the blood of Christ" (*Smyr.* 6.1). At the least there is

5. Ἀιών, used with reference to the Prince of this world, is characteristic with Ignatius; see *Eph.* 17.1, 19.1; *Mag.* 1.2; *Tral.* 14.2; *Rom.* 7.1; *Phld.* 6.2. Probably *Rom.* 6.1 alone has an historical reference. Twice he uses πρὸ αἰώνων (*Eph.* Ins., *Mag.* 6.1) with the notion of predestination or existence from eternity. Once he speaks of a standard set up εἰς τοὺς αἰῶνας (*Smyr.* 1.2).

6. Jewish belief in angels is at its height in *I Enoch* 6.1 ff., 20–21, and passim. For the doctrine of judgment on the wicked angels see also ibid., 90. For a list of orders see *Test. Levi* 3.

7. See, e.g., M. Dibelius, *Die Geisterwelt im Glauben des Paulus*, Göttingen, 1909.

judgment for them if they do not believe. Since this is so, we must conclude that they are for him the deceived, not the deceivers, for they can receive the new power of grace that came into the world through Christ. Certainly they are not identical with the emanations from the godhead of later gnosticism, nor do they seem to be similar to the planet-sons of Ruha of the Mandaean writings.[8] They are apparently led away by the conceits of the Prince of this world, and they are open to the help of God as the devil himself is not.

This world-view is in no sense an original creation, for it was widely shared by generations who preceded Ignatius and by his contemporaries. It might be illustrated from countless writings, but it is interesting to observe its forms in the writings prized by groups with whom we believe Ignatius was associated, Essene-Christians and the ones that used the *Odes of Solomon* and the Fourth Gospel.

The *Manual of Discipline* presents a comparable *Weltanschauung*, although it has elements that do not appear in the Ignatian letters. God is one, and from him comes "all that is and will be," and the creation remains completely in his control (*DSD* 3.15,17). It is within this world created by God that man's life is played out, and the *Manual* holds the doctrine of the two spirits created by God: those of truth and of perversion, or error, or deceit (3.25). The Parables of *I Enoch* have a different explanation of the origin of the spirit of evil, and rest it on the wicked perverseness of the angels who would "do as if they were the Lord"[9] and who therefore fell like stars into darkness, and on earth remained as the tempters and harassers of men. Whether or not *I Enoch* was known to the Essene-Christians, speculation about the rise of evil must have been widespread. Whatever its origin, evil operates against the purposes of God, and God hates it and its ways (*DSD* 4.1). It is

8. So Reitzenstein, *Iranisches Erlösungsmysterium*, p. 234, referring to the myth in *Qol.* xiv; see Lidzbarski, *Mandäische Liturgien*, pp. 184 f. Schlier, pp. 6 f., quotes it.

9. *I Enoch* 68.4. The sinning of the angels with the daughters of men is everywhere in *Enoch*, e.g. 6.1–6; to them is ascribed the origin of the sin of men, 10.8–16. Cf. Adam as the deliberate originator of sin, *II Baruch* 56. See Charles, ed., *Apocrypha and Pseudepigrapha*, 2, 477 f.

a surd in the otherwise meaningful world of his purposes, for it implies that he condones at least for a season the effective rule of the angel of darkness. The *Manual of Discipline* declares darkly that God does this through the "mysteries of his understanding" (4.18), for the explanation of the act remains hidden. *I Enoch* 68.4 at least removes from God the onus of being the immediate cause of evil.

For the *Odes* and the Fourth Gospel, like Ignatius, the doctrine of the two spirits is lacking, and the Evil One stands out more prominently. In them appears the same figure by different names—Satan, or the Deceiver, or the Prince of this world—performing, as we have seen in part above, precisely this role of the tempter and harasser. In the end God will triumph. Not all the spiritual powers, according to the *Odes*, are hostile to God, for they speak of hosts and elect archangels who have the seal of God (4.7 f.). Sometimes in them the Evil One is represented as Anti-Christ, since he imitates the Beloved (38.11), and once he appears in mythical form as the primordial dragon with the seven heads (22.5). In the Fourth Gospel he is the thief who ravages the flock (10:10) and the Prince of the world who has nothing to do with the Son (14:30). All these notions, whatever their individual differences, are allied to the world-view [10] of *I Enoch* and the *Manual of Discipline,* where rebellious angels or spirits contend with angels of the presence—a struggle of absolute importance for human beings.

The most interesting thing about this widely shared notion of the world is that its dualism is so qualified. There is no doubt that the Father is in control. Men and angels are threat-

10. K. G. Kuhn, "Die in Palästina gefundenen hebräischen Texte und das Neue Testament," *Zeitschrift für Theologie und Kirche, 47* (1950), 205–11, argues that the world view of the Essenes, set in a religion of law and Jewish apocalyptic, is a *Vorform* of gnosis. In his later article, "Die Sektenschrift und die iranische Religion," ibid., *49* (1952), 314 ff., Kuhn abandons his earlier conclusion and relates the thought of the *Manual* to Iranian sources, united with the creation theory of the Old Testament, and he argues that gnosticism exhibits a later stage of influence, impressed on a Greek view of a world of matter, and hence producing the notion of matter as contrary to the divine.

ened by the presence in the world of the Evil Ruler or by rebellious angels, but they will not win in the end. Nor is the
world itself alien to God. There is in the Ignatian letters no
dramatic passage like that in Paul's letter to the Romans where
he declares that "the whole creation groaneth and travaileth
in pain together until now," hoping that "the creation itself
. . . shall be delivered from the bondage of corruption . . ."
(Rom. 8:22 f.); and probably Paul [11] goes farther than Ignatius
would be willing to go, for his sense of the need for redemption, real as it was, was less tragic than that of Paul. We may
wonder whether even the Docetists in Antioch held that the
world was alien to God, for there is no evidence that the creation was under debate.

Although Ignatius' understanding of the world was conventional, his analysis of the plight of men is somewhat more
individual. His conception differs sharply from that of Paul,
for the lively awareness which Paul has of the sinfulness of
human beings is almost lacking. He does not half hypostatize
the principle of sin, as that which in Paul's thinking holds
men enthralled, and incredibly enough only twice in the letters
does the word "sin" occur, as either verb or noun (*Eph.* 14.2,
Smyr. 7.1). This is not to suggest that Ignatius is complacent
about man's own powers or that he feels less strongly the divine
goodness of proffering salvation, but the absence of the notion
of sin arises from a rather different view of the constitution
of man. For him "flesh" is not, as in Paul's thought, doomed
almost by necessity, for in Paul, as Bultmann [12] says, both sin
and flesh are considered "powers to which man has fallen
victim," so that through their corruption the mind itself can
be infected, and the whole self become darkened (e.g. Rom.
1:28).

11. For the Jewish notion of the creation corrupted through Adam's
sin see Strack-Billerbeck, *Kommentar, 3, ad* Rom. 8:20. Bultmann, *Theology, 1,* 227–32, considers that Paul's understanding of the creation owes
something to both Jewish and gnostic views.

12. Bultmann, *Theology, 1,* 244. For a careful discussion of Paul's view
of flesh, sin, and death see ibid., pp. 232–49, 199–203.

For Ignatius, on the contrary, flesh refers to the *actual* or the *natural* man, who is not necessarily dominated by radical evil. Flesh and spirit are certainly different, but they are not inevitably opposed. The flesh can even be said to have a certain dignity and necessity of its own, and a real function to perform, for by means of it men have traffic with the ordinary sensible things and the world. "For this reason you are of flesh and of spirit, that you may deal graciously with the things which are before your eyes; and as for the invisible things pray that they may become apparent to you . . ." (*Poly.* 2.2). He acknowledges that in general flesh and spirit have different spheres: "They who are of the flesh cannot do spiritual things, neither can they who are of the spirit do carnal things . . ." (*Eph.* 8.2). It might be thought that this sentence suggests an acceptance of the gnostic division of men into *sarkikoi* and *pneumatikoi*, but Ignatius quite clearly does not hold this. He says that even the Christians who are *pneumatikoi* are still *natural*, still enmeshed in flesh, for they do things κατὰ σάρκα. And for them the flesh and the spirit are not opposed principles, with the flesh a constant pitfall and temptation for the spirit: "Whatever you do even according to the flesh is spiritual, for you do all things in Jesus Christ" (*Eph.* 8.2). The same idea holds concerning the resurrection of Jesus Christ. He was raised both flesh and spirit (*Smyr.* 3.2), and one must doubt that Ignatius would have been willing, as Paul was, to say that the risen bodies of his followers would be spiritual. Although after the resurrection Jesus Christ was able to eat and drink with his disciples, thus showing that he was completely embodied, he was nevertheless spiritually united with the Father. The presence of the flesh was in no way a barrier to spiritual union.

Although the opposition between flesh and spirit is not radical, spirit belongs to God as flesh does not. This is partly the result of Ignatius' conviction that the Holy Spirit may take over and dominate a man (*Phld.* 7.2), and in this sense it is the human spirit that is possessed by the Holy Spirit. But whether the Holy Spirit dominates or not, the heart of the matter is that God should be the focus of man's life. Thus Ignatius contrasts care for the neighbor "according to the flesh" with loving him "in Jesus Christ" *(Mag.* 6.2), and he brings to an end the contrast between those who are of the flesh and therefore cannot do the things of the spirit, and those who are of the spirit and therefore cannot do the things of the flesh by saying that what is done "according to the flesh" is spiritual, when it is done "in Jesus Christ" *(Mag.* 8.2). We shall consider this again in Chapter 8, but such phrases make it clear that flesh is not radically inimical to spirit. It is the necessary basis for the self, and for that reason would seem to be neutral, potentially the seat either of a natural or a redeemed person. The goal is that the self, composed of flesh and spirit in unity,[13] shall be dominated by spirit and united with God. There is here no flesh-spirit dualism like that which characterizes later gnostic thought,[14] nor is flesh ever spoken of as particularly vulnerable to the onslaught of the Prince of this world. Clearly for Ignatius the reason for man's need for salvation is not his connection with matter.

What makes men dependent upon God for salvation is their tendency toward division. It is this which for Ignatius constantly threatens men and takes the place of the more dynamic "sin." The notion includes all the kinds of separateness that can occur. Men are divided from one another and from the church in factionalism and anger; they are split within themselves by pride and boasting, so that they depend upon themselves and do not live "in Jesus Christ." It is because of this vulnerability that the wiles of the devil, which may make a man "wise in his own conceit" are so dangerous, for so long as he is split within himself he is not united with God. Flesh itself, separated

13. Only once does Ignatius use the tripartite analysis of man as flesh, soul, and spirit *(Phld.* 11.2). Once *(Phld.* 1.2) he speaks of himself as ψυχή, but characteristically it is as πνεῦμα *(Eph.* 18.1, *Tral.* 13.3, *Rom.* 9.3, *Phld.* 7.1, *Smyr.* 10.2). Σῶμα always means the physical body *(Rom.* 4.2 *bis,* 5.3). It is clear that he is not very self-conscious about terms. One may surmise that the Docetists did not stress the tripartite division. See Jonas, *Gnosis,* *I,* 212–14.

14. For excellent short statements of the motifs of gnosticism see Bultmann, *Theology, I,* 165–72, and *Das Urchristentum im Rahmen der antiken Religionen* (Zurich, 1949), pp. 181–92; H. Jonas, *The Gnostic Religion* (Boston, 1958), chaps. 2, 3.

from spirit and become dominant in a man, may be the worst hazard. Without divine aid men are left vulnerable to outward attack and to their own weakness.

As we have seen above, it is by Christ alone that salvation comes to the world. Judaism claimed to offer salvation, but Ignatius declares that it is grossly inadequate, since it is incomplete.[15] The prophets, who were central especially for sectarian Judaism, lived not according to Judaism but in the light of the Gospel, and thus anticipated the great reality of the incarnation. They above all would have had salvation if Judaism could have given it, but they knew its consummation only at the coming of Christ. It is he who is the Door of the Father through whom patriarchs and prophets and the whole church (*Phld.* 9.1) enter in. He and he alone brings salvation to the men in the churches and to the spiritual powers of the heavens.

For all of Ignatius' certainty that redemption comes only in Christ, there is in the letters no fully developed doctrine of the saving work. Single insights lie everywhere on the surface, but they are never built into a unified structure of thought. The notion of the οἰκονομία θεοῦ is the most vivid of his pictures, and here is presented the divine drama of salvation to the men and powers subject to the hostility of Satan. The Son came forth from the Father, and the historical life as a whole is the effective act. That Ignatius thinks of it, somewhat unreflectively, as a whole is shown clearly by his groupings of the essential events, although there is no single formula in the letters expressing them. *Eph.* 19.1 mentions the three mysteries of the "virginity of Mary, and her giving birth, and the death of the Lord." The ἀρχεῖα, the ultimate foundations, on the other hand, are the "cross, the death, and the resurrection" (*Phld.* 8.2), and in still a third passage the central events are listed as the "coming and passion and resurrection" (*Phld.* 9.2). The constituent parts of the whole seem to be the coming or the birth (*Mag.* 11.1), with its attendant marvels, and the passion or death, and the resurrection. But since the passion and resurrection are so often linked together, we are justified in reducing to two the main strands

15. See above, Chap. 3.

in Ignatius' thought, although there is some overlapping. One emphasizes the coming of the Lord, and connected with that is the notion that by his coming, grace and life have been made available. The other is the affirmation that the cross and the passion gave salvation and life. Before we examine the significance of these two strands of Ignatius' thought about salvation, we must explore the meaning for him of "grace" and "life."

One must conclude that Ignatius thought of grace as having become available to man in the incarnate life as a whole. It simply has "come to us" (*Smyr.* 6.2). He contrasts it, as a present possession, with the wrath which is to come (*Eph.* 11.1), and he clearly holds that before Christ came it was lacking. This is implied by the passage, "if we are living according to Judaism we confess that we have not received grace" (*Mag.* 8.1). The prophets had received grace, but this was because they already lived according to the Gospel and were not typical of the world.

Grace [16] is thus essentially a soteriological word, for it means the divine help extended to men for their salvation. Sometimes it is loosely used as the equivalent for the whole saving event (*Phld.* 11.1), but usually it carries more specific meaning. It is by the grace of Jesus Christ that men can be loosed from the bonds of ignorance that make them susceptible to the false teachings (*Phld.* 8.1). Ignatius himself hopes for grace that will help him to endure the violent death of martyrdom (*Rom.* 1.2), but it is also the ground of the holiness of the bishop Polycarp (*Poly.* 1.2). Again, it is by the grace of God that Ignatius received the sentence of death which offers him the chance to "attain unto God" (*Smyr.* 11.1), and here it seems to mean

16. Grace must be mentioned in this connection, but cannot be fully evaluated until we observe Ignatius' thought about love and unity. T. F. Torrance, *The Doctrine of Grace in the Apostolic Fathers* (London, 1948), esp. pp. 65, 69–77. Torrance, in his excellent essay on Ignatius presents grace as "the groundwork for the doctrine of *gratia inherens et infusa*" (p. 76). Ignatius avoids the magical overtones that mark the thought of some gnostics. See J. Moffatt, *Grace in the New Testament* (New York, 1932), pp. 377 ff. For grace in Paul, as in Ignatius, as the definition of the saving act see also G. P. Wetter, *Charis* (Leipzig, 1913), pp. 78–87.

rather the graciousness of God. It is usually, however, the power that makes for steadfastness and for the relationships within the community which are truly Christian.

Life, almost as often as grace, carries the thought of the gift of Christ to men, and in similar fashion he sometimes equates it with the whole saving work. "God appeared as man to bring in the newness of eternal life" (*Eph.* 19.3), or again he is "true life in death" (*Eph.* 7.2). This is the point of the incarnation. Jesus Christ is the "inseparable life" of the churches (*Eph.* 3.2), and again "Jesus Christ, our true life, has power" over the problematical repentance of the false teachers (*Smyr.* 4.1). It is "in Christ Jesus" that Ignatius hopes he may be "found unto true life" (*Eph.* 11.1). Christ bestows life as well as being life in himself, and in these passages life is not clearly distinguishable from grace.

The *Odes* and the Fourth Gospel [17] express clearly what Ignatius implies throughout but never directly says: that life is the hallmark of deity. The *Odes* state explicitly that the gift of life comes from the Living One:

> For he that is joined to Him that is immortal,
> Will himself also become immortal.
>
> And he that hath pleasure in the Living One,
> Will become living. [3.8, 9]
>
> For I was ready before destruction came;
> And I have been set on His immortal pinions;
>
> And deathless life embraced me
> And kissed me.
>
> And from that (life) is the Spirit within me;
> And it cannot die, for it lives. [28.5–7]

The Fourth Gospel expresses the same idea even more clearly; for it life is the very being of God. "For as the Father hath life in himself, even so gave he to the Son also to have life in himself . . ." (John 5:26). And the purpose of the incarnation

17. Dodd, *Fourth Gospel*, pp. 144–50, interprets the idea of ζωή αἰώνιος as similar to that of Philo, with Plato in the background. The emphasis is on "eternal" rather than "life."

was that life might be imparted to men: "I came that they may
have life, and may have it abundantly" (John 10:10). ". . . He
that heareth my word, and believeth him that sent me hath
eternal life, and cometh not into judgment but hath passed
out of death into life" (John 5:24). In Ignatius' letters the
statement that "newness of eternal life" would help to abolish
death (*Eph.* 19.3) is an example of the same kind of thinking.

The fact that God is life, and that he gives life to men goes far
to explain the importance of the incarnation for both Ignatius
and the Fourth Gospel. "And the Word became flesh and dwelt
among us, and we beheld his glory . . ." The words are the
climax of the prologue to the Fourth Gospel. "There is one
physician, both of flesh and of spirit, born and yet existing un-
born, God in man, true life in death . . ." (*Eph.* 7). It is
supremely important that the incarnation be "true," for only
when God became available to men could they gain life.

But to say that is not to imply that Ignatius or the Fourth
Evangelist came on simply rational grounds to the thought
of deity as the source of life. It is an idea that permeates the
period, and they appropriated it and its corollary light, although
the latter is not characteristic for Ignatius. The twin concepts
have already been well developed on Jewish soil. In the cosmo-
logical speculation of *I Enoch* the tree of life that grows beside
the throne of God (24–25) is a kind of mythological ap-
purtenance of deity. It is "He that liveth forever" (*I Enoch* 5.1),
who is the source and guarantor of life. In the parables of
I Enoch life and light are more frequent. In 62.16 garments
of life are given to the righteous after the judgment by the
Lord of Spirits (cf. *DSD* 4.8). God is the source of light, which
appears now as a synonym for the good spirit that works in the
world (63.6) or again the mark of the righteous "as fiery lights"
before God (39.7b). One gathers that they are lights at least
partly because they have achieved the status of living in the
presence of God. This is not unfamiliar terminology in the Old
Testament, for light was the first creation of God, and fiery light
is a symbol for God in the visions of Ezekiel and in later
apocalyptic, but in these still later writings light becomes
associated with him almost as a description of his nature. In the

Testament of Zebulun 9.8 God is himself described as the "Light of righteousness" and in the *Manual of Discipline* he is the "life-giving Light" (3.7). Although the latter affirms stoutly that God created the spirits of both light and darkness, it goes on to say, "The one, God has loved for all the duration of the ages; and in all its activities he delights forever" [18] (*DSD* 3.26 f.). Many comparable passages could be cited. Life and Light, then, are the ultimate gifts to men because they come from God who is Life and Light. A marginal gloss in *Test. Jud.* 24.4 uses the divine description as a messianic title: "this Fountain giving life unto all." It is with these notions that we find ourselves on the threshold of the thought of Ignatius, the Fourth Gospel and the *Odes*. The prologue of the Gospel brings the two together in declaring of the Logos that "In him was life and the life was the light of men," and in the body of the Gospel Christ declares himself to be "the light of the world" (8:12). In the Ignatian letters light appears only once, in a passage referring to martyrdom. Ignatius says that his death will mean "being born into life" ($\zeta\tilde{\eta}\sigma\alpha\iota$)," or, in quick parallelism, receiving "the pure light" (*Rom.* 6.2). Even this one passage bears witness that light and life are aspects of deity, since by the martyr's death Ignatius expects to "attain unto God."

The *Odes*, too, make full use of these notions. The Lord purposes the everlasting life of men (9.4, 6.9–18). The Odist declares

> The Lord hath directed my mouth by His Word
> And He hath opened my heart by His Light.
>
> And He hath caused to dwell in me His deathless life;
> And gave me to speak the fruit of His peace . . .
>
> [10.1, 2]

and Christ answers antiphonally that "traces of the light" were given to men, and they "walked in my life" (10.6). There is everywhere the same notion that in redemption life is given to men (cf. Ode 3), and light is also important. "The mouth of the Lord is the true Word, and the door of his Light" (12.3);

18. Brownlee's translation.

here Light and Word are equated (cf. 10.1). The redeemed spirit is "possessed by His light" (11.11). There is no need to list further passages.

It will be apparent that this common stock of ideas about the nature of deity is widely used. That in the different circles they are modified by their association with other ideas no one would deny. But in all of them the notion exists of the God upon whom men are dependent for life, not only in creation but in salvation. Life and light are divine gifts that transform human existence. As long as "life" means only life after death—more life quantitatively—it is an idea consonant with late Old Testament thought. But when the gift is of that which is the very nature of God himself, a further step has been taken. Obedience to commands, entering into covenant, may continue to be important, but a new element has been added that will transform the understanding of human life, introducing both danger and riches.

Life and Not-life are primordial categories in Iranian thought and must surely stand behind the belief in the two spirits, the opposition of life and death, which appears in the Essene writings and was taken up into Christianity. Judaism and developing Christianity continued to affirm stoutly that God is finally in control; the dualism is only relative. But because God allows the two spirits, or even creates them, it becomes more difficult to affirm his righteousness. It is rather his being that must be affirmed. "Eternal Being is the support of my right hand" [19] (*DSD* 11.4). A few lines farther on, the psalm speaks of "His marvelous mysteries in Eternal Being" (11.5). To press the translation here would make rigid what is very tentative. Emphasis on the righteousness of God is in no way abated. But the God who eternally *is*, who is the source of *life*

19. So translated by Brownlee with, *ad loc.* n. 8, a possible alternative, "He Who is forever," but Brownlee rightly calls attention to Philo's use of ὁ ὤν and τὸ ὄν. Dupont-Sommer, *The Jewish Sect of Qumran*, pp. 143 f., translates this and the next reference, respectively, "And the Eternal Being is the prop of my right hand"; and "The light in my heart comes from His marvellous Mysteries; In the Eternal Being my eye has beheld wisdom."

and *light,* is in subtle ways different from him who spoke upon
Mt. Sinai. The notions about God in the pseudepigraphic and
some of the Essene writings foreshadow the ideas that appear in
Christian thinking at the very end of the first century. The God
of being and life, whose mysteries are beyond men, is that one
who manifested himself in the Son for the redemption of the
world. It is at this point that revelation becomes redemption.

These passages not only show the importance of the ideas of
grace and life and light for Ignatius and his age, but also make
understandable the background for his emphasis on the *coming* [20] of Christ as one of the two great aspects of God's act.
"God was manifest as man for the newness of eternal life" (*Eph.*
19.3). Because he was God, and hence himself Light and Life
and Grace, by his *parousia* he brought them to men. And with
this idea Ignatius shows himself in agreement with the Docetists,
although unlike them he struggles to maintain that it is through
true incarnation that the gift is effectually made. He maintains a balance, but there is no denying that he walks a tight-
rope, for with only one more step the "coming" could have
been divorced from history by emphasis on the events that
preceded his entry into human life.

With the alternative events associated with the saving work—
the cross and passion and resurrection—Ignatius occupies more
traditional ground. He is as sure as those who had preceded
him in the church that real life has been made available
through the tragic and triumphant events. Here the emphasis
is not on deity as itself the source of life but on acts performed
on the scene of history which were the means by which life became available.

The life which is salvation comes to men through the dying
and rising again of Christ. On the Lord's day, says Ignatius,
"our life welled up through him and his death" (*Mag.* 9.1).

20. The use of *parousia* by Ignatius to mean the historical coming is
significant of his belief that this was a definitive and absolute event fully
consummated. It also shows his abandonment of the notion of the second
coming, which is throughout the N.T. the meaning of the word. See the
article s.v. by Oepke in Kittel, *Theologisches Wörterbuch.*

Here it is primarily the resurrection which is in his mind. But the cross, too, however much it is a stumbling block" to unbelievers, is to Christians "salvation and life eternal" (*Eph.* 18.1). Again, "unless we decide voluntarily by his help to die and so to reproduce his passion, his life is not in us" (*Mag.* 5.2), and having faith in Jesus Christ is the basis for resurrection for Christians. "Without him we have no true life" (*Tral.* 9.2). Most dramatically Ignatius cries out, "The passion . . . is our resurrection" (*Smyr.* 5.3). The vivid figures of speech belong here also, in which he affirms the effective power of the cross. It is the planting of the Father, and its branches bear the imperishable fruit of Christian lives that will escape death (*Tral.* 11.2, *Smyr.* 1.2). Here the cross is a tree, perhaps akin to the mythical tree of life. The cross is furthermore the machine of Jesus Christ that raises Christians, like stones for the building of God, to their place (*Eph.* 9.1). Or he suggests the powerful attraction that the cross or the passion has for disciples of the Lord. He writes to the Romans begging to be allowed "to imitate the passion" of his God (*Rom.* 6.3). The cross is a standard that draws all men to it in devotion (*Smyr.* 1.2), and Christ calls them that are his by the cross, through his passion (*Tral.* 11).

That the preaching of the cross and death of Christ continued to be a "stumbling-block to unbelievers" (*Eph.* 18.1) need not surprise us, and Ignatius indicates why the docetic thinkers who were his opponents were repelled by it. In Ignatius' mind it was the final and incontrovertible proof that Christ truly became man and entered the scene of history. He was nailed in the flesh to the cross "for our sakes" (*Smyr.* 1.2). The docetic thinkers found it possible to dodge the full implication of human birth by emphasizing its painless character,[21] but the cross and the death could be treated only by silence. Ignatius says that the false teachers must "repent concerning the passion" (*Smyr.* 5.3); this is the crux of their stubborn twisting of the historical tradition.

Partly in opposition to docetic doctrine but more fundamentally to preach clearly the means of redemption, Ignatius

21. As in the *Ascension of Isaiah* 11.8–14, and Ode 19, esp. 8 f.

returns again and again to the passion. The cross is "for our sake," and in one strange lapse into an abstraction it is for "the faith of God" that Jesus Christ was crucified (*Eph.* 16.2). There is no escape from his conviction in many passages that if it had not been for the death on the cross, salvation would not have been effected. It was the essential means by which God worked. The "prize" of Christian living is for him "incorruption and eternal life" (*Poly.* 2.3), and again he speaks of the cross as "salvation and eternal life" (*Eph.* 18.2). As with Christ the righteous prophets rose from the dead, just so did the Christians hope to attain life in the presence of God. Men who had touched Christ's risen body were so infected by his quality of deathlessness that they became immune to death (*Smyr.* 3.2), but for the later Christians there was still hope through a mystical identification with him. They would by that means become fruit of the cross. One may wonder whether the use of the word μυστήριον in *Mag.* 9.1 suggests the means of identification, in a technical sense—that is, that in a mystery drama men entered so closely into the passion that they were identified with Christ. "Our life sprang up through him and his death." There is difficulty in being sure what Ignatius means, but the connotations of the passage are those not of the repeated action of a "mystery" but of the once-for-all event of the resurrection.

One other idea is connected with the ultimate identification of the Christian and his Lord. Ignatius in thinking of his own death by which he will "become a man" says that the "Perfect Man empowers" him (*Smyr.* 4.2). Here is the suggestion that Christ is representative Man, to whom men can join themselves, and this idea we shall explore further in Chapter 9.

When Ignatius considers the passion and crucifixion as the deliberate act of Christ, and in some other connections, too, he implies without ever developing it the notion that it is a sacrifice. Nothing else can explain the emphasis that they were done "for us." He suffered "for our sins" (*Smyr.* 7.1). The emphasis on the altar [22] in the church, indeed its very existence, would

22. In *Eph.* 5.2 and *Tral.* 7.2 he uses the word θυσιαστήριον to mean the part of the church containing the altar, or perhaps the whole meeting room.

suggest that the notion of sacrifice was embedded in the liturgy; "therefore, there is one flesh of our Lord Jesus Christ, and one cup for union with his blood, one altar (θυσιαστήριον) as there is one bishop" (*Phld.* 4.1, cf. *Mag.* 7.2). The realism of his expression in this passage, which we shall consider fully in the next chapter, makes it difficult to avoid the conviction that he thought of the death as a sacrifice,[23] although there is here a clear reference to the eucharist. And since he considers his own coming death as in some sense a sacrifice, it is difficult to hold that the supreme Passion was less than his. He writes to the Romans, "Grant me no more than to be poured out as a libation to God, while an altar is still ready . . ." (*Rom.* 2.2). He thinks of his death as an oblation, though he changes the figure so quickly to the brilliant word—"It is good to set to the world directed towards God, that I may rise to him"—that one must wonder how much weight his figure of oblation will bear. He hopes, however, to become a "sacrifice" by means of the beasts which he expects will devour his body. (*Rom.* 4.2). He never expressly states that the death of Christ is a sacrifice, and one can hold only by inference that it is a part of his thinking, but it seems nevertheless to mirror Old Testament concepts, as do I Cor. 5:7, and N.T. Eph. 5:2, and Hebrews. In any case it is not a dominant motif for interpreting the death of Christ.

It is this ambiguous treatment of the idea of sacrifice that makes us aware of the curious incompleteness of Ignatius' thought about redemption. For the notion of reconciliation with God is absent. Redemption changes men, empowers them, gives them the divine grace of true life; Christ brought life, he died as sacrifice, his suffering was an expression of love. But he did not atone to God on behalf of sinning man. Paul on the contrary sums up the whole work of Christ as reconciliation— "God was in Christ reconciling the world unto himself"—and with that insight he achieves a depth that Ignatius misses. For both men the cross is crucial for the saving of men. But for

23. Richardson, *Christianity*, p. 101, n. 99, maintains the opposite. Bartsch, *GG*, pp. 82 f., holds that the doctrine of the Passion as a sacrifice is not really grounded in Ignatius' thought but is an echo of community tradition.

Paul [24] the cross is not merely the necessary prelude to the resurrection; it is a propitiation (Rom. 3:24 f.), and the means of reconciliation to God (Rom. 5:10), and the symbolic victory over the principles of sin and death (Rom. 6:6 ff.) that through their mortal bodies held men in thrall.

This shift in emphasis is a subtle one not to be explained as a result of any single factor. Most obviously it follows from Ignatius' anthropology, which included no very lively belief in the sinfulness of man, and hence his estrangement from God. The separateness and self-will that mark men are rather their misfortune than an affront to God. The tragic element is lacking. Another factor in his thought, which must have blinded him to this lack, is the importance of the "coming" in the incarnation. Love and life were given because Christ was God; and since that was so, the passion did not hold the unique place that it did for Paul.

A somewhat similar ambiguity appears in Ignatius' eschatology. As we have seen above, he holds to the doctrine of the availability of grace but also admits that the wrath of God is still to be encountered. He even speaks of the ultimate punishment of the false teachers as the experience of "unquenchable fire" (*Eph.* 16.2). And judgment will fall even on the spiritual powers if they do not believe in the blood of Christ. There is an end for all, and the stark choice between life and death faces all men. "Each man must go to his own place" (*Mag.* 5.1). Here are at least the trappings of Jewish eschatology with the notion of an approaching judgment; yet one remains doubtful that there is a *single* last Assize that Ignatius looks forward to and we conclude that what is implied is the idea that judgment occurs as men exclude themselves from unity with God and therefore fail to lay hold on deathlessness.

The prologue of the Fourth Gospel suggests the latter idea when it says that "his own" in failing to receive the Word made flesh remained in darkness. Ignatius is not so definite, but when he declares that these are the last times, he goes on to

24. For Paul's interpretation of the death of Christ see V. Taylor, *The Atonement in New Testament Teaching* (2d ed. London, 1950), pp. 82–101; Bultmann, *Theology*, *1*, 292 ff., esp. 297.

say that by its very existence the mercy of God may become our own "judgment" (*Eph.* 11.1). The merciful act of sending the Gift which is Christ can be a judgment only if man turns away. He suggests this in a phrase and then swiftly contrasts the Wrath with the Grace: objective future testing, and the self-exclusion of a present refusal to "love the Grace which is present." But the conclusion of this pregnant sentence is a denial that notions of eschatology are important, for he pleads: "only let us be found in Christ Jesus unto true life" (ibid.). We argued in Chapter 3 that the Docetists maintained that grace had already come. There is no evidence other than this passage that the Essene-Christians preserved a belief in Jewish apocalyptic, though it would be entirely consistent with Essene belief.[25] Ignatius knows both beliefs, and we may assume that he had met them both in Antioch, is willing to accept either, and therefore reaches this state of uneasy indecision, but he is able to endure it because he is utterly certain that the matter is not an essential part of the Christian gospel about which a man must think truly if he is to be saved. Christ is God become manifest at the end of time (*Mag.* 6.1), but the emphasis is not on the last phrase but on the salvation event itself.

Throughout our examination of Ignatius' beliefs about salvation it has been apparent that he is holding in balance views that are not always easily related to each other, and that there are inevitable points of strain. From one point of view, for instance, the coming of the Saviour was not wholly unexpected, for it had been announced by the prophets. They taught about him, had faith in him (*Phld.* 5.2) and even received grace from him (*Mag.* 8.2). They are so fully of the new dispensation that there is no suggestion that Ignatius holds with Paul a sharp division of history into an age of law which was superseded by one of grace, for more than promise is received by the prophets. On the other hand the events of the incarnation are marked by a revolutionary novelty such that their

25. Judgment is central for all Essene writings. See *DSD* 3.23, 4.18–21, 9.23, 10.13 for the sense of waiting for judgment; the anathemas, *DSD* 2.6–9, 15. It is everywhere in *I Enoch* and frequent in the *Habakkuk Commentary*.

meaning eludes the Prince of this world. Similarly, there are points of strain in trying to reconcile the *coming* and the *passion* as important in salvation. Ignatius attempts to do this by saying that all the events in the incarnate life must be considered together, but this strategy of inclusiveness does not lead to intellectual clarity. We see a similar difficulty when he tries to reconcile the notion of judgment with the continuing opportunity of life and grace proffered in the incarnation. These ambiguities are important because they show Ignatius' problem and the problem of all of his generation of Christians, in using ideas that came from two different worlds. They are not merely incidental failures on his part to think out one or another of the doctrines, but arise from the disparateness of the elements he is trying to join together.

As we have seen in earlier chapters, the important recent studies of Ignatius represent him as influenced by gnostic thought. Schlier's *Religionsgeschichtliche Untersuchungen zu den Ignatiusbriefen* was the first full-length study of the letters against their contemporary background and its central argument is that Ignatius' thought of Christ bears the unmistakable mark of pre-Valentinian and Mandaean gnosis. Before we analyze Schlier's thought in detail it will be profitable to recall the general outlines of the background myth.

In the *Ascension of Isaiah* [26] (which we have in a form worked over by a Christian editor), in the *Ginza* of the Mandaeans, in the *Excerpta ex Theodoto,* and elsewhere in writings of the second and third centuries there appear variants of the myth of a redeemer who descends from the region of the Sovereign God to earth, to save mankind from the enmity of the power of this

26. The relevant sections are in the *Vision of Isaiah* 9.7–10.31. R. H. Charles, *The Ascension of Isaiah* (London, 1900), p. xlv, holds that Ignatius knows the *Vision* (*Ascension* 6.1–11.40) and bases his judgment on the "similarity" between *Eph.* 19 and *Vis.* 11.16: "This hath escaped all the heavens and all the princes and all the gods of this world." This does not seem to me to imply knowledge of the Vision but rather a natural conclusion based on a similar world-view. Flemming and Duensing in Hennecke, *Neutestmentliche Apokryphen* (2d ed. Tübingen, 1924), p. 303, date the *Vision* in the second century.

world. He is unknown to that power, as in some of the versions
he is unknown to the rulers of the heavens through which he
passes on his descent. By struggle he wins out over the Ruler
of earth, who holds enslaved the human beings who are related
to the Sovereign God because they are light-souls embedded in
a material body. The redeemer, then, in glory and in a form
that makes his identity known to all, ascends through the
heavens to his father. Schlier [27] argues that Ignatius knows this
myth in some form, though since the details vary greatly it is not
clear in what form Schlier believes he knew it, since he maintains only that it stands "im Hintergrund."

The crux of the proof rests on the discovery in *Eph.* 19 of a
number of the motifs of the myth: the secrecy that marks the
descent, the ignorance of the Prince of this world, warfare
against him which issues in the freeing of men, and an ascent in
glory: [28]

> And the virginity of Mary and her childbearing escaped
> the notice of the ruler of this world just as did the death
> of the Lord—three mysteries of a cry wrought in the still-
> ness of God. 2 How then was he set forth to the ages? A star
> in heaven shone brilliant beyond all the stars, and its light
> was indescribable, and its newness caused amazement, 2b
> and all the rest of the stars with the sun and moon formed
> in choral dance around the star, but its light was beyond
> measure greater than theirs. And there was perplexity,
> whence came the new one, so unlike them. 3 By this event
> all magic was undone, and every hold of wickedness dis-
> appeared, ignorance was purged away, the old kingdom
> was destroyed, for God appeared as man to bring in the
> newness of eternal life and that which had been made ready
> by God was set in motion. Thereupon everything was dis-
> turbed because the destruction of death was being taken
> in hand.   [*Eph.* 19]

27. For the gnostic redeemer in Ignatius see Reitzenstein, *Iranische
Erlösungsmysterium*, pp. 86 n. 3, 234 ff.; Bultmann, *Theology, 1,* esp. 179–
80; Schlier, *Relig. Untersuch.,* passim.

28. See Schlier, esp. chap. 1. Bartsch, *GG*, pp. 154–59, also criticizes
Schlier's treatment of the text, but in my opinion by pressing detailed connections much too closely.

Schlier begins his analysis by maintaining that since the threefold mystery was unknown to the Prince of this world, the chapter opens with a gnostic motif. A second important step is the appearance of the word αἰών in the plural, which Schlier reads as indicating that the appearance or announcement of Christ was "to the aions," or spiritual powers, whether the rulers of the heavens or the beings of the pleroma itself. Then by reading the chapter as composed of three parts he moves to establish the three stages: first, hidden descent; second, manifestation to men and warfare against evil powers; and finally, the open ascent in glory. Of the hidden descent, all that remains is the fact that the redeemer was not known by the Prince. The second stage is discovered by inverting *Eph.* 19.2 and 19.3 and therefore reading next the last part of the chapter. Here there is mention of the "manifestation" of God as man, and the results of the incarnation in the dissolution of magic, the removal of "bonds of wickedness," the destruction of ignorance, and finally the "abolition of death." Then Schlier turns back to Part II of *Eph.* 19 and in effect discards 2b on the ground that it is an intrusion, since it has nothing to do with the myth which he is postulating.[29] With 2b out of the way, the light of the star then becomes the glory of the *ascending* redeemer.

There are grave difficulties in the way of this interpretation of the chapter. There is no doubt at all that the salvation drama of the οἰκονομία θεοῦ initiated the stage of direct divine action which was *new,* and unknown to the Ruler of the Age. But this element of his ignorance does not seem in any way the equivalent of a detailed story of descent, and it might rather be said to follow from the world-view of Ignatius. Of course the Enemy of God was not party to events wrought as mysteries in God's silence. Nor is there any suggestion that the redeemer appeared to successive ranks of heavenly powers, for the mysteries, which take place on the scene of history, are grouped together precisely as the events are grouped in the passages which we have discussed above in which Ignatius summarizes the key events of the redemptive life of Christ. The details differ, and

29. Schlier, pp. 29, 31, agreeing with Reitzenstein, *Iranische Erlös.,* p. 234, n. 3. Bartsch, *GG,* criticizes this treatment of the text, pp. 154 ff.

the motifs of the virginity of Mary and something unique in her manner of giving birth might well appeal to the Docetists—but even here there is the stubborn inclusion of the *death* of the Lord. It is exceedingly difficult to find evidence of the descending redeemer.

The plural form of αἰών is by itself not very conclusive. Schlier's interpretation of it as "spiritual powers" here and elsewhere seems less natural than the meaning "ages"—certainly in the passage where the cross is an "ensign for all the ages" (*Smyr.* 1.2) and in *Mag.* 6.1, where the existence of Christ with the Father "before the ages" is contrasted with his manifestation "at the end." Πρὸ αἰώνων surely is balanced by ἐν τέλει and to read it as referring to the spiritual powers would be artificial. *Eph.* Ins. lacks the contrast but deals with the same notion of eternity. The passages which Schlier emphasizes most are *Eph.* 19.1 and 8.1, the latter of which he reads as "the church well known to the aions." [30] To insist here on a technical gnostic meaning seems extreme, and justified only if there are related facts. Ignatius after all names powers (*Tral.* 5.2, *Smyr.* 6.1), and it is in such passages that we should expect to find mention of the aions if Ignatius uses the word in a gnostic way.

The necessity of excluding 2b from *Eph.* 19 as well as the inversion of the order of parts in the chapter is a sign of weakness. I see no reason for the excision of 2b, for parallelism is natural to anyone who knows the psalms, and Ignatius is particularly fond of it. 2b uses, as we shall see below, symbols that are important in the pseudepigrapha, and the "perplexity" of the star powers stands as a barrier to reading any reference to the ascent of the gnostic redeemer, since the ascent was supposed to be known to all. Elimination of 2b can only be on a priori grounds. Admission by Schlier that one cannot expect

30. Reitzenstein, *Iranische Erlös.*, p. 236 n. 2, translates *Eph.* 8.1 as the "church well-spoken of to the aions," and concludes that Ignatius uses the word for spiritual beings. Schlier, p. 28, so translates the word in *Eph.* 19.2. I consider that in both instances the word is used in the time sense, as in *Smyr.* 1.2. See the article on αἰών by H. Sasse in Kittel, *Theolog. Wörterbuch, 1,* for the teaching of the Two Ages and for the tendency to the use of plurals.

the motifs to hold stable forms or places in the myth does not serve to establish conviction any more securely.

Unfortunately for the argument that we have echoes of the Mandaean redeemer, the events of *Eph.* 19.3 cannot be paralleled in the *Ginza* very successfully. The *Odes of Solomon* have references which reflect thought similar to the removal of bonds of wickedness and the destruction of ignorance, and the "abolition of death" strikes a strongly Pauline note. What remains is the *fact* of victory over the "old kingdom" in a cosmic setting, but no close resemblance to the other myths.

It is also worth remarking that there is no appearance of the word for ascension in the Ignatian letters. Schlier maintains that the idea exists, though in a hidden form, for he believes that Ignatius held the view that the dead prophets [31] waited for the coming of Christ not under the earth but in a place in the air, somewhere between earth and the heavens. Mention of preaching to them therefore involves an ascent. He points out that the passages dealing with the prophets do not have a place reference, nor do they indicate the time when the preaching took place, and he marshals parallels from later writings and from the Mandaean writings to show the greater likelihood that Ignatius also believes that the dead "wait" between heaven and earth.

It is far simpler to believe that Ignatius shared with Matthew and the later New Testament writers the notion of a descent into Sheol.

Ode 42 has the same tradition about the preaching to the dead and in much the same stage of development as in the Ignatian letters; although in it the interest is not solely in the prophets, and many more details appear than Ignatius suggests. It also assumes a descent to Sheol.

Sheol saw me and was in distress;
Death cast me up and many along with me . . .
And I made a congregation of living men amongst his dead
  men;

31. Schlier, pp. 19–23. Pp. 72–76 cite comparable usage, but the parallels all seem too late to have affected Ignatius.

And I spake with them by living lips:
In order that my word may not be void.

And those who had died ran towards me;
And they cried and said, Son of God, have pity on us;

And do with us according to thy kindness;
And bring us out from the bonds of darkness . . .

And I set my name upon their heads;
For they are free men and they are mine.   [42.11, 14–16, 20]

The statement in the *Vision of Isaiah* 9.16 that Christ "plundered the angel of death" echoes the idea in the Ode of the enmity between Christ and the powers of death which is lacking in Ignatius in connection with the teaching of the prophets, though it is abundantly present in other connections, as we shall see below.

In N.T. Eph. 4:9 we find the statement that Jesus Christ descended into "the lower parts of the earth," and I Peter 4:6 says that "the gospel was preached even to the dead." Matthew (27:52 f.) alone of the canonical gospels has the story that the graves were thrown open at the convulsion of the world when the Lord died, though it is presented in such an elliptical form that it is uncertain whether the raising of the saints from the dead took place at his death or, as it says immediately afterward in verse 53, "after his resurrection." The ambiguity occurs perhaps because the author was unsuccessfully attempting to conflate two rather different traditions. Rev. 1:18 perhaps refers to the descent into hell when it mentions the "keys of death and of Hades." In the Ignatian letters there is admittedly no specific mention of descent, but it is more likely than not that it was assumed. Christ "raised" the prophets from the dead (*Mag.* 9.2). When to this is joined the passage which says that "he was truly crucified and died as the denizens of heaven and earth *and the underworld* saw" (*Tral.* 9), one must believe that the descent into Hades is the most natural inference; and if this is admitted, Schlier's attempt to find evidence outside of *Eph.* 19 for an *ascent* is fruitless, and the whole proof rests on the unspeakable light of the star.

The debate over symbolism in *Eph.* 19 will perhaps never

be exhausted, but the materials from the Qumran library point in a different direction from the speculations about the descending and ascending redeemer. In the Essene writings and the pseudepigrapha the star figure is a not infrequent symbol, used sometimes with and sometimes without messianic reference. The source of all the messianic star passages seems to be Balaam's prophecy in Num. 24:17, "There shall come forth a star out of Jacob, and a sceptre shall rise out of Israel." Since the star and the sceptre stand in parallel construction, the reference is unmistakably to a messianic ruler or leader, and confirmation of the importance of the passage is offered by the inclusion of Num. 24:15–17 in the leaf of a Testimony Book found at Qumran.[32] The *Damascus Document* 9.8 declares that the Star is "he who studied the Law," and Charles [33] holds he is the leader of the covenanters who went up to Damascus.

Comparable passages are found in *Test. Levi* 18.2 ff. and *Test. Judah* 24.1. In the latter passage the star is itself the Messiah: [34]

> And after these things shall a star arise to you from
> Jacob in peace
> And a man shall arise [from my seed] like the sun of
> righteousness,
> Walking with the sons of men in meekness and right-
> eousness . . .

In *Test. Levi* 18.2–4, on the other hand, it is unlikely that the star is a messianic figure; it is rather the announcer or an accompanying sign, as in the gospel of Matthew:

> Then shall the Lord raise up a new priest.
> And to him all the words of the Lord shall be revealed;
> And he shall execute a righteous judgment upon the
> earth for a multitude of days.

32. See Burrows, *More Light on the Scrolls*, p. 400.

33. *Ad loc.* For the discussion about the flight to Damascus see Burrows, *Dead Sea Scrolls*, pp. 198–202; and in *More Light on the Scrolls*, pp. 219–27, Burrows holds that "Damascus" is Qumran.

34. This translation is from Charles, *Apocrypha and Pseudepigrapha*, 2, *following MSS αβS'*.

And his star shall arise in heaven as of a king.
Lighting up the light of knowledge as the sun the day,
And he shall be magnified in the world.

He shall shine forth as the sun on the earth . . .

Even if these Greek *Testaments* are Christian, as their absence
from Qumran suggests, the star symbol which they use is the
direct successor of the star speculation of the Essenes. They must
have been written by just such an Essene-Christian as Ignatius
knew in Antioch.

It is clear that the star is a flexible symbol, one which can
be used in a variety of ways, and its existence in both Ignatius
and Matthew in Antioch must now be placed against this
deeper background provided by the writings possessed by
Essene-Christians. In *Eph.* 19 it is certainly a symbol of the
Son, or Word, not merely an accompanying sign, since by it
the effective power of the new age began, and through it God
was "revealed." That it appeared from heaven is of course true,
but the emphasis is on *appearance* and the beginning of cata-
clysmic changes, not primarily on its relation to other spiritual
powers. The star references in the pseudepigrapha and also in
Eph. 19 never quite shake off their origin in the poems glorying
in the stars of the heavens as the wonders of God; and of
course stars, like the sun and the moon, are particularly successful in connecting truth and light. It is likely that these connotations of the symbol were equally familiar to Ignatius and
it is therefore unnecessary to read this as an allegorical reference to the ignorant heavenly powers of Valentinian gnosis.

Schlier admits his failure to find in Mandaean gnosis parallels
to the destruction of magic. But they can be found in the
pseudepigrapha. *I Enoch* 65.6 (cf. 7.1) declares that the decree
of judgment went out at the time of Noah on the men whose
"ruin is accomplished because they have learned all the secrets
of the angels and all the violence of the Satans, and all their
powers—the most secret ones—and all the power of those who
practise sorcery, and the power of witchcraft . . ." Although
this magic is predicated of the period before the Noahic judgment, we may carry over the same thing to the impending

judgment, since it is implied that these are the powers of the "satans" who still rule.[35]

Ignatius seems, in other words, to be composing freely, drawing on figures of speech that abounded in his intellectual background. In *Eph.* 19 he is suggesting a salvation drama, but he uses mythological material much nearer to Jewish thought than to Mandaean or pre-Valentinian gnosis.

The main points that Schlier makes about the gnostic redeemer *outside* of *Eph.* 19 deal with the meaning of Logos as utterance, and *Sigé* as foreshadowing the Valentinian use of silence as one of the aions, in part with figures of speech, such as planter, for Christ, or the Lord as the bringer of gnosis, and finally his conviction that the historical elements of the suffering, crucifixion, and death of Christ have been reduced to formulae by Ignatius in order to fit them into the myth of the descending and ascending redeemer.

The notion of the revealing Logos as the spoken Word rather than the ground of the Creative and Ruling powers of God, as in Philo, is held in very different circles—among them the Fourth Gospel, Ignatius, the Mandaeans, and various Syrian-Christians. But this fact and the connection of *Sigé* and Logos do not establish the priority of a pre-Valentinian gnosis. Schlier refers to the views of Marcus, who shares this conception, but he was certainly later than the Fourth Gospel and Ignatius. That there was a common usage in Syria seems likely from the similarities in the *Odes,* but that we can postulate a clear common source is doubtful. In similar fashion Silence as it is used by Ignatius as a designation of *deus absconditus* is very different from the Silence that is the name of one among several of the late Valentinian aions, or even, as Schlier holds, the divine pleroma itself. Not all Valentinians [36] held that the feminine principle Silence was wedded to the Father to produce the ideal world, and none of them apparently was willing

35. Although in the passages referring to the punishment of the magic-working angels the Elect One or Son of Man is not mentioned, in various passages in the Parables judgment is connected with him, e.g. *I Enoch* 38.2 ff.; 46.4 ff.; 48.8, 9.

36. Hippolytus, *Ref.* 6.24.

to apply the name to the Father. The Unknown Father in the
Gospel of Truth is not so described.

The notion of Christ as the planter, or the one planted by
the Father, and the believers as plants fits with the Johannine
figure of the vine. Schlier has marshaled the parallels.[37] A
related sort of thinking occurs frequently in the *Odes,* where
the baptismal circlet, the cross, and many other symbols seem
to have the power of growth. The figure can, however, be
traced as far back as Is. 60:21, where the people are described
as "the branch of my planting, the work of my hands"; and in
61:3 the meek and broken-hearted are called "trees of righteousness, the planting of the Lord." This symbol was widely
used, as we have shown in the third chapter, and it is certainly not clear that the Old Testament use of it is "nur
Gleichnisbedeutung," [38] in any sense different from its use by
Ignatius.

But none of these is as important as the discussion of the
final fate of the Redeemer. Here is material from the original
Christian preaching, which cannot be found elsewhere save in
Christian gnosis, since it was no part of the original myth
postulated. Schlier tends to depreciate the importance of these
elements. Thus he affirms of the crucifixion [39] that it "plays no
great role," and of the death that it appears throughout "in
a formalized or unemphasized form of thought." But since there
is no *repeated* list that appears as a kind of formula, it seems
the more probable that Ignatius' mind came freshly to the
affirmation of the points which he held to be the structure of
the Christian gospel itself.

That Ignatius uses some of these as, so to speak, *doctrinal*
references rather than as vivid historical reminiscences must be
granted. But they do not stand in abstract form, except the
reference to the suffering, which may be held to be in some
instances a simple doctrinal term. The description, for instance, of the ἀρχεῖα or authoritative records as dominated by

37. Schlier, pp. 48–54.

38. Ibid., p. 54 n. 1, gives Persian and Indian examples of the original
tree.

39. Ibid., pp. 67 f.

the "cross, and death, and resurrection" (*Phld.* 8.2) seems to carry direct memory of the one who hung on the cross, and died, and rose, and even though the list ends with the "faith which is through him," we seem to be not on the dry soil of doctrinal orthodoxy but on that of passionate living faith. And his emphasis that the Lord "truly" was persecuted and crucified, died, and was raised (*Tral.* 9), although antidocetic and therefore doctrinal, is nonetheless possessed of a sure grasp of history. The allied passages we have already considered in the discussion of history in Chapter 4. In my judgment Ignatius' emphasis on the real events that took place in history in the incarnation and suffering and death of Christ makes it impossible to dispose of them as formulae. Their occurrence in rhythmical passages is not the quotation of traditional phrases, but is better explained as the speech of the spirit-inspired preacher who, like the old prophets, or the psalmists of his own day, put into short rhythmical strophes the aspects of belief that were most precious. Our newly stimulated awareness that psalms and odes were much admired makes it easy to see that Ignatius, as a preacher "in the spirit" might well be expected to compose rhythmically.

To summarize, the attempt to interpret the redemption drama in Ignatius by seeing elements of the Mandaean or "pre-Valentinian" redeemer figure seems to me forced and unconvincing. Still less convincing is the attempt to read the letters as so strongly interested in the cosmic drama that the historical events of the life of Christ are subordinated. If there is one thing which Ignatius emphasized it is precisely the reality of the human life, and the numerous passages in which he points out that the death is *for men* can be read only as passionate affirmations of the costliness of that historical experience, although a slight ambiguity has entered his thought with the notion of the *parousia*.

It is interesting to compare and contrast the redemption drama of the *Gospel of Truth* with that of Ignatius. They differ sharply with respect to anthropology and world-view. For the *Gospel* creation was in a sense incomplete. God produced creatures of some freedom, for they could "of their own volition" go

out from him (22.27–33), and of great potentiality, for their end
was knowledge of him (37.38 f.). After their wandering this
could be brought about only by the act of a redeemer. These
men lacked both name and knowledge: they could become full
beings only through knowledge of the Father.

It is not only that these creatures of the Father are ignorant—
they endure torment and anguish as they dwell in a world of
matter, which was fashioned by Error. (17.15). This world is
appearance not reality—it is a kind of delusion (πλάσμα)—for
Error itself has no knowledge of truth or being, and hence
cannot truly create (17.15–24). It has no "root" (17.29 f.), and
both the world and the creatures it produced are mere appearances of Falsehood (17.24 f.). But here in this world of Anguish
live not merely the empty men created by Error but also those
who are from the Father (21.23), although they lack knowledge
of him. The appearances of Error will be destroyed with the
world (21.35 ff.), for they can never be like the others who will
come to know "whence they have come and whither they go"
(22.13 ff.). Here is the gnostic anthropology with its familiar
division.

The world depicted in the *Gospel* is marked by strife and
deficiency. Error fashioned it, and there he works against "Those
of the Center" (17.34), until on the coming of the Saviour they
learn their names (21.25–29), and their nature as members of
the Father (18.39 f.), and reascend to him (21.10 f.). But what for
them is blessedness is for Error the end. When Truth is declared by the Saviour, Error "becomes, at that very instant, non-
existent" (18.10 f.), and since this is so dread a fate, Error "persecuted . . . oppressed . . . and annihilated" the Son on his
appearance (18.22 ff.). The matter of the world is only a fiction,
unrelated to truth. It is vividly described once as "terror's empty
spaces" (20.35).

The Son is a gnostic redeemer, unrelated to the world in any
essential way. He is clothed in a docetic "similitude of flesh"
(31.5); and although the *Gospel* declares at some length the
events of the crucifixion (20.25 ff.), it is clear that the sacrifice
and death are as unreal as the world in which they take place.

The *Gospel* has a unique combination of interests, psycho-

logical, mythological and metaphysical, which blend in sometimes confusing fashion. Its presentation of life in the world as
a prolonged nightmare has convincing horror, and the picture
of the misery of the ignorant creatures of God is powerful. It
uses familiar gnostic mythological notions like the pleroma, the
emanations from the Father (if that is what the Coptic word
means which gives the translators trouble), and aions or
"spaces." But the discussions of the act of the Father in bestow-
ing his Name and sending his Son lack a detailed doctrine of
emanations, and certainly any notion of a fallen Sophia is
wanting. The concern of the *Gospel* with the metaphysical
ground of the universe is striking. Only the Father is real, and
redemption means a change that is ontological in nature. Behind the mythology are the conceptions of idealistic monism.
The emphasis on knowledge, and the Mind and Will of the
Father, suggests that his nature is consciousness, or the ground
of consciousness. But in spite of this monism, from a soteriological view the thought is dualistic. Nonbeing "exists" in a
subordinate, secondary sense, since its world of matter or error
is at least real enough to hold captive the creatures of the
Father. Here is the familiar difficulty of every monistic system
that must accommodate the disparities of ordinary experience.

The *Gospel* is fully gnostic in its redemption drama, with a
horror of a world of matter, and a division of men into classes,
some of whom perish while others are saved by the knowledge
of their origin imparted by the Saviour who is the Logos, the
Name, the Son. For Ignatius, on the other hand, the world is
real because it belongs to God.[40] Men are exhorted to act to
accept the redemption proffered by the truly incarnate Lord.
The fact that Ignatius and the Fourth Gospel present the life
of Christ as a redemption drama shows that they are influenced
by contemporary speculation, some of which is the early form
of gnosticism of the Docetists. Ignatius is undeniably attracted
by the cosmic sweep of the drama, but for him its elements are
pre-existence, manifestation in a true incarnation, death, and

40. Lack of creation doctrine in Ignatius is pressed by T. Preiss, "La
Mystique de l'imitation et de l'unité," *Revue d'histoire et de philosophie
religieuses, 18* (1938), 221–25.

resurrection. The significance of the whole is the revelation of God himself, among men undermined by division, and the giving of life to men through the "coming," the cross, and the resurrection. The notions shared by the *Gospel* and Ignatius with many of their century serve to accentuate the important differences and underline for us the extraordinary variety of thought that existed. We may well be cautious about granting the availability of any single myth, and even of a dominant cosmic dualism. Even gnostic speculation seems to have been more fluid in those years than some of the German scholars associated with the religious-historical movement have been willing to grant.[41]

41. Arguments against the widespread early influence of a Mandaean form of gnosticism stand in Dodd, *Fourth Gospel,* esp. pp. 121–30; C. H. Kraeling, *John the Baptist* (New York, 1951), pp. 106 ff.; and R. P. Casey, "Gnosis, Gnosticism and the New Testament," in W. D. Davies and D. Daube, *The Background of the New Testament and Its Eschatology,* esp. pp. 76–80.

7. The Church and the Sacraments

IGNATIUS' chief concern, as he faced his own death, was to strengthen the church, and this not because he had an overwhelming interest in administrative matters but because he believed that salvation would by most men be achieved, if at all, within the church. It is for this reason that he warns against the teachers of false doctrine, and urges submission to deacons and presbyters and bishop. But he tells Polycarp to keep before men's eyes the goal of salvation (*Poly.* 1.2) precisely because he knows so well that inside the church as well as outside it men may be led astray by factionalism or pride, and hence lose sight of the end. He saw the church realistically in sober colors, and yet he held that it was a more than human institution.

Like other parts of his thinking Ignatius' thought about the church begins, at least, on the scene of history—the ordinary, everyday, frequently discouraging movement called Christianity. Four out of the five instances of the use of that word in the Apostolic Fathers [1] occur in his letters, and his use of it suggests his ability to look at the church in historical perspective and his acceptance of the fact, for better or worse, that it was a competitor with other faiths.

Sometimes he turns his attention on Christianity as it were objectively, and contrasts it with Judaism. In this sense both are movements, with beliefs, ethical standards, writings, and institutional structure; but as we have seen, he believes that Judaism is incomplete and inadequate, whereas Christianity is full and final. He describes the two as historical movements, but when he comes to judge them he speaks from within faith.

He is conscious of Christianity also as opposed [2] to "the

1. *Mag.* 10.1, 3 *bis; Rom.* 3.3; *Phld.* 6.1; cf. *Martyrdom of Polycarp.* 10.1.
2. Once (*Rom.* 6.2) κόσμος is connected with ὕλη, but Ignatius does not consider the world evil *qua* matter, but because historically and through the rule of the Prince of the age it is in opposition to God. For the

world," and here he seems to mean the vast complex society of non-Christians (*Rom.* 3.3, cf. *Mag.* 5.2). Christianity is, like "the world," open to all men. Even when the church is as struggling and unimpressive as we know it to have been early in the second century, Ignatius sees it as the competitor of "the world." Their values are different: one ceases to love the world when he becomes God's (*Rom.* 2.2, 6.2). And it is because of their sharing alike the hatred of the world, and the hope of the glorious destiny of those who had been "born into life" (*Rom.* 6.2) that the little churches in far-flung cities had a sense of fellowship with each other, exchanging greetings in letters, sustaining those on their way to martyrdom, sending messengers to rejoice at the achievement of peace. He thinks of the bishops established in τὰ πέρατα, the far corners of the world, but united in the mind of Christ (*Eph.* 3.2).

It is not surprising that Ignatius uses the word "catholic," or "universal" to describe the church, though he is the first to do so. By it he certainly means no particular institutional structure, but something which has as its touchstone the presence of the Lord. "Wherever Jesus Christ is, there is the catholic church" (*Smyr.* 8.1). The word does not mark the orthodox church as set over against heretical bodies, for as we have seen in Chapter 3 he does not seem to consider the perverse parties as institutions, or entities, in the sense in which Christianity is, but groups of men who in their error have lost relationship with Christ and have slipped back into "the world."

Neither does he mean by the "universal church" an ideal pattern existing in a heavenly world, for it is significant that he uses the word in the middle of a discussion of church problems. Even the struggling local churches are grounded in the purpose of God. That is what marks them out from the encroaching poisonous growths of the false teachers, the plants which may not be eaten without fatal results, for the churches are the "planting of the Father" and are tended by Jesus. If one can take the inscription of the Ephesian letter as doctrine

opposite view see Schlier, *Relig. Untersuch.*, p. 148. For the view of the world in the Fourth Gospel see Bultmann, *Evangelium des Johannes*, pp. 424 ff., and *Theology*, 2, 26–32.

and not simply as extravagant praise (and probably elements of both are present), the Ephesian church is "endowed with greatness in the fullness of God the Father, ordained before time to live forever in glory enduring and unchanging, united and chosen in a true passion by the will of the Father and Jesus Christ our God . . ." This proclaims his confidence that it is not in some abstract ideal church that true holiness and glory lie, but in these local congregations, with all their persistent difficulties which as bishop he had known so well. The Church is *in* the churches, transforming the ugly and the ephemeral into the noble and the eternal. The churches, thus, are more than human institutions, for they are carrying out the divine intent, and are touched with the divine glory. This is high doctrine.

In a number of ways Ignatius expresses conviction that the church is the outworking of the purpose of God. The inscriptions of the letters make his thought on this matter clear. For he says the church is "ordained before time" to do its work (*Eph.* Ins.) and is "elect," (*Eph.* Ins., *Tral.* Ins.) or called out for its task. It is interesting that never but once in the letters does Ignatius apply the word "elect" to an individual, and then it is to Rheus Agathopus (*Phld.* 11.1), who may even have been "chosen" for the path of martyrdom like Ignatius himself, since he is described as having "said farewell to this life." But it is the church that is called to its destiny, as individual men and women are not. No clearer indication could be given that Ignatius thought of it as implementing the divine purpose to save men. Not only is it elect, but it has received from the divine fullness (*Eph.* Ins.) blessings of different sorts.

Here Ignatius uses the word "pleroma,"[3] which became a technical term for the Valentinians and Basilides, but for him it

---

3. N.T. Eph. 1:23, 3:19, and Col. 1:19, 2:9 use πλήρωμα to mean the divine perfection. Colossians clearly uses it to mean the fullness of unity of the Father and Christ as opposed to a notion of a πλήρωμα including spiritual powers, which last foreshadows the later use. *Excerp. ex Theod.* shows everywhere the notion of the sphere of divine emanations as comprising the πλήρωμα, to which Christ was drawn again with Sophia and the "seeds" (34, 35). Cf. Jonas, *Gnosis, 1,* 362–69.

means the overpowering "greatness" of God (μεγαλειότητι, *Rom.* Ins.), which he uses as a synonym, which has richly endowed the churches. His imagination takes wing when he thinks of that endowment, for the churches have "found mercy" (*Rom.* Ins., *Phld.* Ins., *Smyr.* Ins.), have been "established in harmony with God" (*Phld.* Ins.), are "enlightened" (*Rom.* Ins.), and "beloved of God" (*Rom.* Ins.), and "bearers of things that are holy" (*Smyr.* Ins.). Here it is quite clear that he has forgotten the churches in their modest and difficult situations and thinks of the Church in its glorious nature and destiny. We may remind ourselves of Ignatius' conviction that the Lord, through his baptism and his anointing, empowered the church in quite particular ways. It is this view of the church that makes understandable his reference to the "universal church."

The churches, in Ignatius' view, are held together by their endowment and mission, but as far as we can see not by any formal organizational ties. It is the devotion to the incarnate Lord that is the core of their fellowship. The gospel is the heritage of all; the eucharist is their common "medicine of · immortality." And the bishops whom Ignatius refers to as having been "appointed in far-flung places" are in harmony "in the mind of Christ" (*Eph.* 3.2). The bishops are the effective means of communication between churches as the lists of representatives from the cities show, but no one of them holds special position—certainly not the bishop of Rome, whom, by strange chance, Ignatius never mentions. He thinks of the Roman church with deep respect,[4] to be sure, as the church of "Peter and Paul" (*Rom.* 4.3), and he gives no evidence of knowing the Petrine tradition which later developed as the basis of the claim of the Roman bishop to primacy.

The sense of mission no doubt varied from one local church to another, but Ignatius would see it as a corollary of the divine calling. For him the church was not, at least when it was living up to its role as elect, a club of those who were enjoying the

4. For the view that Ignatius recognized the "special dignity" of the Roman church see J. Lebreton and J. Zeiller, *History of the Primitive Church* (London, 1949), 2, 424 f. See ibid., n. 18, for the literature on the subject.

privileges of salvation, but a group conscious of obligation [5] to the men of the encroaching world. In this respect the memory of the apostolic activity had not grown dim:

> And for other men pray without ceasing, for there is a hope of repentance for them, that they may even reach God. Allow them, therefore, to be your disciples by your acts at least. In the face of their anger be gentle, in the face of their vaunting words be humble, in answer to their reviling pray, in the face of their erring be established in faith, in the face of their savagery be civilized, and do not seek to repay in kind. Let us be found their brothers by our forbearing dispositions . . .   [*Eph.* 10]

Ignatius believes in the influence of the lives of Christians as well as in the efficacy of their prayers. He seems to contrast two strategies with which to meet the world, the one of persuasiveness (*Rom.* 3.3), the other of courageous witness. For the martyr the latter is inevitable, but persuasiveness, even in the face of hatred, is the method usually open to the church.

Ignatius' thought about the form of the church is deeply marked by his conviction that God has ordained it from eternity. He thinks of it as continuous from the lowest to the highest. There is a structural hierarchy throughout the great church, and the effect of the intermediate steps is not to set apart the higher ranks, but on the contrary to link the humble Christian with God. It is chiefly their place in this structure that makes the position of the clergy so important, not merely the fact that in the churches they acted with authority.

The true head of the church is God, and here Ignatius is characteristically unconcerned whether he speaks of the Father or Jesus Christ or both together. Thus Polycarp of Smyrna "has for his bishop God the Father and the Lord Jesus Christ" (*Poly.* Ins.), and in the Magnesian letter it is the Father of Jesus

5. On the basis of references to "his own," e.g. John 10:4, 12, 14, the Fourth Gospel is frequently interpreted as furthering an exclusive church community. For an interpretation of the theme of the great prayer as "Indirecktheit des Offenbarung," and hence a view of a missionary church similar to Ignatius', see Bultmann, *Evang. des Joh.,* pp. 371–74, 390–92.

Christ who is "bishop of all" (*Mag.* 3.1). Again when Ignatius
thinks of the Antioch church robbed of its bishop, he declares
that it has "God for its bishop in my place. Its bishop shall
be Jesus Christ alone . . ." (*Rom.* 9.1). According to some
versions [6] he also speaks of Onesimus of Ephesus as bishop
ἐν σαρκί (*Eph.* 1.3), and the implication is that it is God who is
bishop in a more fundamental sense. In similar fashion in the
Magnesian letter there is an implicit contrast between the
bishop who is seen and the invisible one (*Mag.* 3.2).

It might be argued that if the church is truly dependent on
God there would be no need for any intermediate ranks between God and men, but Ignatius is fascinated by comparisons
between the ranks in the church, and he tries to construct a
typology. His comparisons are not consistent, but on the contrary fluid and changing, and they do not seem to represent
commonly held doctrine but rather individual speculations
which he is trying to clarify. Whatever the value of any particular typology, Ignatius believes that the three grades in the historical church are *essential.* "Without these the 'church' could
not have its name" (*Tral.* 3.1).

As Ignatius considers the church, he sees it made up of the
Father, Jesus Christ, the Apostles, and then on the historical
scene, the bishops, presbyters, deacons, and the vast group of
lay people. He holds that although all have their places, there
are illuminating interrelations to be seen. "Let everyone respect
the deacons as Jesus Christ, just as the bishop is a type of the
Father, and the presbyters as the council of God and the band
of Apostles" (ibid.). Here is the scheme he seems to favor most:
the bishop compared with the Father, the deacons with Jesus
Christ, and the presbyters with the Apostles. He suggests the
same thing in *Mag.* 6: "For the bishop presides in the place of
God, and the presbyters in the place of the council of the
Apostles, and the deacons have been entrusted with the ministry of Jesus Christ," although in this passage the typology is

6. Included by GL; omitted by ΣAg. Lightfoot, *ad loc.,* brackets the
words as "highly suspicious, both as being absent from some authorities
and as being unmeaning in themselves." The latter part of Lightfoot's
comment overlooks the comparable references to God as bishop.

not maintained to the end, for when he reaches the deacons he turns the sentence into a discussion of function.

Ignatius is so eager to point out the analogies that in these passages his theology becomes uncharacteristic, for he half suggests that Jesus Christ is distinct from the Father in the same way that the Apostles are from him—an idea wholly at variance with most of his thought. It is dangerous ground. Further difficulties show up, also, for if the deacons are similar to Jesus Christ, by virtue of being ministers of the mysteries of Christ, they seem to outrank the presbyters, who are types only of the apostles, although in other references throughout the letters it is the presbyters who with the bishops serve as the heads of the churches. The deacon Zotion, after all, is "subject to the bishop as to the grace of God and to the presbyters as to the law of God" (*Mag.* 2). Here another sort of comparison is suggested, of the bishop likened to the divine grace, and the presbyters to the divine command.

What is unvarying, in the midst of so much that is variable, is Ignatius' conviction that the approach to the structured ranks of the church is by submission. No one in the church escapes that. Thus the laymen at various times are exhorted to submit to the bishop (*Tral.* 13.2, cf. *Phld.* 1.2) and to the deacons (*Smyr.* 8.1) as one might to the commandment, and (as we have just seen) to the presbyters as one might to the laws of Jesus Christ (*Mag.* 2.1). Even the bishop falls into place, since Polycarp must look to God as his bishop (*Poly.* Ins.). And this submission is only partly to superior rank, for the presbyters of the church at Magnesia have deferred to their young bishop "inspired by God's own wisdom, yet not to him, but to the Father of Jesus Christ, to the bishop of all" (*Mag.* 3).

The startling element in the scheme is the place of the Apostles. Ignatius looks back to them with reverence as having given ordinances to the churches—διατάγμα (*Tral.* 7.1) and δόγμα (*Mag.* 13.1)—and in that sense the ruling presbyters are similar to them. He imagines them as acting collectively and formally, for he speaks of them as the Council of God (*Tral.* 3.1) and as the presbytery of the church (*Phld.* 5.1). Here is expressed the reverent imagination of the church as it looks back to the great

leaders of its earliest days, subject to Christ and to the Father
(*Mag.* 13.2). That it is idealized history is of no consequence.
The apostolic tradition is strong in the church at Ephesus, since
Ignatius hopes that he may be "found in the lot of the Ephesian
Christians who with the apostles were ever of one mind in the
might of Jesus Christ" (*Eph.* 11.2). There is no attempt to
define who they were, but we may suppose that Ignatius is using
the word in its usual and wider sense of the established leaders
of the primitive church, since Paul is counted among them
(*Rom.* 4.3).

But that Ignatius is thinking of them in more than the historical sense is made clear by his typology, and by two other
references which ascribe to them truly amazing status. He says
that the Lord "did nothing without the Father either by himself or by the Apostles" (*Mag.* 7.1). Here he is certainly thinking
not of the gospel accounts, where from beginning to end the
disciples are dependent upon their master, but of some suprahistorical reality which he envisages, in which the Apostles have
continuing place in the universal church. Finally he caps all
the other passages by saying (*Tral.* 12.2) that when the Trallians cheer the soul of their bishop, it is to "the honor of the
Father and Jesus Christ *and the Apostles.*" No higher position
can be granted them. In the thought of Ignatius that dignity
has been achieved for which the mother of James and John, the
sons of Zebedee, begged: that they should sit on the right and
the left hands of the Lord in the Kingdom. But here the Kingdom has no longer any vestige of the Jewish Messianic Kingdom; it has become instead the eternal and universal church.

It is only in the light of this doctrine of the church that we
fully understand Ignatius' insistence on the importance of the
bishops and presbyters and deacons. Just as the institution of
the church is thought of as having more than historical significance, as there is real continuity between the visible ranks and
those that are invisible, so there is a sense in which it is true
that only as men are joined with the bishop can they be with
God. The implication is that so and only so does a unified
church result. But that there is a danger introduced Ignatius
seems unaware. In a church that is at once historical and uni-

versal the real possibility of human error is ignored if not implicitly denied, since Ignatius never admits that a bishop might err.

In spite of the existence of different levels in the church, Ignatius' idea is not an echo of Platonic thought, affirming the mirroring of the heavenly in the earthly church, nor is there here the notion of the church as belonging in the pleroma. That the attempt to create a typology is certainly a step in the direction of the Platonic or more immediately the Philonic [7] view of the world no one could deny, but as we have seen above, Ignatius did not hold any particular typology invariably, and even the most frequently suggested pattern is partly at odds with some of his most vigorously held beliefs. The continuity he affirms is something very different from the strict parallelism of the ideal with the actual. He would not deny the difference between the two, for the heavenly church is invisible and certainly pre-eminent, but the earthly church is never considered to have reality only as it mirrors or *participates in* the heavenly. The church has reality in all its parts, whether historical or eternal. It is the place held by the Apostles in the scheme which more than anything else proves that here is no figure of the heavenly church mirrored by the earthly, for the Apostles sometimes appear in memory as historical figures, and sometimes grouped with the Father and Jesus Christ as types for the historical church. The notion of continuity in the church from the lowest to the highest makes place for this ambivalence of the Apostles, whereas an idea of a strict heavenly-earthly parallelism does not.

Continuity of that sort from one rank in the hierarchical structure to another produces unity, and it is within a united community that salvation takes place. It is for that reason that

7. The notion of the intelligible as pattern for the corporeal world was widely held. See, e.g., Heb. 9:24, 10:1, etc.; Philo's *Opif.* (IV)16–19. Von der Goltz, *Ignatius von Antiochien*, p. 66, emphasizes the unity for which Ignatius strives, but believes nonetheless that the earthly community mirrors the heavenly, that "jede Einzelgemeinde das sichtbare irdische Abbild der καθολικὴ ἐκκλησία ist" (ibid., pp. 62 f.). This does not seem to me what Ignatius means by the catholic church, since he clearly includes local churches.

unity of the lay church (τὸ πλῆθος) with the deacons and presbyters and bishop looms so large in Ignatius' mind. He writes,
for instance, to the Ephesians, hoping that "perfectly held together in one submission, submitting yourselves to the bishop
and presbytery, you may be made holy in all respects" (*Eph.*
2.2). He addresses the Philadelphian church in the inscription
"whom I greet . . . more especially if men be at one with the
bishop and the presbyters who are with him." It is a passage
like this one that has laid Ignatius open to the charge that his
goals were primarily organizational,[8] but in the perspective of
the letters as a whole it is clear that the union achieved by submission and obedience is his hope. The Philadelphian inscription goes on to describe the clergy *as a whole* as "ordained after
the purpose of Jesus Christ, and he established them firmly
according to his own will by his Holy Spirit." Since the clergy,
as Ignatius sees it, are as truly a part of the structure of the
church as are the Apostles, the Gospel, and the Commandment,
therefore only as men are joined to them can they belong to
the church and their "establishment" is necessary. Even belonging to God is inconceivable except as one is in unity with
the bishop. "For as many as are of God and of Jesus Christ, they
are with the bishop; and as many as shall repent and come into
the unity of the church these shall be of God that they may be
living according to Jesus Christ" (*Phld.* 3.2). The full range of
his thought about union will be discussed in Chapter 9, but his
concern for the position of the clergy can be rightly understood
only as one sees that it is in his mind prerequisite to union.

We have so far been considering the more abstract parts of
Ignatius' thought about the nature of the church, but he expresses different insights when he views it as a community of
men and women living under God. They are not all saints, for
strife and divergent opinions mark its members, but nevertheless he continues to remind them of the fellowship that is the

8. For a view balanced between the importance of practical organization
and mediating salvation see C. C. Richardson's article, "The Church in
Ignatius of Antioch," *JR, 17* (1937). The interpretation of Ignatius as
concerned with organizational power is stated with psychological trim-
mings in Streeter's *Primitive Church,* pp. 163 ff.

essential mark of the church. Thus by implication they are the "planting of God" (*Tral.* 11.1, *Phld.* 3.1), although he actually uses the figure negatively to deny that the false teachers have any such status. They are "fellow pilgrims" in a triumphal procession (*Eph.* 9.2), they are joined in "one submission" (*Eph.* 2.2); and in *Poly.* 6:1, in a section possibly belonging to the letter to the Smyrnaeans, the long list of verbs compounded with συν- gives evidence of the variety of the experiences they shared.

Here belongs also Ignatius' use of the figure of the church as the body of Christ who is head. The word "body" occurs directly only once, when he says that the resurrection is an ensign "for his saints and faithful ones . . . in one body of his church" (Smyr. 1.2), but the use of "members" is more frequent, and as in I Cor. 12:12 f. it is a figure that presents the relation of the believers to Christ. Once (*Eph.* 4.2) it seems at least as likely that μέλη should be interpreted as choral themes, for it comes at the end of a musical metaphor. But in *Tral.* 11.2 the figure occurs unmistakably. Ignatius says that by the passion the Lord "calls you who are his members," and he continues, "The head therefore cannot be born without members, since God promises union, that is himself." The dependence of the head upon the members certainly takes further the figure of the unity in one body than anything to be found earlier has done, and it brings us face to face with Schlier's interpretation of the implications of this phrase, and his view of Ignatius' teaching about the church.

The thesis which Schlier advances is that as in the case of the figure of the redeemer, so in his view of the church in its relation to Christ Ignatius is influenced by gnostic myths. He presses Ignatius' use of various figures as being *not* similes or metaphors but elements of myth which one can find in developed and connected form in later gnosticism and which one must assume to have existed in much the same form in Ignatius' time. Thus since in the language of gnosticism a reference to "sweet odor" means gnosis or revealed knowledge,[9] so Igna-

9. Schlier, pp. 61–63. Cf. Reitzenstein, *Die hellenistischen Mysterienreligionen,* pp. 395–401.

tius' declaration that Christ received the ointment on his head in order to "breathe incorruption" on the church should be read in that sense. Certainly since he speaks of the "evil odor" of the false teaching of the Ruler of this world (*Eph.* 17), he might well have been willing to speak of the sweet odor of the teaching of Jesus. But that that meaning is central in his reference to the anointing it is hard to see. There seems to be rather an individual bit of exegesis.

It is certainly true that the later gnostics read the word for odor or sweet ointment in a special sense. But as we have seen, the figure is old, and it is variously applied. Ode 11.15 speaks of the "pleasant odor of the Lord," and both Old and New Testament connect the metaphorical with the actual meaning in the sweet savor of sacrifice, and the sweet odor of anointing, and it carries a different meaning still in Paul's declaration that Christians are a "sweet savor of Christ unto God" (II Cor. 2:15). Ignatius' use seems to be still another variant, since by the anointing Christ endows the church with incorruptibility. That the words *could* be read in a technical sense is obvious; that Ignatius did so seems exceedingly doubtful.

In similar fashion Schlier points out that to speak of the church as "enlightened," or "established" is also to use gnostic terminology [10] and that "filtering" came to be a technical term for purification among the gnostics. The *Excerpta ex Theodoto* (41) contains them all. The first two of these words, however, are rather obvious terms of description. The poetic figure of enlightening appears in Psalms 19:8 and 18:28, and it is difficult to see that Eph. 1.18 need be read in any different sense.[11] It is, of course, metaphorical. Again, the notion that God will "establish" his congregation, or his seed, in the world, is an idea that occurs throughout the Old Testament, and in similar sense in Paul. That the church should be "established" is not a strange application of the figure, nor a particularly

10. Schlier, pp. 84–88. Cf. *Rom.* Ins., where the church is described as "beloved and enlightened;" in *Phld.* Ins. it is "established" (*bis*).

11. H. A. A. Kennedy, *St. Paul and the Mystery Religions* (London, 1913), pp. 197 f., points out the dependence of Paul's use of φωτίζειν on LXX descriptions of spiritual illumination.

gnostic idea. One need not call on parallels like the "establishment" of Sophia by Horus.

The words συνδιυλίσθη, as in *Excerpta ex Theodoto* 41, or ἀποδιϋλισμός (*Phld.* 3.1, cf. *Rom.* Ins.) are admittedly rarer, but the uncompounded form occurs in Matt. 23:24 in the figure of "straining out" the gnat. Ignatius describes the unity of both the Roman and the Philadelphian churches as achieved by filtering out the false teaching. Schlier goes on not to press the word itself but to point out that "purification" is a great concern with the Valentinians. Purification, or cleansing, as a means of achieving unity within the group, is not a characteristic Old Testament idea, but one finds in Malachi references to the refiner's fire, and fuller's soap (Mal. 3:3), and the notion of cleansing applied to the nation in Is. 1:16; and certainly an idea similar to that of Ignatius, and not obviously gnostic, is to be found in the figure of the "cleansing" of the vine, and the casting out of the unfruitful branches in the Fourth Gospel (John 15:2–6), as also in the figures of the cutting down of worthless trees and the burning of chaff in the preaching of John the Baptist (Matt. 3:10–12). A similar problem and similar ways of meeting it must surely face every voluntary community, as the detailed commands of the *Manual of Discipline* (7.17–25) about dealing with backsliders clearly show, whether or not the word is used. To sum up, these figures seem much more like normal, rather widespread illustrations here applied with telling and significant effect to the church, than technical terms or even specifically gnostic ideas.

Schlier has an interesting study of the head-members metaphor,[12] and here his conviction is stronger that the use points to a gnostic myth in which in a realistic sense the members are particles of the redeemer. He is convinced that in this usage Ignatius is not dependent on New Testament Ephesians and presses the fact that in Valentinian gnosis the redeemer cannot enter into the pleroma without the redeemed. He considers the Pauline use of the body-members phraseology a *Gleichnis,* and points out that for Paul Christ is never the head of the church, whereas both in New Testament Ephesians (and

12. Schlier, pp. 88–97.

Colossians) and in Ignatius more is assumed. This observation rests in part on the a priori argument that a figure would not be used individually in the ordinary literary sense but that it must point to a generally recognized mythological basis. The early Christians were creating a community not like the Jewish one, based on nationality, and they therefore needed new terminology and conceptions to describe its nature. The body-members notion used by Paul is a rather obvious figure for stating an organic relationship; and once given the figure, it is clear that it can and will be applied in various ways and used freely, as Ignatius does the reference to the Spirit that blows where it will (*Phld.* 7.1).

There is no denying that Ignatius [13] goes much further than Paul does in saying that Christ is related to his followers as the head is united to its members (*Tral.* 11.2). "A head cannot be born without limbs, for God promises union, which is his very nature." In a sense the existence of Christ implies followers. It is a daring kind of thought. But it is a natural development of the figure, although it occurs in a context that makes too swift a transition for clarity from the symbolic notion that the cross cannot be thought of except as bearing immortal fruit to the idea that in a similar fashion the very existence of a head calls for members. Both are necessities, which Ignatius explains by saying that behind both stands the nature of God as himself union and therefore always creating unity. It seems forced to try to read in here the gnostic myth of the light-redeemer able to return to the pleroma only as he recovers from the engulfing darkness of the world the particles that make up his body.

A further step in Schlier's argument rests on Ignatius' de-

13. Bartsch, *GG*, p. 27, emphasizes the fact that what is important in the figure is the idea of unity. An equally daring declaration of necessary relation, although not the head-members terminology, can be found in rabbinic sources. Simeon ben Yohai, a disciple of Akiba, said: "The Scriptures declare, 'Ye are my witnesses and I am God.' This means, 'So long as ye testify to Me, I am God, but if ye cease to testify to me, I am no longer God.'" *Sifre Deut.* 346 (quoted in L. Finkelstein, *Akiba, Scholar, Saint and Martyr*, New York, 1936, p. 213).

scription of the *instrument* [14] of the cross (*Eph.* 9) which, using the Holy Spirit as "rope," hauls into place the stones that are the Christian believers. With this he parallels the machine to be found in the *Acts of Archelaus* 8, a Manichaean document that describes "an instrument of twelve jars which is made to revolve by the sphere [of the sun] and draws up with it the souls of the dying." The instrument also appears as a ship that ferries passengers. Parallels of "drawing up" souls to the place of the light do not seem very close, nor does the notion of the zodiac as a well-wheel, but as far back as the *Upanishads* the well-wheel has been a symbol of *samsara,* driven by the ever-rushing water of the world stream, and it must surely be admitted that here is a figure early enough and widespread enough to enable us to understand Ignatius' use of it in a different connection.

We have not done justice to the very interesting series of parallels that Schlier and the other religious-historical followers of Reitzenstein have collected. When one reads uncritically long pages of such parallels, there is an extraordinary cumulative effect. It is not sustained, however, for at least one reader, when each step in the series is evaluated, and inquiry is made whether the conclusions reached necessarily follow.

We agree profoundly with Schlier that Ignatius in describing the church is thinking of a body that is "ontologically" grounded. It has, as he points out, cosmic significance; it cannot be explained simply on sociological grounds. But by pressing the figures of speech he believes to be gnostic allusions, he all but removes the church from the historical scene. He says that [15] "the earthly church is to the heavenly edifice, which is the church much spoken of by the aions, the highroad (πάροδος) of those who will go up to God" (cf. *Eph.* 12.2). But this translation implies a parallelism of the earthly and the heavenly church that we do not find in the letters and an approving interpretation of the role of the aions that seems contrary to Ignatius' reticence on the matter. In particular we cannot follow Schlier in his conviction that the members of the church, in

14. Schlier, pp. 110–24.
15. Ibid., p. 121.

contrast to the position Ignatius holds as one approaching
martyrdom, are by *nature* redeemed, and hence on a higher
plane than he. As we are arguing in this chapter and in Chapter
9, Ignatius had much too realistic a view of the *need* for salvation of the men in the churches to believe that they were
already saved.

In other words, we find it difficult both in detail and in the
picture of the whole to discover positive influences of particular
gnostic myth on his conception of the church. That the Docetists
held that some men possessed by nature a likeness to the divine
world we have seen in Chapter 3, and Ignatius rejects the idea.
That he shared with them in any degree the notion of Christ as
a light person coming to his own or the church as the body of
those *by nature* redeemed seems to us a misinterpretation. With
them he emphasized the *coming* of Christ, bringing grace and
life to the churches, but over against them Ignatius insists on
the veritable incarnation, and therefore on the grounding of
this event in history. A similar down-to-earth quality seems to
save his teaching about the church from being engulfed in
esoteric details.

But whatever the influences may have been that bore on
Ignatius' thought about the church, there is no gainsaying the
fact that he saw it as the scene and the mediator of salvation.
Within the church, instituted and empowered by God, those
being redeemed were given grace, so that in the end they could
"attain unto God." The crown of this experience came in the
two sacraments, baptism and the eucharist, and we turn now
to consider them.

Of the two, baptism receives much slighter attention in the
letters—too little to allow us to believe we understand Ignatius
fully, although we can get some insight into his thought. As
we have seen in Chapter 4, he starts with the conviction that
the power of baptism rests on the fact that Christ himself had
been baptized. "He was baptized that by experiencing it ($\tau\hat{\wp}$
$\pi\acute{\alpha}\theta\epsilon\iota$) he might purify water" (*Eph.* 18.2). Even if with many
interpreters this be read "that by his passion he might purify
water," a translation that seems difficult in view of the fact that

the passage is concerned with baptism, the light shed on the nature of the sacrament is not affected, for in either reading Christ cleansed water. The phrase, short as it is, conveys several ideas. In the first place, baptism in the church rests on an historical act deliberately performed by Christ. His own baptism, says Ignatius, was accepted or chosen in order to institute the rite which the church performs as sacrament.

This affirmation is the more significant because elsewhere Ignatius quotes Matthew in saying that Christ was baptized "in order to fulfill all righteousness." Because he does quote this saying, one has to read *Eph.* 18.2 as a conscious statement of belief, and may wonder whether here he is differentiating the baptism of the church from other baptisms which he knows.[16] After all, the disciples of Menander, if he was a contemporary, are reported to have had a baptism [17] "into him," and Acts mentions the "baptism of John" (18:25) which Apollos considered an adequate basis for work in the Christian church. Essene baptism was a repeated rite of purification, and Jewish baptism a part of the initiation of the proselyte. We ought perhaps to read *Eph.* 18.2 as identifying the virtue and authority of Christian baptism. In the next place Ignatius implies that he thinks of baptism as in its own nature basically a rite of cleansing; the purified water in some ways conveys its own purity. This notion is rather unexpected and out of character in the light of Ignatius' very slight doctrine of sin, and it suggests that here he is stating something assumed but not very

16. Discussions of baptismal rites are too numerous to cite here extensively. References to the literature as well as important views can be found in the following places: H. H. Rowley, "Jewish Proselyte Baptism and the Baptism of John," *HUCA, 15* (1940), esp. 313–30. R. Reitzenstein, *Die Vorgeschichte der christlichen Taufe* (Leipzig, 1929), and J. Thomas, *Le Mouvement baptiste en Palestine et Syrie* (Gembloux, 1935), argue that immersion rites were widespread in Hellenistic and early Roman Syria. Kraeling, *John the Baptist,* pp. 106–22, criticizes the cogency of the argument for Mandaean influence. The new evidence available in the *Manual of Discipline* is discussed in W. H. Brownlee's essay on "John the Baptist in the New Light of Ancient Scrolls," in *The Scrolls and the New Testament,* ed. K. Stendahl (New York, 1957), pp. 37–44. For the meaning of baptism in the Hellenistic church see Bultmann, *Theology, 1,* 133–44.

17. Irenaeus, *Adv. haer.* 1.23.5.

well grounded in his theology. Cleansing has nothing to do with that division which most worried Ignatius, and represents probably one facet of the initiation asked by the church of those who came into it from a pagan environment.

In this passage and elsewhere there is emphasis on the grounding of the rite in the divine power. Only so could the water be cleansed or the cleansing be transmitted to its recipients. *Eph.* 17–18 dwells in a meditative mood on the aspects of the divine *gift,* and it recites some of the acts of Christ: he received ointment, gave salvation by the cross, was conceived by Mary of the Spirit, was born, was baptized. There is a creedal ring to some phrases of it but it is difficult to believe that *this* particular group of facts was ever made the basis for a creed by any church. There is a perversely individual character about the selection. It begins by saying that Christ received ointment "that he might breathe immortality on the Church" (*Eph.* 17.1) and ends with his receiving baptism "in order to purify the water" (*Eph.* 18.2). We conclude that the performance of the acts by Christ gives them sacramental efficacy, although Ignatius leaves us with unanswered questions.

One of these is whether in the church that he knew the anointing and the water baptism had an obvious connection that is no longer clear to us. The Syrian church used chrism as a part of the baptism service, at least in later centuries, and the swiftness of the transition here suggests that in Ignatius' time also both may have been part of one service. Furthermore at least one meaning of chrism was that it gave power to bring events to pass by breathing. The ceremony in the late *Acts of Judas Thomas* [18] shows the bestowal of power to be used against the enemies of the church. The prayer during the ceremony of anointing says: "Jesu: let his victorious might come and be established in this oil, like as it was established in the tree (wood) that was its kin, even his might at that time, whereof they that crucified thee could not endure the word: let the gift

---

18. *Acts of Thomas,* trans. from M. R. James, *The Apocryphal New Testament* (Oxford, 1924), p. 433; cf. chap. 27, p. 376. See G. Rietschel, *Lehrbuch der Liturgik* (Berlin, 1909), Bd. 2, pp. 27 ff., for the act of *insufflatio* or *exsufflatio* in the baptism.

also come whereby breathing upon his (thine) enemies thou
didst cause them to go backward and fall headlong, and let it
rest upon this oil, whereupon we invoke thine holy name."
The power to breathe destruction upon enemies may very well
be the reverse of the power to breathe ἀφθαρσία upon the
church. I John may refer to chrism (2:20, 27) when it declares
that all have received the "anointing from the Holy One" and
that would best be explained if it was an anointing which had
to do with baptism, since that sacrament alone was the common
experience of all. If the reference to the anointing (*Eph.* 17.1) is
indeed an evidence of chrism as part of the baptism, the gift
of life or immortality comes as the divine seal upon the cleansing.

C. H. Kraeling has suggested [19] that the "speaking waters" of
Ode 11.6 may well be a draught of water at baptism which confers the Spirit, a procedure appearing also later among the
Mandaeans, and he would link with this the "speaking water" of
Rom. 7.2. If this should be so, it would still further underscore
the fact that baptism meant to Ignatius a divine gift, of cleansing, of life, of the Spirit. Elsewhere in a passage strongly
reminiscent of N.T. Eph. 6:13 ff., although like it in no detail,
he implies that baptism is a continuing strength, for in the
figure of the armor of the Christian baptism is listed first. "Let
your baptism remain as your armor, your faith as a helmet,
your love as a spear . . ." (*Poly.* 6). It is a passage that belongs
less to doctrine than to preaching. It is interesting to note that
there is in the letters no mention of the baptism of the believer
"into the death," which is Paul's main interpretation, nor yet
any reference to it as connected with repentance. There is no
justice, however, in emphasizing what Ignatius does *not* say,
but we must concentrate upon his affirmations. Baptism is
essentially a sacrament, performed and guaranteed (*Smyr.* 8.2)
within the church and grounded in the acts of the Lord.

The eucharist appears much more frequently than does baptism and it is obvious that it bulks much the larger in Ignatius'

19. "The Apocalypse of Paul and the 'Iranische Erlösungsmysterium,'"
HTR, 24 (1931), 223 f. Bousset, *Hauptprobleme,* pp. 292–94, suggests the
parallels.

thought about the church, probably because it is a repeated rite, not the door of initiation. Like baptism the eucharist is the gift of God (*Smyr.* 7.1), and indeed so completely does he think of it as a sacrament, coming to men from a divine source, that there are no lengths to which he does not go in describing it. He says the "eucharist is the flesh of our Saviour Jesus Christ who suffered for our sins" (ibid.), and at this point one may well recall his other identification of the flesh of Jesus with the gospel (*Phld.* 5.1). Here he is using metaphorical language to declare that both the eucharist and the gospel are inextricably linked with the Lord as he is encountered by the Christian.

But it is clear from the context of this passage that in the case of the eucharist he intends more than that. He is affirming a realistic doctrine about the nature of the elements, for the reason why "those who have strange opinions" do not come to the eucharist is that it is the very "flesh." As we have seen in Chapter 3, the Docetists feel forced to absent themselves because their repugnance of matter, which precludes any affirmation of the true "flesh," makes them differ sharply from Ignatius. That same realism is expressed almost as directly when Ignatius cries out that for food he desires the bread of God which is the "flesh of Jesus Christ," and for drink, "his blood" (*Rom.* 7.3). To sustain himself as he goes on toward martyrdom, it is the eucharist that he craves.

It is in the last-quoted passage that the problem shows up which dogs any interpretation of Ignatius' thought about the eucharist. Any analysis which attempts to answer the question whether he speaks realistically or symbolically is doomed to defeat, for the fact is, he does both. On the one hand, his realism keeps the Docetist away from the service. On the other hand, he says that the blood of Christ is "love incorruptible" (*Rom.* 7.3). As Lake has pointed out (*ad loc.*), it is wholly possible that here is a play on words that refers at the same time to this ultimate evidence of Christ's love for man, and to the *agape* as a meal. But this is by no means certain, for in *Tral.* 8.1, shortly after mentioning the *thusiasterion* or sanctuary where sacrifice would be made (*Tral.* 7.2), he urges them to renew themselves in "faith which is the flesh of the Lord, and in love which is the blood of Jesus Christ." There is no certainty that this should be understood as a reference to the eucharist, but it follows along with the *Romans* reference where the bread is the flesh and the drink is the blood.

The Fourth Gospel represents very nearly the combination of realism and symbolism that we have found in Ignatius' thinking, and for both the essential terms are flesh and blood, not body and blood, as in Matthew and Paul. In chapter 6 of the Gospel realistic and symbolic ideas are linked together without discrimination: "The bread which I will give is my flesh, for the life of the world . . . Except ye eat the flesh of the Son of man and drink his blood, ye have not life in yourselves . . . for my flesh is meat indeed, and my blood is drink indeed" (6:51, 53, 55). Here is realistic doctrine in an absolute sense.

On the other hand, these passages all stand in the context of Jesus' affirmation that he is the bread of life: "Verily, verily I say unto you, he that believeth hath eternal life. I am the bread of life" (6:47 f.). Here the reference is not to the elements in the sacrament but to the very being of Christ. And the words that are always quoted against a realistic interpretation stand only a bit farther on in the same chapter. "It is the spirit that giveth life: the flesh profiteth nothing: the words that I have spoken unto you are spirit, and are life" (6:63). Ignatius and the Fourth Gospel both seem to be ambiguous in using now realistic terms, now symbolical ones, but they agree that the sacrament binds the Christian to Christ and that it conveys life. Sacramental realism is thus not for either of them the finally important matter, for the sacraments lead on to union with God.

It is possible that there is implied behind Ignatius' phrases the notion that the eucharist is established through the death of Christ, rather than at the Last Supper. Only so could he give his flesh and blood. This view, and this alone, would explain the swift shifts in meaning of the phrase "the blood of Christ." Now it recalls to Ignatius the death (*Smyr.* 12.2, 6.1) of Christ, and his love for men (*Rom.* 7.3), but again it is an element in the eucharistic feast.

As with baptism, what moves Ignatius most about the eu-

charist is that grounded as it is in the compassionate love of
Christ, it is a divine gift. This is to consider it not in an institutional sense but as expressing the divine purpose to redeem
man. He describes it in a much-quoted phrase as the "medicine
of immortality, the antidote given that we die not but live forever in Jesus Christ" (*Eph.* 20.2). This taken out of the context
of his thought suggests something close to magic, as if partaking
of the elements had an irresistible effect, and it is not infrequently so interpreted, but if one reads it in the light of all
that he says about union, such an interpretation seems un-
tenable. It indicates, however, how inextricably close are the
eucharist and the goal of life. It is through the eucharist that
the effects of the passion and resurrection are laid hold upon by
men who did not know Jesus in his lifetime. Ignatius declares
that those who touched his risen body after the resurrection
were effectively changed. "And straightway they touched him
and believed, for they were joined with his flesh and spirit.
Therefore they were contemptuous of death, and were found
to be superior to it" (*Smyr.* 3.2). Within the context of faith the
life which the Lord possessed was participated in by his disciples. It is apparently in similar fashion that the bread that is
the flesh confers immortality on those who partake of it.

He says, furthermore, that by the eucharist the "powers of
Satan are overthrown" (*Eph.* 13.1) and that the warfare "in
heaven and on earth" is made to cease. Elsewhere he makes
clear his belief that to meet in the eucharist (*Phld.* 4)—or, here
by a play on words, to give thanks and glory to God—establishes
the congregation securely in a harmony of faith. Since we know
that he believes passionately that by this kind of harmony the
church is rendered invulnerable to the attempts of Satan to
introduce disunion, one can see that a natural meaning is intended, but when the mention of Satan introduces to Ignatius'
mind the thought of the cosmic warfare in which Satan is involved, the notion of the eucharist as a cosmic instrument becomes an understandable if rather hyperbolic addition.

An important passage that deals directly with the inner
significance of the eucharist is in the letter to the Philadelphians, but one can only regret that it is not more precise.

There Ignatius declares that anyone who walks in perverse doctrine "dissociates himself from the passion" (3.3; 4). And then swiftly he goes on to urge them to use one eucharist, "for there is one flesh of our Lord Jesus Christ and one cup for union in his blood." As we have seen above, Ignatius believes that it is essential to confess that the elements of the eucharist are the veritable flesh and blood of the Lord. Here he seems to be adding that as the Christian participates in the eucharist with this understanding of it, he associates himself with the passion. The eucharist becomes in that sense the means of grace, the final means of achieving union—a word that sums up the further reaches of human experience—the hope that all they do will be done κατὰ θεόν. It does not, however, tell us how this is achieved. We may wonder whether Ignatius had asked the question.

Bartsch has pressed most fully the influence of mystery [20] conceptions in Ignatius' thought about the eucharist, and his argument is therefore for Ignatius most worth examining. Distinguishing [21] between sacrament, which is the magical bestowal of power, and mystery, which involves participation in effective divine action, he believes that some passages can be interpreted only in the second sense. He holds that Paul uses words that came from the mystery cults, but applies them freely to the whole religious life, whereas Ignatius has "relapsed" into real cultic usage, which emphasizes the practically magical results of the rite itself. Taking *Poly.* 7.1, for instance, he interprets [22]

20. The influence of the mysteries has frequently been pressed. See esp. Bousset, *Hauptprobleme*, pp. 305–13; A. Loisy, *Les Mystères païens et le mystère chrétien* (Paris, 1919), chaps. 1, 9; Reitzenstein, *Mysterienreligionen*, passim but esp. pp. 88–91, 240–52; G. P. Wetter, *Altchristlichen Liturgien: Das christliche Mysterien, 1*, Göttingen, 1921 (most material is late but on the early meaning of the eucharist see pp. 45 ff., 66–69, 101–23; for Ignatius, "Das Abendmahl ist ein antikes Todes- und Auferstehungsmysterium auch für diese Christen," p. 123); GG, pp. 99–132. K. G. Kuhn, "The Lord's Supper and the Communal Meal at Qumran," in Stendahl, ed., *The Scrolls and the New Testament*, discusses the Essene tradition, and points out, pp. 75 f., the similarity between the view of the "cup of immortality" in the *Joseph and Asenath* novel and Ignatius' view.

21. GG, pp. 99–102.

22. Ibid., p. 117.

it to mean the hope on the part of Ignatius to "attain through the suffering of God" (ἐάνπερ διὰ τοῦ παθεῖν θεοῦ ἐπιτύχω). But elsewhere in the letters the frequently used phrase θεοῦ ἐπιτυχεῖν is the expression for "attaining unto God," and it is more natural to read it "if through my suffering I may attain to God." Certainly Ignatius hopes to "attain" by martyrdom, but it is in this case by means of his own suffering, and the passage can be a eucharistic allusion only by a forced reading.

Smyr. 7.1, a passage which affirms that the eucharist is "the flesh . . . which the Father raised up," goes on to say that "they who refuse the gift of God . . . are dying; it is better for them to love (ἀγαπᾶν), that they also share in the resurrection." Bartsch [23] interprets this passage as meaning that it is better for them to participate in the eucharist, the result of which is resurrection, then and there. But the passage must be read in context. Ignatius has in *Smyr.* 6.2 bitterly criticized the Docetists because they do not love the needy. In the same mood he sweeps on to their other marks of perversity—they absent themselves from the eucharist, and are therefore perishing— but at the end of the sentence he returns to their imperative need to love. One cannot be sure of all that the resurrection connotes to him, but it is clear at least that the unloving have no part in it, and although ἀγαπᾶν may refer to holding an *agape,* it certainly also reaffirms the criticism of the earlier part of the passage. *Mag.* 5 mentions the choice between death and life that faces all men, and concludes that "unless of our own free will we choose by his help to die, reproducing his passion, his life is not in us." It seems unwarranted to consider that the phrase "reproducing his passion" alludes to a mystery. The choice between "death" and "life" is carried symbolically in the Christian paradox that he who loses life gains it.

Mystery notions were widespread, and there is no antecedent reason why they could *not* have been held by Ignatius. Many of the converts to Christianity must have had a previous experience as members of the cults. The problem for the historian is whether the ideas and practices were taken over unchanged, as Bartsch seems to believe, or whether the influence was a much

23. Ibid., pp. 116 f.

more subtle and general one, affecting Christian thinking just as deeply but in an indirect way, such as the assumptions about the relations between Christ and his followers. Certainly Judaism did not provide ways of thinking useful for that relationship. Gnosticism, or the mysteries, or general oriental thinking did, and we shall see in the next two chapters the forms that it took in Ignatius' thinking. The Christian lays hold of the *results* of the passion, appropriates grace, and participates in life. But is it by means of a passion represented in realistic dramatic form in the eucharist, so that in the liturgy there is a veritable dying and rising? Unfortunate as it is, the passages are not clear enough to give us certainty, although the literal adoption of mystery ideas does not seem likely, and the interpretations on which Bartsch rests his case seem forced.

We must in any case, I believe, differ sharply from Bartsch in his belief that the participant expects to become a Christ, and if this central concept is removed it is very doubtful that the concepts of the mysteries are dominant. Full discussion of the matter must wait for Chapter 9, and here we merely summarize it.

Ignatius uses daring words of his own martyrdom. He says that by it he will "become a man" and a "word of God" (*Rom.* 2.1, 6.2), although in the context he does not by the latter phrase primarily affirm identity with Christ; rather he affirms revelatory meaning as against the mysterious irrationality of an animal. His death will be an oblation on the altar (*Rom.* 2.2). It will imitate the passion of Christ and by it he will "attain unto God." He is affirming his belief that the martyr's death has a real effect on the church, in the sense that it is a sacrifice, and a final affirmation of God. But the result for the individual is not a *Vergottung*.[24] The "attaining," coming only at the end of life, seems to mean something like life in the presence of God, similar to that enjoyed by the Angels of the Presence or the martyrs in Revelation. "Life" could no longer separate the martyr from the love of God—to use Paul's words. Since Bartsch's argument for θεοποίησις rests in the main on the expectation of the martyr that he will become Christ, and this

24. Ibid., pp. 80 ff. But see below, Chap. 9.

can be found only by forced readings, still less can we admit that
in the eucharist the ordinary Christian thought of himself as
becoming a Christ. He receives life and grace; he even experiences union; but all this is not to *become Christ,* nor does
that seem for Ignatius to be the meaning of "being a disciple."

However the inner meaning of the eucharist is interpreted,
one can understand Ignatius' emphasis on validity. Its importance made such a concern inevitable. Only that is a "valid"
sacrament which is celebrated by the bishop, or by someone
whom he appoints (*Smyr.* 8). This stipulation implies the existence of competing rites, and here Ignatius is driven to a
practice of rejecting those not connected with the church by
the approval of the bishop. Here is a note of authority which
seems in some ways antithetic to the warm note of devotion that
glories in the sacraments as the means of union. But there is
another passage which puts even this in a less rigid light. He
thinks of the eucharist not as dependent upon the bishop solely,
but as a sacrament of community, so that it is the community
alone that gives it validity. "If any man be not inside the sanctuary he lacks the bread of God. For, if the prayer of one or two
has such power how much more has that of the bishop and the
whole church?" (*Eph.* 5.2). It is for this reason that faith and
love lead to the "flesh of the Lord . . . and the blood of Jesus
Christ," and therefore to a valid eucharist.

It is clear, then, that both the sacraments have meaning
within *the community.* The eucharist effects a change within
the community itself, as it moves into a deepened experience of
faith and love. By it the individual men and women so live that
whatever is done is "according to God" (*Phld.* 4); by it they
achieve immortality, but it happens to them as they are members of the community and it is mediated by the united
church, as it is symbolized and guarded by the bishop. It is not
the bishop who operates alone even in this central matter of the
eucharist, for it is his prayer along with that of the whole
church—in other words the great praying community—which
makes it possible for a man to have the bread of God. Thus
even in thinking realistically, Ignatius avoids the pitfall of the

formalism of the sacramental act that bedeviled the medieval church, for he has a lively sense of the sacrament as taking place within, and only within, the united church community.

It remains to try to place Ignatius' view of the church and the sacraments in some kind of perspective. Schlier understandably protests against interpreting the letters without knowledge of the contemporary background, and insists that it can only result in modernizing Ignatius. The warning is justified, but Schlier's method of ignoring the pattern of thought as a whole and reading certain phrases and figures in a gnostic sense because in other documents they are so used is quite as misleading. The test of meaning must be whether the gnostic meanings are consistent with *all* Ignatius says, and it is particularly difficult to see that his view of the church fits neatly into gnostic ideas. For it is not made up of those already "established" and "redeemed." The Antioch church had just been split by a fight, and struggle seems to have been rising in the Asia Minor churches. The high doctrine about the church—and it is present —is very carefully grounded in a realistic view of this struggle. The influence of gnosticism is not to be found in the figures of speech.

However, a simple answer to the question of the influences bearing on Ignatius' conception of the church is not easily made. He is clearly close to some of the ideas of the *Manual of Discipline,* where there is similarly high doctrine about the Community. God has given to the men of the Covenant Community knowledge of his "prudent purpose, and righteousness, his strength and glory" (*DSD* 11.6 f.). And the Community itself has eternal meaning.

To those whom God chose He has given them as an eternal
    possession;
And He has given to them an inheritance in the lot of the holy
    ones;
And with the sons of Heaven he has associated their assembly
    for a community council
Their assembly will be in the Holy Abode as an eternal planting
During every period that will be.   [*DSD* 11.7–9]

Here, as for Ignatius, the community is elect of God, and he has ordained that the society of the angels in heaven is the continuation of the Community on earth.[25] All, accordingly, as "members of the eternal assembly," have a relation to their fellows that is similar to what Ignatius describes as life κατὰ κύριον. And also, as in Ignatius' view of the church, this high doctrine is no bar to a careful and down-to-earth description of the ranks in the Council and their obligations in dealing with the most humdrum of everyday matters. The community is elect, but members enter it one by one and must live within its discipline. There is, understandably enough, in the Essene writings mention of submission and of unity, since they are inevitable concerns for any historical community, but they are not emphasized in the *Manual of Discipline* as they are in Ignatius' thought. Unity in the *Manual* is simply one element in a long series of virtues, and the emphasis on the penalties provided against individualism bulks larger. It is clear, however, that whatever the differences, there is much in this view of the community as well as perhaps in actual practice that is similar to Ignatius' view of the church as elect, purposed by God, and continuous from earth to heaven.

But the church as Ignatius sees it is by no means a simple reflection of the Essene community, for it is differently centered. The Essenes are a covenant group, perhaps similar to a mystery in having ranks entered by initiation, but the meaning of the community is not expressed in progressive knowledge, or apparently in an experience of unity, but in the keeping of all the ordinances of Torah. Ignatius, too, recognizes the necessity of forms and ordinances, but the church is not built around

25. Trans. Brownlee. Cf. *Psalm of Thanksgiving* C in trans. Dupont-Sommer, *Dead Sea Scrolls*, p. 72:

> And I knew that there was hope
> for him whom Thou hast formed from the dust (and
> destined) for the eternal Assembly.
> Yea, the perverse spirit hast Thou purified of a great sin
> so that he might mount guard with the
> army of the Saints
> and that he might enter into communion with
> the congregation of the Sons of Heaven.

them. It is Christ and the Father, united in being God, who are the center, and this fact changes the locus of the experience for the Christian. The full consequences of this for the relation of the Christian to God will not be clear until in the next two chapters we discuss the conception of imitation of Christ and of union, but certain things begin to be apparent. In spite of the fact that the gnostic view of the church in the details pressed by Schlier does not seem to be present in Ignatius' thought, there is a less definable way in which the view held by the gnostics is important. The church is no longer a Torah group waiting for the last Judgment, nor even the first Christian modification of that pattern. The "last times" are now present. The church has become a body brought into being by the divine act of grace, and made up of those in the process of being readied for their ultimate attainment. But because "attaining unto God" is a relationship to God, so every step in the process demands relatedness, in submission, by imitation, in faith, in love. The gnostic myth of the light-particles being reclaimed by the redeemer may not be here, but that of the individuals deeply related to each other and to Christ seems to suggest gnostic or perhaps mystery assumptions of the relation of the members to one another and to God.

PART THREE

Christian Life

8. Life According to the Lord

EVEN in the separate and splintered phrases in which it now stands, Ignatius' view of the Christian life has power and vitality. Preached more connectedly it may well have explained his high position of leadership in the church; for lists of virtues, wooden and dull when one comes on them in didactic sermons, are not characteristic of his thinking. Only once does he use such a technique. He puts his conviction simply enough: the important thing is that Christian lives should be *centered in God*. It is as simple as that—and as difficult. Throughout the letters in a variety of ways he underlines the cleavage between the values of God and those which are "human" or "natural," he rejoices with the Ephesians that they "love nothing, by the standards of human life, but God only" (*Eph.* 9.2), and he praises the Trallian church because they do not "live according to men, but according to Jesus Christ" (*Tral.* 2.1, cf. *Rom.* 8.1). The values of God are clearly not those to which a man would come if he accepted unreflectively the ways of the world.

The Christian life is the response of men to the saving act of God that has already taken place in a definitive sense in the "coming and passion and resurrection," as a result of which men have received divine aid. It is not impossible that life should be God-centered, since "grace" and "life" have been proffered by God. But that there is nothing automatic or irresistible about this shows even more clearly in Ignatius' thought about ethics than in his view of the church and the sacraments. The means of salvation are at hand; Ignatius declares dramatically that death is being abolished, and the old kingdom is coming to an end. But unless men reach out, the "newness of eternal life" will not be theirs. It is here that the practical results appear of the differences between his view of the nature of men and the view held by the Docetists. For however they may try to qualify it, the fact that some men are dif-

ferently endowed from others and so are involuntarily destined
for salvation takes the reality out of the ethical life.[1] And for
Ignatius this is not true. As he sees it, God has acted, but now
man has to act, and no person has advantage over any other.
This may be the reason why he practically refuses to call any
person "elect" for as we have seen, Rheus Agathopus alone is so
described, and it is probable that he like Ignatius himself has
entered on the path of martyrdom. Just as Ignatius is quick to
consider his own bondage an evidence of the grace of God
(*Smyr.* 11), so he speaks of this other man as one singled out by
God.

The goal for him is clear, and that it is anything but a conventional statement, embalmed in dull formulae, is shown by
the variety and freshness of the phrases Ignatius uses to describe it. It means to "belong to God,"[2] to "devote your time
to God" (*Poly.* 7.3), to "be full of God" (*Mag.* 14.1), and to be
"in harmony with God" (*Mag.* 6.1, 15.1; *Phld.* Ins.). He expresses this last idea in a figure of speech taken from music,
when he urges them to join in a great chorus of harmonious
praise to God (*Eph.* 3.2–4.1). A person who has achieved this
state of being single-minded in his devotion Ignatius describes
as being marked by "holiness." The infrequency with which he
uses the word "holiness," or "holy," is evidence of his recognition that to be truly committed is very rare. He so describes
Paul (*Eph.* 12.2) and the prophets (*Phld.* 5.2) as men of profound achievement, and once he speaks of the "holy presbyters"
(*Mag.* 3.1), but in general he refuses to apply it lightly to the
ordinary members of the churches. Nevertheless, and paradoxically, it is this high development that he asks and expects of
men.

All of this means that without using the word he places a
strong emphasis on the importance of choice and then persistence in the path chosen. A number of times he speaks of

1. E. Dinkler, "Zum Problem der Ethik bei Paulus," *Zeitschrift für
Theologie und Kirche, 49* (1952), 192, describes the reason for this differently. He says the gnostics tend to identify "Habens und Seins so dass
der Imperativ sachlich bedeutungslos und vom Indikativ verschlungen ist."
2. *Eph.* 8.1, *Mag.* 10, *Phld.* 3.2.

"repentance," which Paul and the author of the Fourth Gospel use rarely if at all, although he usually means by it the *return* [3] of the Christian who has separated himself and therefore an intellectual about-face rather than the original conversion. Once he uses it of the non-Christian who has a "hope of repentance," [4] and once he includes himself in what seems like a homiletic device. For him choice is of paramount importance, and it seems to mean the ultimate commitment of a man. One can be a coin marked by the stamp either of God, or of the world (*Mag.* 5.2), and the choice has momentous consequences. Ignatius puts forcefully the idea elaborated in the doctrine of the Two Ways: that such choice in the last analysis is one between death and life (cf. Deut. 30): "Unless voluntarily we decide by his help to die and so reproduce his passion his life is not in us" (*Mag.* 5.2).[5] The right choice means the possession of the quality of *life* that characterizes the Lord, although it is reached by association with him in his death. The choice is momentous, then, not because objective punishment will ensue if the wrong decision is made but because the wrong choice has deeply tragic results: the mistaken one will fail to receive the gift that lifts him from the plight in which the "natural" man finds himself.

As we saw in our examination of Ignatius' anthropology in Chapter 6, he can emphasize choice because men are free: the dice are not loaded. Men do not enter the race handicapped in either the Pauline or the gnostic sense. They are not peculiarly vulnerable through the *flesh* as the aspect of man's

3. So *Smyr.* 4.1, 5.3. *Phld.* 8.1 and probably *Phld.* 3.2 should be so understood.

4. For these two meanings see *Eph.* 10.1 and *Smyr.* 9.1.

5. The pervasiveness of the influence of late Judaism, particularly in its Essene form, can be seen in the appearance of the doctrine of the well-known Two Ways in Ignatius, *Mag.* 5; the *Didache* 1.1 ff.; *Barnabas* 18–20; cf. *DSD* 3.13 ff. There is a marked difference in the degree to which after decision is made the doctrine of the Two Ways is used to support a legalistic ethic. For Ignatius this is not so. See *Ecclesiasticus* 15.17 ff. for another example of freedom of choice. For the Iranian background of the Two Ways see especially K. G. Kuhn, "Die Sektenschrift und die iranische Religion," *Zeitschrift für Theologie und Kirche, 49* (1952), 296–316.

nature prone to sin,[6] nor will they find themselves among those who are by nature *sarkikoi,* and therefore condemned at birth to error and lack of salvation. In this respect Ignatius differs sharply from the Docetists. For him the God-centered life is open to all men if they will. But to say that is not to suggest that he thinks that right choice and persistence in it are easy. We have seen above how deeply he fears that under the torments of a martyr's death he might not endure and thus at the end betray his dearest hopes. But at least there is nothing that automatically condemns a man to despair. The Christian life can be lived if men choose to appropriate grace.

One of the corollaries of this view is that there is no rigorism of an ascetic nature in his ethic. As we saw above, even what men do "after the flesh" is spiritual if all things are done "in Jesus Christ" (*Eph.* 10.3)—that is, so long as the centering of their lives is clear. It is not that he does not recognize sins of the flesh. He quotes Paul in saying that Christians should keep their bodies as temples of God (*Phld.* 7.2), and quite as one might expect he believes that purity and temperance should be characteristic of the Christian life (*Eph.* 10.3), but sins of the flesh do not burden his mind. He approves of the vow of chastity taken by some of the men in the church at Smyrna, but the reasons for his approval and the ways in which he qualifies that approval are the telling matters. He says it is "to the honor of the flesh of the Lord"—one form, apparently, of the imitation of the Lord, which he urges in many other connections. Since

6. Paul makes a distinction between life simply in the flesh (ἐν σάρκι) or according to the flesh (κάτα σάρκα)—that is, on the one hand, the natural, historical human situation, and on the other, man's living according to flesh, which means accepting the values of the natural, historical sphere, or being "conformed to the world." The predicament of man, as Paul sees it, is that the first makes the second easy and all but inevitable; but in any case willfully living by the norms of the world means sinning against God. In that sense the "mind of the flesh is death" (Rom. 8:6). The best discussion is in Bultmann, *Theology, 1,* 232–53. Ignatius agrees with the descriptive part of this; but perhaps because he is contending with those who mean by "flesh" the "material" or "sensual" and therefore evil aspect of man, he is concerned to present natural life as neutral, potentially dominated either by flesh or spirit. He lacks Paul's sense of the terrible vulnerability of man to sin.

it is the Lord's *flesh* that he emphasizes, it is difficult to find in his mind any disparagement of flesh,[7] and in view of his vigorous affirmation of a true incarnation this is understandable. After giving his approval, he goes on immediately to say that the whole value of their vow of celibacy will be lost if they boast of it; only the bishop is to know. He treats it as a matter on which an individual might wish to make a voluntary act of devotion, but asceticism as such does not interest him. There is no place in his thought for a recognized order of celibates, who would be honored in the church for their abstinence and no fear of the body. The choice, then, arises not from a rejection of the material basis of life but from a positive subjection of all to God.

A further consequence of Ignatius' emphasis on freedom in choosing is the generally optimistic nature of his ethic. He apparently believes that men will choose (as he himself is doing) life—$\zeta\omega\acute{\eta}$ not $\beta\iota\acute{o}s$—not death. This runs through the letters as an unspoken assumption, as the nature of his appeal to his readers demonstrates. On the one hand he congratulates the churches because they are "established," "filtered clear" of every stain and so on. And again he urges them to greater effort to maintain that state. The optimism rests initially on the gracious act of God, but close on it follows Ignatius' hope that men will not betray their trust or throw away their opportunity, though he is not sure enough to be silent on the matter.

He suggests a variety of reasons for choosing life "according to Jesus Christ" instead of "according to the flesh," and by their very differences they give a three-dimensional picture of the church. Among them there is an interesting and rather natural admixture of those which would have meaning primarily for the Christian community and those which speak to the concern of an individual for his own destiny. Ignatius points out, for instance, the fact that unless the members of the Christian

7. In the light of Ignatius' qualified approval of the vow of chastity, it is difficult to see how it can be held that he turns from the world because it is $\H{\upsilon}\lambda\eta$. So, however, Schlier, *Relig. Untersuch.*, pp. 146 ff. on the basis of *Rom.* 6.2. For Ignatius the world is evil because its Ruler wars against God.

church achieve faith, and love, and live in harmony with each
other, not nourishing grudges within the community, Christianity itself will suffer in the eyes of the world. "Give no pretext
to non-Christians, that the congregation of God may not be
reviled for a few stupid men" (*Tral.* 8.2). This is important
because it is through its appearance before the world that the
Christian church must make its initial appeal (*Eph.* 10.1, cf.
Tral. 3.2). It is by achieving a quality of life that arrests attention that Christianity can become persuasive to the world (*Rom*
3.3). Here the missionary interests of the churches are prominent.

He also tries to make them aware of the danger in which
they stand, which is both of an external sort—the special circumstances of the period—and that arising from their own
weakness. He is conscious of living in an age of great testing,
to which his plight as prisoner bears witness, and his sense is
keen that disciplined lives alone are able to withstand the tribulation to which they are exposed.

It is interesting that the appeal to fear is not more often
used, and its infrequency witnesses to the balance of Ignatius.
In spite of the fact that he is on his way to martyrdom, he does
not look at life darkly. He is uncertain about his own courage
as he faces martyrdom, but for the churches it is a positive and
confident hope that marks the letters, rather than a warning
that his readers will fall unless they are steadfast. Nevertheless,
the note of warning is not wholly lacking. He hopes that the
members of the Ephesian church will continue in their "good
order in God," which seems to mean precisely this quality of
disciplined and well-ordered lives. The virtues most frequently
mentioned are endurance, steadfastness, and long-suffering
(*Eph.* 3, 10; *Phld.* 1.2), all of which would be a response to outward pressures. But he sees the disciplined life threatened not
only by persecution but even more frequently by the easy-
going assumption of human beings that what they have expressed in words has been accomplished in fact. Some of Ignatius' most perceptive insights into human nature appear in this
connection, and he points out the central importance of unifying intention and action. The "deed" is no mere matter of

words but "whether one is found to be living by the power of faith, and that to the end. It is better to be silent and be a Christian than to talk about it and not be one" (*Eph.* 14.2–15.1, cf. *Mag.* 4.1).

Once he comes close to appealing to a prudential motive: men had better look to the fruits of their Christian devotion if they hope to be saved. "Let us then not be unconscious of his goodness, for if his actions should be patterned after ours we are lost. For this cause let us be his disciples, and let us learn to live by Christian standards" (*Mag.* 10). But warning though it is, the primary contrast is between God's goodness and men's recalcitrance, and we have no right to press the διὰ τοῦτο and thereby to infer the opposite: that God will save the good.

The most moving and frequent of the appeals is to live Christian lives in order to show a response to the love of God. "It is therefore fitting by every means to give glory to Jesus Christ who has given you glory that you may . . . in all things be sanctified" (*Eph.* 2.2, cf. *Phld.* 10.1). This notion appears so many times and in such a variety of expression that we will not examine it now, but will postpone it to the discussion of the importance of love for God.

The key to Ignatius' view of the Christian life is an understanding of the twin conceptions of discipleship and imitation, for they are central to his thinking. They give content to the choice that he urges, and in following the path that they indicate the Christian life is grounded securely, for it is provided both with an effective motive, in devotion to the Lord, and a pattern for life, in a general sense at least. Ignatius does not use the two notions in precisely the same way, but they carry for him approximately the same meaning. Discipleship implies both devotion to the leader and the following of the pattern; imitation emphasizes the pattern but assumes the devotion.

He may, nevertheless, have made some slight distinction between them for he uses the idea of discipleship more casually than that of imitation. Not infrequently he points out that Christians may become disciples of those further advanced in

the spiritual life than they are themselves, and he writes to
Polycarp that he hopes that he himself will be found at the
resurrection to be Polycarp's disciple [8] (*Poly.* 7.1). He believes
that others too might well take a lesson from the bishops (*Tral.*
3.2, *Eph.* 1.3), for those bishops whom he has met seem to him
men of spiritual gifts. Non-Christians may even become the
disciples of Christians (*Eph.* 10.1). But however real may be
this lesser discipleship, one gathers that it has validity because
there is a reflection of the greater in the lesser. These more
spiritually developed men reflect at least in part the master
whom they serve.

More characteristically he hopes that Christians will become
disciples of Jesus Christ,[9] and hence learn to live godly lives,
or "to live according to the standards of Christianity" (*Mag.*
10.1). Here there is the very definite notion of patterning
lives [10] after that of Christ. The prophets were his disciples
(*Mag.* 9.2) and he their teacher in the Spirit, as he is the only
teacher of his living disciples (*Mag.* 9.1). This implies an interesting combination of devotion to the Lord and learning

8. GL read ἀναστάσει. Bauer, *Die Briefe, ad loc.,* and Lightfoot prefer
αἰτήσει, witnessed to by gA, the latter both because *Smyr.* 11 seems to
parallel this passage and because the reading of A shows that it was in the
text before the fourth-century interpolation. Bartsch, *GG,* pp. 117 ff., reads
with GL but interprets the resurrection as "die Auferstehung im Auge, die
der Gläubige im Kult erlebt . . ." (p. 118), but this seems perverse in the
light of the future reference in *Tral.* 9.2, which can hardly be to the
eucharist.

9. The Ignatian letters have more references to imitation and discipleship than all the other Apostolic Fathers together. This is evidence of
Ignatius' warm Christ-centered piety. In the N.T. the word for imitation of
Jesus Christ is rare; it occurs only in I Cor. 11:1, Eph. 5:1, I Thess. 1:6,
though the theme is carried by other expressions, e.g. I Pet. 2:21, II Cor.
10:1. Discipleship, in Ignatius' sense, is lacking in the N.T., probably
because the word still connoted the earliest followers of the historical
Jesus.

10. For imitation in the rabbinical tradition see G. F. Moore, *Judaism,*
2, 109 ff; I. Abrahams, *Studies in Pharisaism and the Gospels* (2d ser.
Cambridge, 1924), pp. 138–82. For its place in early Christianity, C. H.
Dodd, *Gospel and Law* (New York, 1951), pp. 39–42.

from his acts, for the devotion of the disciple to the Lord is presupposed as the ground for learning. And, contrary to much that Schlier holds, there seems to be a clear intention on Ignatius' part to place in the center of the Christian churches an effective memory of the historical Lord.

Discipleship provides a pattern both in death and in life, for on the one hand it is a figure that prepares men for whatever suffering may come, and on the other hand it points to specific attitudes toward other men that come into play in the ordinary events of life. One of the most frequent notes is Ignatius' interpretation of persecution and the martyr's death as imitation, or discipleship. "For this reason we endure steadfastly, that we may be found disciples of Jesus Christ our only teacher" (*Mag.* 9.1, cf. *Rom.* 5.3). He cries out that he hopes to be an "imitator of the passion of my God" (*Rom.* 6.3), or again, that discipleship offers for the ordinary Christian in his difficulties with the antagonism of non-Christians a figure of endurance (*Eph.* 10.2).

There is implied also a pattern for living based on the goodness, gentleness, and benevolence of the Lord. Ignatius praises the Ephesians for being "imitators of God" (*Eph.* 1.1) and goes on to suggest that they have shown him, and no doubt others, a perfect expression of brotherly kindness. Again he writes to the Trallians that it was their "godly good will" that made him know that they were "imitators of God" (*Tral.* 1.2).

Both the devotion that leads to imitation and the pattern implied appear in another passage: "Therefore let us not be unconscious of his goodness. For if his actions should be patterned after ours we are lost" (*Mag.* 10.1). Here it is not altogether clear whether the "goodness" is that shown supremely in the passion or in some other aspect of the historical life, but there is a passage discussing attitudes toward non-Christians, where he is urging imitation of the gentleness of the human life of the Lord. "For in the face of their anger be gentle, in the face of their vaunting words be humble . . . before their savagery be civilized, and do not seek to repay in kind. Let us be found their brothers by our forbearing dispositions, and let us be imitators of the Lord and seek who may be the more un-

justly treated, or robbed, who the more scorned . . ." (*Eph.*
10.2).[11] This is the effective memory carried in the church.
Ignatius acknowledges that kindly action will not necessarily
awaken a like response, for the overtures are seen as repulsed
with scorn. The imitation of the compassion of the Lord results
almost inevitably in the imitation of his suffering, through the
perversity of the unredeemed and natural world. But Ignatius
never suggests that there are utilitarian reasons for imitating
him.

It is perhaps inevitable that the notions of discipleship and
imitation of the Lord involve a radical perfectionism,[12] and
Ignatius gives frequent illustration of it. In fact, to achieve
either of these goals seems as one reads the letters to be almost
beyond the powers of men. Ignatius more than once speaks of
himself as merely "beginning to be a disciple" (*Rom.* 5.3, *Eph.*
3.1). Truly to be a disciple (*Eph.* 1.2, *Rom.* 4.2) or to be "per-
fected in Jesus Christ" (*Eph.* 3.1) is a goal to be reached only
when a martyr's death shall proclaim that a man was able to
endure to the full.[13] Here he reflects, and perhaps generalizes
on, his own fear that his determination may not prove strong
enough to endure. Ignatius speaks out against his opponents
when he declares that no esoteric knowledge of "heavenly

11. There is no quotation here of Is. 53, but surely a general reminiscence of the Suffering Servant. Cf. I. Pet. 2:22–24. E. G. Selwyn, *First
Epistle of St. Peter* (London, 1947), pp. 90–101, connects the meekness and
the death. Perhaps the tradition of the "lawless men" present in Acts 2:23
here receives some attention.

12. This is not unique in Ignatius. For different meanings of τέλειος and
their part in the ethical thought of Judaism, Paul, and Stoicism see
H. Preisker, *Das Ethos des Urchristentum* (Gütersloh, 1949), pp. 129–39.

13. T. Preiss, "La Mystique de l'imitation et de l'unité," *Revue d'histoire
et de philosophie religieuses, 18* (1938), 199–210, contrasts Paul's idea of
participation throughout life in the sufferings of Christ with the desire of
Ignatius to imitate him in the actual Passion, which Preiss sees (p. 209) as
"possession de son maître," and as leading to the desire "lui devient
quasiment identique" (p. 211). Here he seems to press Ignatius' vivid
figures with unwarranted literalness. The contrast between the two men
seems rather to arise from the immediacy of the sufferings facing Ignatius.
We do not know Paul under such circumstances, in spite of Philippians.

things and the orders of the angels, and the associations of the principalities—things seen and unseen" (*Tral.* 5.2) makes a man a disciple, for knowledge has nothing to do with it. It is the ultimate commitment called for in imitating the Lord that is alone effective.

One passage suggests how far this conception reaches: "Do nothing apart from the bishop, watch over your bodies as the temple of God, love unity, flee divisions, be imitators of Jesus Christ as he was also of his Father" (*Phld.* 7.2). Here he declares in effect that the imitation of Christ can be achieved only within the church community, and with this step it becomes practically a synonym for the experience of salvation which likewise normally occurs within the fostering care of the church. The degree of perfectionism involved is indicated also by the fact that he half suggests that they press on to be imitators of the Father. He does not actually drive his thought so far, for the subordinate clause does not have to carry that meaning, any more than the gospel of Luke must be understood as demanding the achievement of divine mercy in the saying "Be ye therefore merciful, as your heavenly Father is merciful"; but in both the norm is absolute for commitment if not for achievement.[14]

It is the fact that discipleship will be complete for Ignatius only as he follows the passion of his Lord that suggests to Bartsch that the concept is a primarily "cultic" notion, rather than an idea grounded in ethics. This is true if what he means is that the perfectionism of the demand has removed it from moralism, so that it becomes endurable only as Ignatius is bound by worship as well as by other aspects of experience in a close bond to his Lord in the death or suffering. He is never the follower in a mechanical sense, earnestly performing acts according to pattern, but he will "rise free *in* Jesus Christ" (*Rom.* 4.3). And overtones of this ultimate hope no doubt are

14. Preisker, p. 225, does not observe this distinction and considers that Ignatius has narrowed his conception of Christ by believing in him as norm for life, and teacher. He fails to comment on the passages in which Ignatius declares that he is not yet a disciple.

present whenever Ignatius thinks of discipleship and imitation. But when Bartsch [15] maintains that "imitation" for the ordinary believer is controlled by thought of a eucharistic μίμησις, we find him hard to follow. The suggestion of ethical imitation is too strongly present in the passages he cites.

The very absoluteness of the standard implied for measuring lives precludes the possibility that the ethic could become moralistic. That moralism was a genuine possibility one must recognize, since it is the Gospel of Matthew that influenced Ignatius so deeply, and in Matthew the teachings of Jesus are presented as the extension and completion of the Torah and *might* therefore be read as subtler and even more difficult moral achievement: "You have heard that it was said to them of old time . . . but I say unto you." Here the teachings can be interpreted as a new law, as they are in the epistle of Barnabas (2.6). At first sight, indeed, Ignatius seems to echo that view, although on closer examination one can see that he escapes legalism, and moralism. As we have seen in Chapter 3 in several passages he refers to the commandment (*Mag.* 4, *Tral.* 13.2, *Smyr.* 8.1) or the commandments (*Eph.* 9.2, *Rom.* Ins., *Phld.* 1.2), and once to the law of Jesus Christ (*Mag.* 2.1). By these words he sums up the notion of Jesus Christ as authoritative lawgiver, although once he may have had in mind specifically the two commandments of Matthew. There is a related reference to the teachings of Christ. There can be little doubt that he considers that the commandments were lived out perfectly by Jesus Christ. In that sense and to that degree they suggest that the pattern of the ethical life is well known and that the obligation to follow it has been laid upon all Christians.

But he escapes moralism because, one may surmise, under the influence of the notions of discipleship and imitation he thinks of the life of Christ as a whole and even the commandments as a kind of mystery in which the whole historical life is gathered up. Thus he praises the Romans because they are "in flesh and spirit united in all of [Jesus Christ's] commandments" (*Rom.* Ins.), suggests that the teachings of Christ are the basis of unity within the churches (*Phld.* 8.2), and hopes that the

15. GG, p. 124, referring to *Eph.* 10.1, *Phld.* 7.2, *Tral.* 1.2.

Ephesian church will be "adorned in every way with the commandments of Jesus Christ" (*Eph.* 9.2). Only once is there a reference to a particular commandment (*Mag.* 4) and then to one that cannot be precisely identified. The followers of strange doctrine are not coming together in "valid meetings according to the commandment." It would therefore be false to conclude from his references to the commandments that he held an idea of the Christian life as one to be achieved by careful observance [16] of law. The imitation of Christ, being disciples of him or of the more spiritually developed Christian leaders, or being adorned with the commandments of Jesus Christ are all ways of thinking which emphasize the unity of the whole person, who is in harmony with God (cf. *Phld.* 1.2).

A further result of this ethic of imitation is the success with which he avoids an overemphasis either on intention or on deeds as alone sufficient. He avoids the dangers both of spiritualizing the ethic,[17] as the Docetists did, and of suggesting that goodness is to be achieved by the accumulation of separate good acts. The goal is to conform life to the divine. "All of you pattern yourselves after God; respect one another, and may no one look on his neighbor according to natural values, but love one another in Jesus Christ always" (*Mag.* 6.2). Giving one's time to God means doing "the work of God" (*Poly.* 7.3, cf. *Mag.* 10.1, 2). There is no sentimentality here. Devotion to God leads on to appropriate action.

It is somewhat startling at first to realize how frequently

16. The Essene ethic at its best certainly tried in similar sense to ground its emphasis on specific acts in a devotion to God. Thus in *DSD* 1.12 ff., where men are "not to transgress a single one of all God's provisions," the result of coming into the Community of God will be to "clarify their mind by the truth of God's ordinances, and to direct their strength according to the perfection of His ways . . ." But the emphasis on the act and the law is nevertheless pervasive.

17. Ignatius gives two inadequate clues to their ethic: they lack *agape* (*Smyr.* 6.2), and they do not respond to the sufferings of the martyr (*Smyr.* 5.1). These are negative criticisms, and one can infer the positive position only tentatively. Both suggest an ascetic withdrawal from life and so great an emphasis on spirit that flesh and matter are despised. See Jonas, *Gnosis,* 2, 24–29. For the choice for gnostics between antinomian and ascetic ethics see K. E. Kirk, *Vision of God* (London, 1932), pp. 208–17.

Ignatius speaks of deeds or works, particularly in view of Paul's
contrast between works and faith. Certainly it is a word much
more subject to misinterpretation than Paul's "gifts of the
Spirit." But an analysis of his usage makes it clear that the
ethical life is never identified with works. In some cases when
he speaks of deeds it is in connection with a specific act which
he considers of great importance, such as the acceptance by the
Roman church of his decision not to try to be freed (*Rom.* 2.1)
or the sending of a delegate to Antioch (*Poly.* 8.1, *Smyr.* 11.2).
It is obvious that he would urge such deeds. Three times he
seems almost to equate the word with "Christianity" (*Rom.*
3.3, *Eph.* 14.2 *bis*) in a connection in which he momentarily
looks at Christianity from the point of view of the nonbeliever,
who, of course, can see only the outward consequences of the
Christian's commitment. In none of these cases does it seem
fair to accuse him of suggesting that action is what tells in a
man's relationship to God. Only once in the letters does the
word carry that meaning, and that is in the elaborate metaphor
of the Christian life as that of the soldier:

> Please him in whose army you serve, from whom you get
> your pay. May none of you be found a deserter. May your
> baptism continue to be your armor, faith the helmet, love
> the spear, endurance the heavy armor; may your works
> serve as your deposits, that you may receive the discharge
> pay due you.   [*Poly.* 6.2]

Here the *works* are compared to the fund deposited from his
own pay to the credit of the legionnaire so that when and if he
was separated from the army he left with some money. In the
sense that the soldier might consider with satisfaction his
deposita, so the *works* seem to be ground here for gratification.
Although there is no detail in which the two passages are
similar, it inevitably recalls N.T. Eph. 6:13 ff.[18] But precisely
because the form of the allegory drove its creator on to be

18. That this is a favorite if hackneyed form of moral teaching shows
in the fact that it can be found at least as early as Is. 59:17. Cf. also *Test.
Levi* 8.1.

realistic about the soldier's life—in details expressed in technical Latin words perhaps learned on the journey—and thus to ingenuity in including as many aspects of it as possible, it is difficult to press his figures at any point, especially if they run counter to his characteristic usage. It remains true that the *works* of the Christian are not what determine his relationship with God, but they are the result of the relationship.

Although the core of the matter is discipleship and imitation, Ignatius does not remain wholly silent on the detailed qualities which he hopes will mark the lives of Christians. Even when he does not directly relate them to the incarnate life, one can discern that tradition in the background, although Ignatius' particular emphasis arises from his reading of the needs of the times. If from the early church only his letters had survived, we should not have a very complete notion of the characteristics which the churches tried to build up in their members,[19] for the letters are not exhaustive treatises and Ignatius takes for granted an understanding on the part of his hearers of what the Christian must do. They had the Pauline letters, and no doubt one or more of the gospels, and each of the little churches was nurtured by its own leaders. The situation had changed since the earlier days, when Paul found it necessary to give considerable attention to the contrasting works of the Spirit and of the flesh. We find no lists of virtues except that in the pedestrian allegory just quoted of the Christian as soldier, but in one passage or another he reveals a good deal about the qualities to be displayed or avoided, and we may assume both the baptismal teaching of the convert and the ordinary moral teaching of the lay church.

Those most to be avoided are sins of the spirit—the variants of the overweening pride and egotism that are the source of

19. The literature on the moral teaching in the church is voluminous, and only a few examples can be named. Dodd, *Gospel and Law*, pp. 10–24; P. Carrington, *The Primitive Christian Catechism*, Cambridge, 1940; Kirk, *The Vision of God*, pp. 111–30. See Preisker, pp. 145–48, for the shift of emphasis in N.T. virtue lists from those of the spirit-filled life as in Gal. 5:22 and II Cor. 6:6 to the strongly Hellenistic list of II Pet. 1:6 f., which includes virtue, knowledge, self-control.

division in the community.[20] Ignatius scores the tendency to set oneself above the common lot (ὑπερφαίνω), to consider oneself a special case (*Eph.* 5, *Smyr.* 10.2, *Poly.* 4.3). It is that which leads a man to ignore the bishop, to cut himself off from the community, and therefore to lose contact with God. He quotes approvingly, "God resisteth the proud" (Prov. 3:34). Along with that goes a temptation to buttress one's self-esteem by boasting (*Tral.* 4, *Poly.* 5.2) or by indulging in that aptly described sin, "vain-glory" (κενοδοξία—*Phld.* 1.1). Here also belongs self-importance, or being "puffed up" (*Mag.* 12.1; *Tral.* 4.1, 7.1; *Smyr.* 6.1; *Poly.* 4.3). Ignatius understood very well the ambitious, self-willed mind. And he knew that these qualities are the inevitable prelude to division and anger, which above everything else shatter the communities (*Phld.* 8.1, cf. *Phld.* 3.1, 7.2; *Smyr.* 7.2) in which he hoped love and mutual forbearance would grow. More importantly still, they are the qualities which cut a man, secure in his own independence, off from God.

As one might expect, it is the reverse of these aspects of the sin of pride that he enjoins upon his hearers. Gentleness (*Tral.* 8.1) and humility (*Tral.* 3, 4.2; *Poly.* 2.1, 6.2) are qualities to be cultivated precisely because they make a man open and teachable. Such a disposition, and it alone, makes possible the submission (ὑποτάσσομαι—*Eph.* 2.2) or the obedience, which belongs to the disciplined and ordered spirit, which proclaims the freedom of a man from willfulness. Ignatius sums all of this up in his almost wistful description of the bishop of Philadelphia, in which he comments on "his mind, turned Godward, recognizing its goodness and perfection, and the unruffled and serene temper by which he lives in all godly patience" (*Phld.* 1.2). Serenity and strength and gentleness are, one must suspect, the qualities Ignatius most coveted for himself—the first and last of which were hardly consonant with his temperament.

But meekness and gentleness are not enough. For in the dangerous world of the early second century there had to be a core of steel in the Christian character, and it is this Ignatius refers

20. For an excellent discussion of Paul's treatment of these see Bultmann, *Theology, 1,* 241–43.

to when he speaks frequently of "endurance" [21] (*Poly.* 3.1, *Tral.* 1.1). Polycarp must "stand firm as an anvil which is struck" (*Poly.* 3.1); or to change the figure, the great athlete is the one who can take punishment—the Greek suggests that almost literally—and yet win (ibid.).

If these are the inner characteristics of the individual, there are others that express his relation to the community. They are the ones that might be expected—benevolence (εὐνοίαν—*Tral.* 1.1) and Christian charity. Love for the widow, the orphan, the distressed, the prisoner, the poor man just released from prison—in short for the hungry and thirsty of the world (*Smyr.* 6.2)—are expected of all. It is absence of these concerns which proves that the beliefs of men who hold strange doctrine are wrong. Frequently, as we shall see below, Ignatius speaks of love, without specifying its object, but in this passage he makes abundantly clear his belief that love was not to be expressed simply within the Christian community, but that it must be offered to those in need of kindness, and of practical help. In this respect Ignatius is more universally minded than is the Fourth Gospel, in which the injunction to "love one another" seems, in spite of the missionary obligation, to ignore the non-Christian world.

But beyond the warmth of devotion and the suggestions of pattern expressed in the conceptions of discipleship and imitation, Ignatius' favorite concepts are faith and love. These two words express his deep convictions about the character of the Christian life, and they occur constantly throughout the letters, sometimes separately, more often in conjunction. If they were to be considered simply two "virtues" added to the qualities we have discussed above we should grossly misunderstand Ignatius, for although the ideas occur as nouns far more frequently than as verbs, it is clear that faith and love initially

---

21. Either as verb or noun, ὑπομονή occurs thirteen times in the letters, but the emphasis is not unusual in early Christianity. It does not, however, appear in virtue lists until the deutero-Pauline and post-Pauline writings. Cf. I Tim. 6:11, Rev. 2:19, II Pet. 1:6 ff.

describe the ways in which the disciple is related to the Lord
and to his fellows in the church, for both are words that express
relatedness. They carry the thought of Ignatius farther than
the more abstract notions of discipleship and imitation: they
try to state what the nature of the relation is, and by them
he can express relation to God the Father as well as to the incarnate Lord. Both involve the whole man, not merely his
mind or his feelings, or a pattern of activity, and both have
meaning only as they are the experience of the man whose life is
centered in God. Ignatius never defines them, since they have
been from the beginning characteristic of the community into
which he and all other Christians are bound, but he uses them
in a unique way to describe the life of the Christian. He says
once, "Faith is the beginning and love is the end of life" (*Eph.*
14.1). They are thus opposite ends of one process—not really
to be separated from each other. Since he thinks of them so, it
is not surprising that it is hard to discover what the exact differences between them are.

"Faith is the beginning." Certain aspects of his thought appear clearly enough for us to be able to gather why he affirms
faith's primacy. Faith is the response of man to what God has
already done. It wells up in man because God has acted in the
death and resurrection of Jesus Christ. Thus Ignatius says that
God has set up in the resurrection a standard for the saints and
faithful people (*Smyr.* 1.2); his redeeming acts attract men.
Again he speaks of the mystery of the death of Jesus Christ by
which men have received faith (*Mag.* 9.1, cf. *Tral.* 2.1). Quite
clearly the Christian responds because God acted through Jesus
Christ. It is not God as performing the great works of creation
who evoked this response, or God who revealed his will to the
prophets, but the redeeming God revealed in the mysteries of
the death and resurrection.

It is therefore inevitable that Ignatius should hold that faith
involves the *belief that* these events occurred and were supremely meaningful. Faith in this sense is an affirmation of the
reality of the οἰκονομία θεοῦ, the efficacy of the divine redemption.
As we have seen, there is sound reason for Ignatius' emphasis on
right belief, for the docetic teachers were denying the reality of

these events by "spiritualizing" them. Their interpretation removed the action of God from ordinary life as men knew it. There is among some in our time a tendency to look with suspicion on the rational aspect of faith, and "faith-belief" is contrasted to its own disfavor with "faith-trust," which is held to be the only vital meaning of the word. To judge Ignatius on these grounds is to miss both the desperateness of the situation which he faced, and the fact that faith-belief for him is meaningless apart from trust. Faith as the response of men to the redeeming God was central, but right understanding [22] of the acts of God was only a degree less important. Even belief can be said to come "through" Christ, as the result of his acts (*Phld.* 8.2), although this passage can also be read with the meaning of trust. And for men and spiritual powers alike it is essential to "believe in" the blood of Christ if they would escape judgment. Ignatius declares that such right belief, held in common by Christians (*Eph.* 13.1) in an undisturbed meeting, is the necessary ground for finding the eucharist the medicine of immortality (*Eph.* 20.1). He would have them remain steadfast and immovable in that faith (*Eph.* 10.2):

> being fully assured with respect to our Lord that he is in truth of the line of David according to the flesh, the son of God by the will and power of God, truly born of a Virgin, baptised by John that "all righteousness might be fulfilled by him," for our sakes truly nailed to the cross in the flesh under Pontius Pilate and Herod the Tetrarch . . . that he might set up a standard for all ages by his Resurrection . . .   [*Smyr.* 1.1, 2]

Once he goes so far as to say that it was for the "faith of God" that Jesus Christ was crucified (*Eph.* 16.2), a startling and elliptical witness to his belief that the correct understanding by men must be said to be a part of the very purpose of God. It is the passage that certainly comes closest to the use of faith

---

22. Πιστεύειν εἰς appears some five times, always with the connotation of intellectual assent (*Tral.* 2.1, *Smyr.* 6.1, *Mag.* 10.3 thrice). Πιστεύειν ἐν or πιστεύειν without a preposition are used for either conviction or trust.

characteristic of his age,[23] either as one virtue alongside other virtues, or the intellectual affirmations of the church without mention, at least, of trust. But it is significant that for Ignatius even this is related to the suffering of the Lord, and is saved from abstraction by that fact.

But however important he held this right understanding to be, Ignatius characteristically speaks of faith as a personal relationship to Christ. By having trust in him (*Phld.* 5.2) men are saved. The Father will raise up "in Christ Jesus" those who believe in or have trust in him (*Tral.* 9.2). Faith *in* him (ἐν— *Eph.* 1.1) or *through* him (διά—*Phld.* 8.2), or *towards* him (εἰς— *Eph.* 14.1) are different phrases for expressing the many-sidedness of the one experience of relatedness.[24]

The result of this orientation in faith is a radical change in the life of the Christian. "No one professing faith sins" (*Eph.* 14.1). There is a real ethical change. Or again he declares that "Faith cannot do the works of unfaithfulness" (*Eph.* 8.2). The transformation is so deep that an abyss can almost be said to yawn between the faithful and the unfaithful—those related to Christ and those alien to him (*Mag.* 5). One must suppose that in these affirmations about transformation Ignatius expresses hope more than fact; as we have seen, few are truly disciples. But the opposition between those grounded in Jesus Christ and the Father and those dominated by pride and egotism appears in the church threatened by intellectual strife.

If faith is the beginning "love is the end" of the Christian life (*Eph.* 14.1). Ignatius suggests here that the life of trust

23. The general decline from Paul's use of faith as trust in God needs no comment. See I Timothy's connection of good conscience and faith (1:5, 19; 3:9); of faith and good doctrine (4:6), or faith as one of the characteristics of the godly life (6:11); faith as the opposite of doubt (Jas. 1:6); faith as the crown of a good life (*I Clem.* 5.6, 26.1); a good work: faith and hospitality (10.7; 12). *Barnabas* is closer to the thought of Ignatius, for faith, promise, wisdom, and teaching are at least acts of God (16.9), and man is nourished by promise and word (6.17). In general Ignatius shares Paul's insight that faith is a personal relationship, although sometimes, as in *Eph.* 3.1, it appears in a list: faith, reproof, endurance, long-suffering.

24. For a discussion of life "in Christ" see below, Chap. 9.

leads on to a still more outgoing and active form of self-giving. Love is the devotion of the whole man to God.[25] Men are to "love nothing but God alone" (*Eph.* 9.2). He alone can serve as the center of a life. It is wholly "right" that men should love Christ (*Eph.* 15.3). Ignatius does not define love [26] any more than he does faith, but he makes it clear that love for God is the antithesis of a self-regarding disposition. It is not even dependent on the assurance of God's presence and so is related to adoration rather than mystical union, although paradoxically love creates the assurance which it assumes: "Let us therefore do all things as though he were dwelling in us, that we may be his temples, and he our God in us. This is the fact, and it will appear clearly to us by the love which we rightly have for him" (*Eph.* 15.3). Love, then, seems to be the "end" both in a temporal and in a teleological sense. It is a state of complete devotion which one must suppose could not be attained at the beginning of the Christian life, and it is the fullest form of human experience and hence a τέλος.

The love of the Christian for God occurs within the context of God's love for men. He urges Polycarp to persuade men "to love their wives as the Lord loved the Church" (*Poly.* 5.2). He speaks at a deeper level when he declares that the blood of Christ is "love incorruptible" (*Rom.* 7.3, *Tral.* 8.1). The passion can be understood only as expressing in an ultimate sense the love of God for man. He declares that the church is "beloved and enlightened by the will of him who wills everything that exists" (*Rom.* Ins.). Nowhere occurs anything as plain as we

25. For expression of love for man in Essene Judaism see *DSD* 10.26; in the *Testaments of the Twelve* see *Test. Gad* 3.6 f., 6.1–4; for the love of God for men, *Test. Jos.* 1.4 ff. For a view of love comparable to that of Ignatius, *I Clem.* 49. Nevertheless, Essene teaching emphasized primarily love within the community: see G. Quell and E. Stauffer, *Love*, trans. J. R. Coates from the article in Kittel's *Theologisches Wörterbuch*, p. 41, and for Ignatius as exceptional among the Apostolic Fathers because love was directed even toward the world, see Preisker, pp. 228 f. For the characteristic limitation of *agape* by *nomos* at that period see A. Nygren, *Agape and Eros, I* (London, 1938), 44–48.

26. He uses ἀγάπη and ἀγαπᾶν throughout the epistles except in *Rom.* 7.2, when he repudiates ἔρως and πῦρ φιλοϋλον.

find in I John, "We love him because he first loved us," but it is quite clear that man's love is his response to the searching and redeeming love of God.

Love for Christ gathers all lesser relations up into it and gives them meaning. To change the figure, it is the ground for all human experience of community. Christians should "love one another in Christ Jesus" (*Mag.* 6.2) and they are to "love one another with an undivided heart" (*Tral.* 13)—a heart undivided, one may surmise, because it is God-centered. The bishop's ministry for his people is "in the love of God the Father and the Lord Jesus Christ" (*Phld.* 1.1), and Ignatius reaches out for their "united prayer and love in God" (*Mag.* 14). This again is similar to the Johannine exhortation that "he who loves God should love his brother also" (I John 4:21), but surely it is also love that is expressed for the non-Christian community when they are met with gentleness and forbearance (*Eph.* 10).

However much one may try to understand the different connotations of "faith" and "love" in Ignatius' letters it is clear that the two conceptions are more alike than different. The number of times they are used together, as though they were mutually dependent, is the evidence of this relatedness.[27] Thus "faith is the windlass and love the ramp" (*Eph.* 9.1), by which men move up to God. And those who "hold the faith in love" (ἐν ἀγάπῃ πιστεύητε—*Phld.* 9.2) find all things good. In similar fashion the "faithful in love" bear the mark of God the Father through Jesus Christ (*Mag.* 5.2). Faith and love seem to be practically identified. More than once they comprise an inevitable pair, partly distinguishable but necessarily complementary, which stands with other pairs or triplets in rhythmical sequence. "Hasten therefore . . . in order that you may prosper in everything that you do, outwardly and inwardly, in faith and love, in the Son and the Father and the Spirit, at the be-

27. Cf. Gal. 5:6 for the two together. The combination of faith and love appears elsewhere in contemporary writings but not with the importance it has for Ignatius except in *Poly. Phil.* 3.3. Cf. I Tim. 1:5,14; II Tim. 1:13; *II Clem.* 15.2; *Barn.* 1.4; Hermas, *Mand.* 8.9; *Sim.* 9.17.4, 9.18.4.

ginning and at the end . . ." (*Mag.* 13.1). Ignatius is fond of pairs and paradoxes, but this is more than a trick of style. Faith and love are the distinguishing marks of Christian life, since both are the expression of relatedness to Christ. Faith is the flesh of the Lord and love his blood (*Tral.* 8.1). Ignatius even declares that "faith and love are everything, and nothing is to be preferred to them" (*Smyr.* 6.1).

In two or three pregnant passages we have the material for conjecturing a little more surely what is in Ignatius' mind when he uses such extravagant language. Faith and love hold such a place in his thought about the Christian life because he believes that they are of a suprahuman nature; their source is the spiritual world. Thus the inscription of the letter to the church at Smyrna praises it for having "received mercy in every gift, being filled with faith and love and lacking no grace." One cannot escape the conviction that the faith and love which mark the church are, like the mercy of God, *charismata,* freely given to men. In similar vein he writes to the Ephesians that the cross of Jesus Christ, the working of the Holy Spirit, and their faith and love are respectively the engine, the rope, the windlass, and the ramp by which, like great stones, they are drawn into place in the building of God (*Eph.* 9.1). Here faith and love seem to be divinely offered, rather than human achievements. To be sure, it is a figure of speech, and one that strains the meaning of language. It is faith that fits into this figure least easily; but that faith itself is "received" of men Ignatius declares quite directly (*Mag.* 9.1), in a passage that suggests both *trust* and *right belief,* since it is faith through the mystery of the death and resurrection.

The most extreme of his statements ends with the declaration that faith and love in unity "are God" (θεός ἐστιν—*Eph.* 14.1):

> None of these things has escaped you if you have perfect faith and love towards Jesus Christ, for these are the beginning and end of life. Faith is the beginning and love is the end, but when the two are in unity it is God himself, and all other things follow them, to the end of nobility and goodness.

It is not easy to know how to understand such a passage. Certainly one must not read it with dry literalism; nevertheless, it can no more be read as mere metaphor than can the great Johannine exclamation which it so strongly suggests, "God is love" (I John 4:8). It is poetic in form, and one meets in it the deepest beliefs of the writer. It is the declaration that faith and love for Jesus Christ, in perfect fullness, bring one into the very presence of God; there God is. It is surely more than to cry out that "it is simply divine to have a full faith and love for the Lord Jesus Christ." [28] It recalls other passages when in a comparable surge of conviction he declares that perfect hope or knowledge *is* Jesus Christ (cf. *Eph.* 17.2, *Mag.* 7.1, *Smyr.* 10.2). They also are poetic, and they express in language that is religious, not metaphysical, a conviction that in devotion, in faith, in hope man finds God acting upon him, and enters into him. This kind of language is possible to Ignatius because he believes so profoundly that faith and love are the basis for union. In one sense they are the end of life, but in a deeper sense they are instrumental: "Faith and love are everything and nothing is preferred before them" (*Smyr.* 6.1). But with that we must put the passage that expresses his belief that even faith and love lead beyond themselves and become the basis for union. He prays, he says, that in the churches there may be "a union with the flesh and spirit of Jesus Christ, who is our life forever, a union of faith and love, than which nothing is to be preferred, and more than all a union with Jesus and with the Father" (*Mag.* 1.2).

It is clear from these last-mentioned passages that Ignatius is not willing to describe the Christian life simply as ethical obedience to Jesus Christ. This, of course, he assumes, but in the enthusiasm of devotion Ignatius lifts this aspect of his thought to a new level. To live as imitators of Christ and in conformity with God affirms the ethical nature of the demands of God upon the Christian, but faith and love in fullness imply that there is more than that. Ignatius expresses his thought about the final goal in his discussion of union, and that we must

28. J. Moffatt, "Ignatius of Antioch—a Study in Personal Religion," *JR, 10* (1930), 178.

defer until the next chapter. But even in our examination of his thought about life κατὰ κύριον, we have seen that he passes beyond the ordinary bounds.

Although it is not so obviously controversial in its intent, Ignatius' view of the ethical life may have been as effective a weapon against his opponents in the church as any part of his thinking. Indeed in certain ways it was more sharply differentiated from theirs than was his view on salvation, although it is actually the practical outcome of that view.

We may conclude that the docetist ethic in its presumed ascetic form had little relevance to the needs of a community that must live in the world, and the reasons are not hard to discover. In the first place the Docetists' emphasis on the power of the Saviour Christ who by his spiritual coming brought grace to the world was more unqualified than was that of Ignatius. They seem to have thought of it as effective in an all but magical way, and possessed of irresistible power, and in the degree to which that is true they concentrated on knowledge about it. A second idea that weakened the need to develop an ethic of love was their view of men as divided between *sarkikoi* and *pneumatikoi*. As we have said above, if men by their very nature were assured of salvation, their perception of the mercy of the redeeming act was reduced. Salvation became their right; hence the ground for a response of love and faith was insecure. Since, as we saw above, love for God and a full expression of Christian love toward the needy are linked closely together, it is not surprising that Ignatius scores the Docetists for being unconcerned about the expression of *agape*. They probably valued purity above love.

He, on the contrary, held that the life of relationships lived by a Christian was of supreme importance, and the very well-knit and sturdy ethic we have traced above was the result. It is based on discipleship to the historical and incarnate Lord, and it is noteworthy that Ignatius holds that the historical life is as central an issue in ethics as in theology, for it alone serves as the ground for a real experience of discipleship. Christ remains the Lord and Saviour, bringing life and grace, but perhaps precisely because Ignatius remembers him, through the teaching of those who had known him, as living in history, the response to him has an earthy quality. Men do not expect magic. And there is no notion of any advantage that precludes the necessity of action on the part of all: hence decision is absolutely necessary. Men are neither *pneumatikoi* nor *sarkikoi;* they live or die according to whether they reach out to appropriate what is offered, and respond in faith and love.

Here, as we have seen, the life of absolute commitment is considered so difficult that it must be said to be achieved only by the few. It remains as the ideal which draws men on, and even in its difficulty it must have served as a challenge to the docetist notion of esoteric knowledge. Here Ignatius gives interesting evidence of one reason at least for the power of Christianity against its rivals. Different as he is in various important ways from Paul, he has fashioned an impressive ethical doctrine.

9. Union

IGNATIUS describes himself in the letter to Philadelphia as a man "completely given over to union" (*Phld.* 8.1). Although in the context this indicates primarily his concern with the troubling factions which the Philadelphian church seems to have been trying to ignore, in a more important sense it could be taken as affirming what he holds to be the deepest experiences of human life. References to union run through the letters, and they cannot be subordinated to the interest in imitation and discipleship we have just considered. As we saw in the last chapter, some of Ignatius' expressions point beyond themselves to further experience. When he speaks of being "imitators of Jesus Christ as he was of his Father," or declares that "faith and love . . . in unity are God," it is clear he is trying to say something for which the ordinary categories of ethical experience are inadequate. His understanding of these further reaches of thought is carried in the several words harmony (ὁμόνοια), unity (ἑνότης), and, most important of all, union (ἕνωσις).

As a basis for interpreting his concern we may remind ourselves that his view of the predicament of humanity stresses not *sin* but *division*. Although this does not seem to him an offense against God, its consequences are so dangerous that men must be aware of the nature of their plight and act to change it. To say this does not mean that men act in isolation, for as we have seen in the last chapter they respond to the act of God already performed. Nevertheless, the bridging of the separations of life occurs only when appropriate decisions are made. Men are divided, within themselves, from one another, and from God. It is this tragic lack of unity that makes them vulnerable to the temptations of the Prince of this world, temptations evidenced in the conflicts within communities and in the unwillingness of the individual to submit himself to discipline.

The greatest danger assailing men arises not from outward acts of persecution but from the tendency toward separateness that undermines them. The core of Ignatius' preaching is that this disunity can be transcended.

More significant than either the individual's inner disunity or the factiousness of the churches, both of which we shall consider below, is the separation of individual and community from God. This is the fundamental problem. Ignatius never directly declares it, but the implications of his hopes for union and his horror of division make the conclusion inevitable. He describes Christ as the inseparable (ἀδιάκριτον) life of the churches (*Eph.* 3.2) and thus suggests elliptically that only in Christ is the divisiveness overcome. At the close of the Magnesian letter Ignatius prays that they may "possess an undivided spirit, for this is Jesus Christ" (*Mag.* 15.1). It is, then, from God[1] that unity comes, and conversely one must suppose from this and many other passages that the lack of it is the mark of lives that are separated from him. He is the source of the unity that heals divisions, and it is for this reason that separation from God is the most disastrous privation that can threaten human beings; nothing but an established relationship to God gives life.

At this level of Ignatius' thought the lack of a systematic use of terms is serious, and we are forced as we have been before to follow whatever clues he offers to discover the connections in his mind between related conceptions. One clue to understanding the importance of union seems to be offered by his view of the fate of the martyr, though in all the letters except *Romans* that takes second place and his chief concern is with the life of the ordinary men and women in the churches, most of whom will never face martyrdom. Not once does Ignatius use the words "unity" and "union" of his fate, and yet, as we shall see, it is his interpretation of his own experience that furnishes perspective for understanding his thought about union. In

1. Bartsch, *GG,* passim, correctly emphasizes the importance of this conception. As we have argued in Chapter 5, the notion of the unity of God is not as abstract as Bartsch would make it, for it is associated always with the conviction that there is no other God. He is certainly right, however, in pointing out that Ignatius does not think of God primarily as righteous, but as the One from whom men are separated: ibid., p. 82.

order to get that perspective we shall have to examine with care the ideas he uses in interpreting the martyr's lot.

Under the experience of persecution the church developed a considerable body of thought and practice about the fate of the martyr,[2] and even in the New Testament its outlines are apparent. The white-robed multitude who stood before God in the vision of Revelation had "come out of great tribulation." Their glory is to "serve God" and to "see his face" (Rev. 22:3 f.). Phrase after phrase depicts their future reward. They will "eat of the tree of life" (Rev. 2:7), they will receive the "crown of life" (Rev. 2:10), and have their names in the book of life (Rev. 3:5). They will reign with Christ for the thousand years after the first judgment, and they will not be harmed by the "second death" (Rev. 2:11, 20:4). According to the Book of Revelation all this comes as the reward of the martyr's death. I Peter thinks of confessors as having partaken of the sufferings of Christ (4:13).

Ignatius' approach differs from that of Revelation, for he does not dwell on the details of the final goal, although he faces it personally. But his letters are the most significant early source for revealing the nature of the experience from the inside, and thus for demonstrating which of the beliefs had most power to sustain. He accepts the indications of his imprisonment as honorable signs. The chains, which he describes perhaps with wry humor as "spiritual pearls" (*Eph.* 11.2), are signs both of the future perfecting of his lot and of his steadfastness in the preliminary stages. He glories in his godly name as prisoner of Christ which his "bonds" justify (*Mag.* 1.2), and he declares that Polycarp has "loved them" (*Poly.* 2.3). It is without doubt his status as one approaching martyrdom that partly explains the

2. Schlier, *Relig. Untersuch.* pp. 152–65, in spite of strong emphasis on gnostic influence on the conception of the martyr, holds that as Christian, Ignatius had something distinctive in the pattern of the Lord's actual death, whereas gnosticism early spiritualized the Passion; H. F. von Campenhausen, *Die Idee des Martyriums* (Göttingen, 1936), esp. pp. 65–79; H.-W. Surkau, *Martyrien in jüdischer und frühchristlicher Zeit* (Göttingen, 1938), emphasizes the Jewish antecedents of Christian teaching about martyrdom; Bartsch, *GG,* pp. 80–99, emphasizes the importance of the story of the Passion in the eucharist. For a sociological study see D. W. Riddle, *The Martyrs, a Study in Social Control,* Chicago, 1931.

honor shown to him, though we must suppose that both the quality of life of the man and his position as leader of the great church of Antioch must also have contributed. There is no evidence that for him they indicate symbols of a condemnation not before a court but before God [3]—he expected at death to attain unto God—and still less easy is it to read his comments on them as allusions to the gnostic idea of the imprisonment of the person in matter.[4] They may in a realistic way be considered distinctions, for they are indications that at least throughout his trial Ignatius had refused to deny his loyalties, but he will not consider them in any definitive sense as ultimate achievements. "For I myself, also, although I am in chains and can know heavenly things and the orders of the angels . . . I myself am not yet a disciple" (*Tral.* 5.2). The adulation of church leaders remains a temptation to him to become self-congratulatory and boastful (*Tral.* 4).

He sees himself in the martyr's role as playing a dramatic and profoundly important part in the life of the church. He says he will be poured out like an oblation, when the altar is ready and while the church forms itself into a great choir (*Rom.* 2.2), and that he will be a sacrifice [5] (*Rom.* 4.2). And lest anyone should think his death a matter of compulsion, he declares that he dies willingly for the sake of God (*Rom.* 4.1). He sees the sufferings of confessors as having persuasive power in the work of the church, along with the prophecies and the law of Moses and the gospel (*Smyr.* 5.1). The martyr's death, although ultimately a lonely experience, takes place in the full sight of the church, and the martyr plays a most honored role.

3. So Bauer, *Die Briefe, ad Eph.* 12.1.

4. Schlier, p. 154, considers that Ignatius believes his imprisonment a sign that he still belongs to the "old kingdom" and was not redeemed, an echo of the idea that he is still bound to matter. Bartsch, *GG*, pp. 92 ff., rightly points out that Ignatius glories in his chains, but argues that the "unworthiness" rests in the fact that as prisoner he is deprived of the sacrament.

5. On Ignatius' view of his death as a sacrifice see above, p. 172. For Jewish views of death as a sacrifice see *Wisd. Sol.* 3.6; "as a whole burnt offering he accepted" the righteous: *IV Mac.* 6.27–29, 17.20–22. On expiatory suffering see Moore, *Judaism, I,* 546–52.

In a more personal sense his death will be important not be-cause it is supported by the church [6] and important as an ex-ample, but because in it the meaning of his own life is per-fected. Because through it he achieves participation in the suf-ferings of Christ, Ignatius will find him (*Rom.* 6.1). We have observed more than once his desire to imitate the passion (*Rom.* 6.3), to die in Jesus Christ (*Rom.* 6.1). That suffering he de-clares is the means to full discipleship: "And why then have I wholly given myself up to death, to fire, to the sword, to wild beasts? But near to the sword, near to God; with wild beasts, with God. Only it is in the name of Jesus Christ that I endure everything, that I may suffer with him" (*Smyr.* 4.2). He thinks of the whole experience of his death and all the events leading up to it as a search [7] for Jesus Christ: "Him I seek who died for us; him I desire who rose for our sake" (*Rom.* 6.1).

This idea is very different from Paul's conviction that in baptism all Christians are baptized into the death of Christ, so that they may be said to have been buried with him, and therefore to have resurrection assured to them (Rom. 6:4, 8). It is a real death of the "old man" or the "body of sin" (Rom. 6:6), and the result is that even now they "walk in newness of life" and are "new creatures" (II Cor. 5:17, Gal. 6:15). The Christian chooses voluntarily to be so "crucified": "they that are of Christ have crucified the flesh with the passions and the lusts thereof . . ." (Gal. 5:24). All this is absent from Ignatius' thought, to the real loss of depth, but one must observe that Ignatius holds in a full Pauline sense the notion of living "in Christ." The nuances are inevitably different, for Ignatius' own death looms upon him in a matter of weeks, and he fears not the absence of the grace of God but his own steadfastness before torture. He knows that in a new and different sense the Perfect

6. So esp. Riddle, *The Martyrs.*

7. Preiss, "La Mystique de l'imitation et de l'unité," *Revue d'histoire et de philosophie religieuses, 18* (1938), 205 ff., contrasts the theocentric mysticism of Paul, who lives "in Christ" as a result of the divine act, with the active search of Ignatius, to the disfavor of the latter. There is no doubt that Ignatius saw his death as a martyr through the developing martyr-theory of the church. As martyr both he and the church would gain. It is in that light that we may see the drive toward death.

Man will have to empower him to meet that trial, and he affirms his faith that it will be so. Even Paul makes a distinction between living in Christ and what he surmises he may face if he dies a martyr. In the late letter to the Philippians he cries out his desire to "know him, and the power of his resurrection, and the fellowship of his sufferings, becoming conformed into his death" that he may "attain unto the resurrection from the dead" (N.T. Phil. 3:10 f.). His own coming death, which imagination painted in less lurid colors than in Ignatius' case because persecutions had not yet become so standard that one knew what he would face, still lay between him and the resurrection.

The decisive moment for Ignatius will come if he persists to the point of death, for then, as he says frequently, he will "attain unto God," or "unto Jesus Christ." [8] His word, ἐπιτυχεῖν or τυχεῖν, is always used of this consummation of life, and even when he varies the form and speaks of attaining to his inheritance or to his lot (*Phld.* 5.1, *Rom.* 1.2),[9] or merely of "attaining" (*Rom.* 8.3), it is clear that he means the same thing. If the Roman church does not accept his decision not to ask for mercy, he will fall short of this achievement (*Rom.* 2.1). He sees it as so desirable—so much the perfecting of life—that things visible and invisible may well envy him (*Rom.* 5.3). Although his interest is not in the details of the final state, he leaves us in no doubt whatsoever that it is a supremely blessed experience, as he shows in his short description of Paul, who was "a man of holy life and a martyr's death who was worthy to be blessed, in whose steps may I be found when I shall attain unto God" (*Eph.* 12.2). As martyr he expected to be finally and irrevocably brought into the presence of God: "God has considered the bishop of Syria worthy to be found at the setting of the sun, having summoned him from the sun's rising. It is good to set to the world facing towards God, that I may rise to him" (*Rom.* 2.2).

In a number of brilliant figures of speech he exults in the

8. *Eph.* 12.2; *Mag.* 14.1; *Tral.* 13.3; *Rom.* 1.2, 2.1, 4.1, 5.3 *bis*, 9.2; *Smyr.* 11.1.

9. ΑΣ imply πέρατος. See Lightfoot, *Apostolic Fathers*, note *ad Rom.* 1.2.

completeness of the change that will come about in "attaining to God." All of them indicate that this experience is the ultimate one—by comparison with it, all life has to offer is empty. He says that by death he will become "a freedman of Jesus Christ" (*Rom.* 4.3); it will let him "receive the pure light" (*Rom.* 6.2). He will be "wheat ground by the teeth of the beasts," to become "pure bread of Christ" (*Rom.* 4.1).

Here the daring of the figure will be apparent if we recall his affirmations that the bread of God is the flesh of Christ; it is reminiscent at once of the eucharist and of the passion. He says he is "being born into life" [10] (ζῆσαι—*Rom.* 6.2), and again one recalls that Christ is the *life* of the churches. Perhaps most significant, it is through his death that Ignatius hopes to "become a man" (*Rom.* 6.2), and by it he will be a word, not an inchoate cry (*Rom.* 2.1). When we recall his description of Christ both as Perfect Man and as the Word of God, the daring of the figures stands out in startling sharpness. In another letter he has said "Only it is in the name of Jesus Christ that I endure everything that I may suffer with him, and the Perfect Man himself strengthens me" (*Smyr.* 4.2). Here is the suggestion that Christ is the representative of the human race in its completeness.[11] And in the moment of "attaining," Ignatius, too, expects at last to reach the stature of true humanity. The metaphor declares that humanity reaches maturity or completeness [12] only in relation to God, and at the same time suggests the paradoxical kinship between the divine and the human that was the living core of so much of Ignatius' Christianity. This is not θεοπόιησις, but ἀνθρωποπόιησις made the more daring because it is Jesus Christ who is at the same time Perfect Man and God. We do not understand that Ignatius declares that in attaining he will be identified with Christ,[13] but most of the metaphors

10. I owe the translation to James Moffatt, from unpublished lectures.

11. The Anthropos figure is suggested by the phrase, though in what form we cannot know. See above, Chap. 4.

12. It may be that the λόγος-φωνή (*Rom.* 2.1) contrast carries this connotation, since λόγος implies meaningful human discourse, and φωνή the cry of an animal.

13. So, e.g., *GG*, p. 80.

indicate that union with him will result. The absolute character of the transformation at the martyr's death can hardly be put more sharply. "Then shall I truly be a disciple of Jesus Christ when the world shall not see my body" (*Rom.* 4.2, cf. *Eph.* 1.2, *Rom.* 5.1).

Religious-historical parallels between Ignatius' view of his fate as martyr and the general gnostic view of the redemption of the *pneumatikoi* are widely discussed. Thus Schlier rejects the idea that Ignatius' protestations of unworthiness are to be explained partly by historical circumstances in the church of Antioch and partly by his own fear that at the end he would lack courage. He explains them rather as half-conscious echoes of the gnostic contrast between the redeemed and the persecuted redeemer; [14] and he holds that in describing himself as ἔκτρωμα [15]—an abortion—Ignatius recalls the myth of the lower Sophia thrown out from the pleroma, while his desire to "be someone" echoes the desire of Sophia to return.

These seem very far-fetched notions indeed, no matter how much *im Hintergrund* they are alleged to stand. Rather, we see the background of his willingness to endure the martyr's death as having Jewish and Christian influences: the Jewish beliefs, from the time of the Maccabees on, that martyrdom effects something both for the martyr and the people, and the change in locus of the thought of suffering, from the periphery to the center, brought about by the passion of Christ. Finally, Paul's interpretation of Christian life as being "conformed unto his death" had driven all men deeply influenced by Paul's thought to consider what that "conformation" might mean. No one of these notions explains the development of Ignatius' view, but at least they give the background of his attempt to relate the experience of the ordinary Christian and the martyr, or to put it another way, his own experience in the years of work as bishop of Antioch, and the martyrdom that lay ahead.

For the martyr's death may be the surest path, but it is not the only one for attaining to God. Ignatius implies that in writing to the Romans, "It is hard for me to attain to God if you

14. Schlier, p. 152.
15. Ibid., pp. 156 ff.

do not spare me" (*Rom.* 1.2). One cannot understand this sentence to mean that it will be difficult for him to be condemned again to martyrdom; it can only mean that although that is the straight road, there are others one can travel. And in the letter addressed to Polycarp, Ignatius writes, "The season . . . demands of you to attain to God" (*Poly.* 2.3). In this letter he is certainly not urging Polycarp to seek martyrdom, but rather to redouble his efforts to establish the church at Smyrna in the face of the dangers of possible disunity. He writes to the Smyrnaeans, "May God reward you, and if for his sake you endure all things you shall attain unto him" (*Smyr.* 9.1).

Endurance is by no means a word used only of the martyr's death. In these passages, as in those we discussed earlier, the goal of attaining to God must probably be thought of as achieved only at death, and only then if the road has been followed which leads to that end. In one passage he states clearly that it is through the achievement of union during life that this will be: "I sing the praise of the churches . . . in which I pray there may be a union with the flesh and spirit of Jesus Christ, who is our life forever, a union of faith and love, to which nothing is preferable, and (above all else) a union with Jesus Christ and the Father. If in him we endure all the wanton insolence of the Prince of this world and escape, we shall attain unto God" (*Mag.* 1.2). We shall return to this passage later, but only after we have examined Ignatius' use of related words. It affirms unmistakably, however, that the experience of union as well as the road of the martyr makes a man ready to "attain." But the "attainment" comes, one must suppose, in death; the tense is future. Through union the undramatic lives of men in the churches are laid hold of in an experience that takes them beyond themselves and overcomes the separation that yawns between man and man, and man and God.

Just as light was thrown on the martyr's experience by several related notions, so it is with Ignatius' thought about unity and union. It is as though he thought of a series of preliminary stages, a school of union as it were.

One of these steps is submission or obedience which he considers the ground of a deeper unity in the church. Practically, as we have seen, it appears as submission to the bishop or to the bishop and other leaders in the church. Such obedience, of course, has important results in institutional harmony, but Ignatius values it for the more important reason that it leads to holiness (*Eph.* 2.2). It is the evidence of lives lived according to the standards of Jesus Christ, not those of human society (*Tral.* 2.1). It is even, he seems to suggest, the kind of discipline necessary for the healing of the disunities of flesh and spirit. "Subordinate yourselves to the bishop and to one another as Jesus Christ did to the Father according to the flesh [16] and as the Apostles did to Christ and to the Father and to the Spirit, in order that there may be union of flesh and of spirit" (*Mag.* 13.2). Submission is so important that it is inherent even in the relation of the Son to the Father. Furthermore, as we have pointed out above, Ignatius' concern for obedience does not arise from his interest in a sturdy organization, since the obedience that he craves for them is to one another as well as to the bishop. By submission to the bishops or to one another, men come to be "subject to God" (*Eph.* 5.3) and "have their heritage in God" (*Poly.* 6.1). Obedience is thus in the last analysis a way of being related to God. One may venture the guess that Ignatius might even be willing to say that the bishops and other ministers exist because it is in just such a structured church that obedience can be learned.

Related notions are expressed in the idea of being "in Jesus Christ." They are difficult to evaluate, for Ignatius uses the phrase in many contexts. Sometimes it seems to be little more than a pious convention as it stands in greetings (e.g. *Mag.* Ins., *Eph.* Ins.), farewells (*Eph.* 21.2, *Tral.* 13), and the description of the delegate to the now peaceful Antiochene church as "blessed in Jesus Christ" (*Phld.* 10.1). In two cases he describes the Christian life in its fullness as that of being related to Jesus Christ. Thus he hopes to be "perfected in Jesus Christ" (*Eph.* 3.1) and after suffering to "rise free in him" (*Rom.* 4.3). More frequently he speaks of the action which results from being

16. Accepting the reading of GL. See above, pp. 138 f.

so grounded. "What you do even after the manner of the flesh is spiritual, for you do all things in Jesus Christ" (*Eph.* 8.2). More pungently, he begs them to "be salted in him, that none among you spoil . . ." (*Mag.* 10.1). A whole life characterized by "abiding in" (*Eph.* 10.3) or "living in" him will mean that at death they will be "found in him" (*Eph.* 11.1, *Tral.* 2.2) and will "live forever in Jesus Christ" (*Eph.* 20.2). It is difficult to find here anything not in agreement with Pauline usage.

Less frequently Ignatius uses the reverse figure, that God may be in man. The Magnesians are described as "having Jesus Christ in" themselves (*Mag.* 12.1). Here belongs the familiar figure of the Christian church as the temple in which God dwells (*Eph.* 9.1). The phrase refers now to a group, now to an individual (cf. *Eph.* 15.3). Ignatius appeals to any man in the Roman church who "has Jesus Christ in himself" to understand his own determination to accept the martyr's death, and so to "attain to God" (*Rom.* 6.3). But to say that it applies to the individual is not to suggest that it has taken place except within the community of the church. To have God in oneself does not seem to be essentially different from being "in God." Both expressions mean lives conformed to the mind of Jesus Christ. They seem to imply not mystical experience but rather orientation of will and life toward God, and in that sense they are similar to the obedience which leads on to becoming "subject to God."

As we have seen in the last chapter, faith and love in unity are the supreme expressions of lives related both to God and to others in the church. Faith and love should then be placed alongside obedience and the quality of being "in Christ" as practical evidences of unity. But although all are evidences of unity of a sort, Ignatius holds that they are also means of achieving still further experience. They are chiefly important because the unity within the church, which they evidence, important as it is in itself is an effective foundation for a greater unity still.

Before that final experience of union occurs, a number of factors must be present. Each of the churches must be knit into the unity Ignatius describes as a synthesis of flesh and spirit. He trusts that the church at Tralles may have "peace in flesh and spirit through the passion of Jesus Christ . . ." [17] (*Tral.* Ins.), and that in all the churches there may be "union with the flesh and the spirit of Jesus Christ" (*Mag.* 1.2). This means that the churches must be dominated by spiritual concerns, not by the interests of the world. Outwardly and inwardly they must be clear and without stain. The "flesh" of the church, which is its outward activity and organization, must be dominated by its divine life.

Union of flesh and spirit is more clearly stated as it applies to the healing of divisions within individual persons, and this too is an essential preparation for final union. As we have seen in Chapter 6, although there are no necessary ethical contradictions between flesh and spirit in Ignatius' thought, nevertheless the flesh and the spirit of a man are not important in the same way. For the unredeemed man there is either division between flesh and spirit, which suggests instability, or integration at the level of the flesh, and only as a man enters into the unity of the church and hence is possessed of the mind of God is unity of flesh and spirit completed, for then they are united in the service of God. If a man believes falsely about the divine source of life, he "perishes by his questionings." What Ignatius looks forward to is not life in the spirit alone but the unity of both flesh and spirit in Jesus Christ. It is significant that he *never* speaks of living κατὰ πνεῦμα but rather κατὰ κύριον. What he suggests, rather, is the need within the individual that spirit and flesh, desire and achievement, word and action become synthesized. The real life within history is the scene of higher insight and redemption. "For this reason you are of flesh and spirit that you may deal graciously with the things which are before your eyes; and pray . . . that you want nothing, and have in abundance all spiritual gifts" (*Poly.* 2.2). A new power comes with the unity.

The unity within the human being is thought of as presaged by and dependent upon the unity of flesh and spirit that marked Jesus Christ. It was apparent even after his death and resurrec-

17. Following Lightfoot, I accept the reading of g rather than GLA. See Lightfoot's note *ad loc.*

tion, and the fusion was so complete that the flesh did not act as a drag upon the spirit: "And at once they touched him and believed, being joined to his flesh and spirit. And after the resurrection he ate and drank with them as one in the flesh, though spiritually he was united with the Father" (*Smyr.* 3.2). It is this unity of flesh and spirit within each man and therefore with Jesus Christ that Ignatius hopes for within the church communities.

Our examination of his usage has shown how rich are the connotations of unity and union and how central the conceptions in his thought. But it must be admitted that we have reached something less than full understanding. One cannot say with assurance that all aspects of unity are necessary steps in the development of the mature experience of the Christian within the church, nor can one say with certainty that any of the phrases that he uses is precisely synonymous with any other. For Ignatius obedience, living in Jesus Christ, the union of faith and love, unity of flesh and spirit—these are all ways of expressing his convictions about the preliminary experiences of unity. The gaps in our understanding are probably inevitable, for these are roads of the spirit not easily charted. The only fact that stands out unmistakably is that all of them are unifying experiences, and that taken together they are instrumental to the final union of the Christian with God.

Whether Ignatius conceived of a union that was more than a unity in will or obedience to God is a matter of controversy.[18] It seems difficult, in the face of the evidence we have observed to avoid the conclusion that although unity of will is necessary, more than that is involved, and he speaks of mystical union. It must be admitted, however, that the difficulties are real, since Ignatius does not use words with precision, and since, furthermore, there are problems about translating some of the Greek genitives into English. The heart of the problem is reached when one tries to discover the precise denotation of the words "unity" (ἑνότης) and "union" (ἕνωσις). Ordinarily he draws a distinction between them, reserving the second for what seems

18. Richardson, *Christianity of Ignatius*, pp. 38 f., argues for "moral likeness."

to be the ultimate in human experience and using it with a transcendental reference. But occasionally he varies this usage.

When Ignatius speaks of the unity of God (ἑνότης θεοῦ), he does not ordinarily mean more than the divine unity which is the mark of the Christian community. "For as many as are of God and Jesus Christ they are with the bishop; and as many as shall repent and come into the unity of the church, these shall be of God . . ." (*Phld.* 3.2). It is obvious that "being of God" and "being with the bishop" are inseparable and mean the same thing.

A similar meaning is expressed later in the letter to Philadelphia. "Now the Lord forgives all who repent if in their repentance they come into the unity of God and to the council of the bishop" (*Phld.* 8.1). The "unity of God" is here a synonym for unity in the church, as it is in the passage which declares that the patriarchs and the prophets and the Apostles and the whole church "are held together in the unity of God" (*Phld.* 9.1). However, even when he uses the phrase "unity of God" Ignatius sometimes means more than this, and gives evidence of an objective reference. *Smyr.* 12.2 is an example, for it presents a series of double groupings in which, for all the close linking, neither of the poles is ever quite a synonym for the other. "I greet . . . all of you individually and collectively, in the name of Jesus Christ, and in his flesh and blood, in his passion and resurrection, which was both carnal and spiritual, in the unity of God and of yourselves." Here the "unity of God" is joined to unity within the group but is certainly not synonymous with it. Even if one considers the genitives to be subjective, there is still an oblique kind of objective reference. The "unity of God" is something more than the unity of the group, or the two would have no place in these pairs of concepts, where there is affirmed the unity of what is at least partly distinguishable.

The clearest passage in which Ignatius speaks of unity between the Christian and God makes use of ἕνωσις rather than ἑνότης. It is extremely difficult to interpret the sentence and avoid the objective reference to God. The climax of his thought is the bridging of the ultimate separation between God and man. Ignatius prays that in the churches there may be:

> a union (ἕνωσις) with the flesh and spirit of Jesus Christ, who is our everlasting life, a union of faith and love, to which nothing is preferable, and—above everything else— a union with Jesus and with the Father. If in him we endure all the wanton insolence of the Prince of this world and escape we shall attain unto God. [*Mag.* 1.2]

It is difficult to translate this passage except by reading the genitives as having objective reference. The union that exists between Jesus Christ and the Father is one of the cardinal points of Ignatius' belief and quite beyond doubt. It would therefore be meaningless for him to pray that in the churches there may be a union *of* Jesus Christ and the Father. The passage is throughout affirming the union of what is not always joined. Union of believers with God is, therefore, the most reasonable translation. Finally, consciousness of the daring of the hope is shown by the crescendo in terms, and by the halt just before he reaches the end: "and what is more than all."

By means of that ἕνωσις a man may come into union even with the Father. This is the consummation of the purpose of God: Jesus Christ who manifests the Father to the world does away with the ultimate separation. Revelation has reached its appointed end in the redemption of men into unity with God. Ignatius is not alone in affirming this paradox of the hidden Father, whom, nevertheless, men may know in mystical union, for the Fourth Gospel has a similar doctrine: "No man hath seen God at any time; the only begotten God who is in the bosom of the Father, he hath declared him" (John 1:18). "Neither for these only do I pray, but for them also that believe on me through their word; that they may all be one; even as thou, Father, art in me and I in thee, that they also may be in us . . ." (John 17:20 f.).

There are two other passages in which Ignatius suggests another facet of his thought about unity and union, to both of which we have referred in other connections. "None of these things has escaped you, if you have perfect faith and love towards Jesus Christ, for these are the beginning and end of life—faith is the beginning and love is the end—but when the two are in unity it is God himself . . ." *(Eph.* 14.1). That this is a figure we may not question, but that it speaks Ignatius' most profound conviction is equally certain.

A more conclusive passage is *Tral.* 11.2, "A head cannot be born without members, since God offers union, and this union is himself." Here Ignatius steps momentarily from suggesting the nature of the experience to analysis of its theological ground, for he is declaring his conviction that the principle of union in the universe and therefore in the church is God himself. It is for this reason that any partial and preliminary experience of unity leads on to final union with God, for God must be said to be the ground of union in the world. Here is suggested neither the Father God nor the incarnate Lord of the church, but God as suprapersonal. It is in him and through him that union comes, that separations are bridged. In this passage Ignatius is declaring in other words the union with Jesus Christ and with the Father.

It is probable that one other passage should be placed beside these two, though it makes use of a different metaphor and can be interpreted with less confidence. In the Ephesian letter (4.2) Ignatius writes: "It is therefore profitable for you to be in blameless unity in order that you may always have a portion in God." Although one cannot affirm identity of meaning between this and *Tral.* 11.2 and *Mag.* 1.2, there is the same emphasis on the unity in the church that makes possible a more ultimate experience with God. A mystical union with God seems here, too, to be the most probable interpretation.

There are certain things that can be said about this experience which Ignatius holds is the summit of life in this world. Union with God takes place only within the church: "Then all of you pattern yourselves after God, respect one another . . . and love one another in Jesus Christ always. May there be nothing among you which shall have power to divide you, but be united (ἐνώθητε) with the bishop and with them

who rank above you as a type and a lesson of incorruptibility"
(*Mag.* 6.2). In this passage he does not mention the experience
that is "more than all," but he indicates clearly enough what
the preliminaries are. The "type" of incorruptibility is the picture that suggests the reality of life which will be reached when
men have "attained unto God." And if one puts together this
passage and *Mag* 1.2, the relationships become apparent.

Schweitzer, in his *Mysticism of St. Paul,* recognizes the central importance of the conception of union, and argues that in
emphasizing it Ignatius is "Hellenizing" Christianity [19] and
taking in effect the step Paul never needed to take because
within the apocalyptic framework of thought he had defined
salvation as living "in Christ" in this world. Ignatius, says
Schweitzer, uses the formula of the mystical living "in Christ,"
but gives it a non-Pauline content by the doctrine that the flesh
and spirit of the Christian are effectually united in the experience in the church, and that hence the same kind of resurrection, that of flesh and spirit, is assured for his followers that
characterized Christ himself (cf. *Smyr.* 3.1).

The theory has the advantage of pointing up the importance
of the church in which alone union takes place, but it does not
seem to identify correctly the place that union of flesh and
spirit has in the scheme of Ignatius. For although it is true
that he holds a different view from Paul of the place of the
flesh in the resurrection, it is not for him the union of flesh and
spirit that is "above everything else." Such union, whether of
the church groups or of individuals within them, is what we
have described as one of the preparatory or anticipatory stages,
and at the summit stands union "with Christ and the Father."
To say that this is within reach in this life is to emphasize
union, as Paul indeed did in the doctrine of being "in Christ,"
but now with a different connotation. For Paul's living "in
Christ" seems to mean having the *mind* of Christ, and it is
therefore a union of will, which meant participation in the
spirit of Christ. For Ignatius the very need for new terminology
seems to mark a difference. It is union with Christ and the

19. A. Schweitzer, *The Mysticism of Paul the Apostle* (New York, 1931),
pp. 334–48.

Father that becomes the central concern. The new words "union" and "unity" make it possible to include the Father, as Paul would not have done explicitly, and to suggest a closeness of being that nevertheless is something other than absorption.

We must still ask why this is of such importance for Ignatius, for as we have shown above, in calling God Silence and at the same time affirming the possibility of union even with the Father, Ignatius is declaring a paradox that verges close on true contradiction. The explanation seems to lie in his conviction that God is also Life. And in describing the giving of life Ignatius comes dangerously close to physical terms. He uses for instance the strange verb κεράννυμι, which means to mix or mingle and would not normally be used of personal relations (*Smyr.* 3.1). Christ came for the "newness of life eternal," and is "our life" also because he rose again. He is in the deepest sense Life, and it is that which makes union with him necessary in the eucharist, and in all the preliminary stages. Only by this closest association can men lay hold on life. But to admit the persuasive influence of the idea of life as characterizing divine Being is not at all to say that there is an irresistible transfer of life from God to man, by participation or in any other way. It is this which makes us most skeptical of the mystery analogies as sufficient ground for the eucharist. For at any stage men may stop. In union they encounter by anticipation the God who *is* Union, and Life. But without the preliminary stages this will never happen.

There is further difficulty that arises from the interpretation of the eucharist as in a radical sense a Christian mystery. Bartsch everywhere deprecates the notion that the imitation of Christ by the Christian means ethical conformity—a belief that in itself is certainly inadequate—and it is significant that nowhere in his book does he discuss ethics. But love is both an ethical notion and a word that implies relatedness and leads on to mystical union. It is their lack of love which marks the Docetists as much as their withdrawal from the eucharist, and neither difficulty can be subordinated to the other. Faith and love are not qualities by which merit is earned. But except as unity in submission and love is present, the final union is not reached, and attaining to God at death would be impossible. This ethical-mystical foundation for the climax that comes in the eucharist adds so much to the notion of participation that it may fairly be questioned whether it is at all true to Ignatius' thought to press literally the echoes of mystery thinking.

Union is possible, then, only within the community. It is not the experience of the isolated individual. The full evidence for that appears when one observes that for Ignatius the eucharist, which above all else presupposes the church fellowship, serves as an occasion for the fullest participation in union with God. It offers the moment when the separation between man and God is most likely to be transcended. "Let every man of you join together in meeting in the grace of the Name, in one faith and in Jesus Christ who was of the line of David according to the flesh, the Son of Man and the Son of God, that you may obey the bishop and the presbytery with an undivided mind; breaking one bread which is the medicine of immortality and the antidote for death, that we may live forever in Jesus Christ" (*Eph.* 20.2).

A parallel thought is suggested in the letter to the Philadelphians, where he urges them to "Be concerned to use one eucharist, for there is one flesh of our Lord Jesus Christ, and one cup for union with his blood, one altar and one bishop . . ." (*Phld.* 4). The eucharist bestows deathlessness and eternal life because in it the worshiper comes into the presence of the divine source of life. The condition for this is community meeting, in submission to the bishop, so that with an "undivided mind" they may enter into the sacramental experience.[20] The allusion to the "undivided mind" suggests the psychological quiet, with critical reason and every other sort of striving in abeyance, that might become the occasion for mystical union.

But when it has been affirmed that Ignatius believes in the

20. *GG*, pp. 101 f., finds much in Ignatius' thought that emphasizes the power-giving sacramental experience, but believes that Ignatius identifies ἕνωσις with the "mysterienhaft" experience, in accordance with his theory that participation in Christ occurs through a re-enacted death and rising. Ignatius certainly is not conscious of these distinctions, however, as Bartsch has to admit when he recognizes that they are blended in a good many passages, and it is doubtful that they apply usefully to his thought.

possibility of a mystical union, within the fellowship of the
church, and at least sometimes on the occasion of the eucharist,
it is still necessary to ask what that means. There are certain
things that apparently it does *not* mean. It is not the mysticism
in which the worshiper is absorbed by the divine, nor could
one find any early Christian for whom such a belief was possible. Ignatius uses many words that express relation, and the
transcendence of separateness, but "union in faith and love"
would hardly be meaningful without the persistence of different individualities. Although love is deeper than feeling and
seems to imply a transformation of the self-centered individual,
as Ignatius suggests in the cry that faith and love in unity are
very God, there is no phrase in the letters which suggests that
union involves becoming God, nor in his anthropology does
Ignatius think of the nature of men as either different from or
like that of the divine. He does not, for instance, characteristically describe the redeemed life as that lived "in the Spirit."
He is not interested in the nature of men in a metaphysical
sense, but he addresses himself to the indubitable fact of separateness. In ecstasy the barriers between man and God fall
away temporarily, but there is no suggestion that man *becomes*
God, although he may become a logos of God. For all his freedom in using the word *theos,* nothing in Ignatius' terminology
suggests anything like the words of Clement [21] that "the Word
of God became man in order that from man even you may learn
how man may become a god," even if by that Clement means
no more than immortality after death.[22] For Ignatius it seems
rather to be the mysticism of adoration,[23] in which the individual rejoices in God but from which in the rhythm of daily

21. *Protrepticus* 1: ἵνα δὴ καὶ σὺ παρὰ ἀνθρώπου μάθῃς πῇ ποτε ἄρα ἄνθρωπος
γένηται θεός. Migne, *Patrologiae,* SG, *8,* col. 64.

22. So G. W. Butterworth, "The Deification of Man in Clement of
Alexandria," *JTS, 17* (1915–16), 169. He maintains, probably correctly, that
θεός should be translated "a" god.

23. Kirk, *Vision of God,* p. 108, describes as the "vision of God" that
which we take Ignatius to mean by ἕνωσις "unbroken personal intercourse
with the divine." Similarly Dodd, *Fourth Gospel,* pp. 194–200, considers
union with God in the gospel to mean "mutual indwelling," a relationship
between persons.

life he must return. For the man who has experienced union there would surely come an ethical change, for henceforth he would abhor disunity and lack of love, whether within himself or in the local congregation; but there is no evidence that Ignatius could consider it θεοποίησις.

Even by allowing ourselves to consider the different kinds of change possible, we imply inevitably but mistakenly that Ignatius was aware of the logical distinctions that later theologians pointed out. The fact is, he never raised the question of the nature of the union between the believer and God, any more than he considered the nature of the union between the Son and the Father. In both cases he is interested simply in the *fact* of union. To say that it was a sacramental union is to point out that he was concerned with the means by which men came to it. He was intent on pointing out that even in this life men could come so fully into the presence of God as to know him without barriers. Returning from such an experience it was inevitable that men should know themselves to be different. If God is life, then entering into God is entering into life. These are the terms that Ignatius seems to have preferred. But throughout the letters the fact stands out that salvation as Ignatius knew it was a gradual process; not to be achieved at one step by baptism or because the passion had once for all offered men a hope of resurrection, but slowly across a lifetime of unity with the church, and with God, through sacramental experiences of faith and love and the eucharist, or by martyrdom. By any of these means men might lay hold on the grace of God, which was expressed in the passion, and so at death "attain" unto him.

And if mystical union with God himself is possible as the final healing of the divisions that mar life, then Ignatius' emphasis on unity and his reiteration of the "one cup," the "one Jesus Christ" becomes more comprehensible. It is the capstone of the arch. It is in this context that the "living and speaking water" cries out to Ignatius, "Come to the Father." It is expressed in theological terms when Ignatius says that "the Lord was united with the Father and did nothing without him" (*Mag.* 7.1), and it explains the joyful urgency of the close of the same passage, "All of you gather together quickly as to one temple of God, as to one altar, to one Jesus Christ, who came forth from the one Father, and abides with the One, and returns to the One." The uniting of the divisions of life, the transcending of the separateness, the giving of life, is the work of the one God in the world. It is because this is his dearest conviction that Ignatius describes himself as a man "completely given over to union." For union is the nature of God himself.

We turn now, in closing, to summarize and set in some perspective the emphases of thought that make his preaching individual and independent, even if not in any radical sense unique. It is difficult to do this, since the letters omit so many of the steps that would be present in systematic writing. But the structure is there; and as we have maintained, it is a structure of thought that was developed to give direction to the church in a period when it was hard to know which insights were creative and which dangerous.

Ignatius' thought of God as Silence or Stillness seems to have accomplished two things. In the first place it provides a ground for the work of Christ, and guards against presenting him as the cult god or the gnostic redeemer. He is "our God," to be sure, but only because he is true God, united with the Father. In the second place the notion provides a firmer basis for the hold that Jews and Christians alike have on the ultimate reality of God. The need for revelation and therefore for the work of Christ becomes clearer if God is thought of as the mysterious ground, but what is revealed is what is ultimately real. Christ as the Logos or the Son reveals in a definitive way the Father who is otherwise never truly apprehended. Functions are differentiated, but the reality and unity of God is not impaired. Ignatius is more extreme than the Fourth Gospel in calling God Silence, but probably less clear than the Evangelist that such a notion calls for increased stress on the importance of the Father, though there is some apprehension on his part of that need for balance.

Equally one may see that to preach Christ as God is to insist, as against rabbinical Judaism or Essene-Christian thinking, that revelation and redemption are intimately and indissolubly joined. Redemption is the gift of God so wholly that Christ, who effects the redemption of men, can be spoken of as himself the gift. This is in part to say that the gift is not Torah. And no matter what view of the Teacher of Righteousness was held, it was not he who in this direct sense was the gift; the covenant remained. God in his compassion would justify men, perhaps even sanctify them, but it was because in his mercy he forgave the man who could not keep the law, not because there was any substitute for law. It remained obligatory, and God's justice and mercy stand opposed to each other in unresolved contradiction. This is the view presented in the *Testaments of the Twelve* and in the *Manual of Discipline*.

Ignatius seems to have perceived the problem and to have solved it in a way not unlike that adopted by Paul, though without the direct attack on Torah. And he goes beyond Paul. His willingness to use the word θεός of Christ may in part represent his awareness that his generation needed something even plainer than the statement that "God was in Christ reconciling the world unto himself." So, in a sense, God might be said to act through the Messiah. But if Christ is indeed Logos, and God, then all previous acts of God, whether by Torah or a Messiah, are superseded. The opposition between the justice and the mercy of God disappears.

Like the gnostics, some of the early Christians saw redemption as a divine drama. But it is the Fourth Evangelist, and less definitely Ignatius, who draws the necessary conclusions from the completion of Christ's work and discards the apocalyptic framework of Judaism. Now, once for all, life and love have been given in the event of the life and death of Christ.

The abandonment of a future tense for the fulfillment of the act of redemption, even if full justice is done to the fact that with the coming of Christ the time was fulfilled, made it necessary in some way to dramatize the uncertainty—the open possibility—in the life of the Christian. For although Christ had come once for all, that did not mean that men were automatically saved. The gnostics came very close to saying that, but Christians avoided the pitfall. For the gnostic had only to take seriously the teaching that the spark which was his real self was of higher stuff. This requires no agony and may even be a subtly gratifying idea. The Christian on the other hand had to struggle in various way to lay hold on grace by the help of God, for his recalcitrant self was prone either to sin, because he still lived in σάρξ, as Paul held, or to division and self-will, as Ignatius saw it. The Docetists, in relaxing the need for human response were unmistakably endangering the Christian message.

It is here that Ignatius performed perhaps his greatest service —in his vision of the church. For all his emphasis on individual choice he never relinquished the conviction that the church as a community is absolutely necessary to the Christian. It is the school of love and of unity, and it is within the church that the final step of union even with God and Christ will be achieved. The eucharist is, of course, of final importance. But it does not take the place the mystery does in the lives of its participants precisely because it is set in a community that emphasizes interdependence of persons in an historical institution as well as in liturgical reality. Perhaps the experiments of the Essenes helped to give the church a pattern of fellowship. For Ignatius makes clear that there was more than a cultic association among the members. In company with one another they had to sub-due the tendencies toward egotism and self-importance—to work toward submission in love which could finally leave the self open to God. The plight of the individual is faced in fullest measure, and a way of meeting it is provided within the community. It is God who redeems, by his gift; it is neither for man's merit nor by his own acts that it comes. But neither is it an act solely on God's part. The word justification is all but absent, perhaps because Ignatius interprets salvation as two separate but complementary steps, only united in the final mo-ment of attaining unto God, or, by anticipation, in ἕνωσις. God's offer is made, his act performed. But for the individual the process of redemption will be completed slowly across a life-time or consummated in the swift moment of the martyr's death.

In many of these respects Ignatius' thought runs parallel to that of the Fourth Gospel and the *Odes,* as the needs which they faced seem to be strikingly similar. But in one important respect he differs sharply, possibly because the letters represent a period a few years later than the other writings. What had been latent when they were written had now become a dangerous threat to the gospel. The chief danger arose not from the side of the Essene-Christians, whose queries were perhaps perennial, but from the Docetists. Before their challenge Ignatius affirms with passion the *truth* of the incarnation. This was no suprahistorical event, woven of the color of myth or built on the cloudy heights of metaphysical speculation, although Ignatius had no fundamental objection to myth. It was sober history, an event which happened here in this world. In making this affirmation Ignatius is opposing not only his enemies but even his friends, for both the *Odes* and the Fourth Gospel show themselves unguarded at this point. Clearly Christian as the *Odes* are, in this respect they are naïvely docetic. They could be read with satisfaction both by those who believed that the Logos truly assumed human nature and by gnostics. The author of the Fourth Gospel could not have foreseen that his emphasis on the other-worldly source of the life of Christ could be used to undermine its reality in the world of men, but the subsequent popularity of the gospel among gnostics bears witness to its ambiguity.

Ignatius saw the peril as the Odist and the Evangelist did not. The hurried writing of the letters need not blind us to the acute intelligence and profound piety behind them. The *only* defense he knew against the dangers which threatened the gospel on every side, and which forced on him the martyr's role, was to stand on the real, corporeal incarnation: "God and man, true life in death." The suffering on the cross was real and the final proof that the grace and love of God are one. History and the world are thus not surrendered to Satan but remain the areas in which God works. Nor is redemption an isolated, profoundly individual moment all but out of time, as the modern existentialists would have it, but a stumbling and wholly human journey in a real world, to find grace in company with others in the church, and in the end to attain unto God.

Bibliography

THIS BIBLIOGRAPHY does not survey all the Ignatian material but is a list of the chief books and articles used.

The literature on the Essenes is voluminous, and it will perhaps be a convenience if I cite separately that part of it to which I am particularly indebted. For the purpose of this study of Ignatius the most important writings are the *Habakkuk Commentary,* the *Manual of Discipline,* the *Hymns of Thanksgiving* and those of the pseudepigraphs most frequently referred to. The American Schools of Oriental Research, under the editorship of M. Burrows, assisted by J. C. Trever and W. H. Brownlee, have published in plates and transcription *The Dead Sea Scrolls of St. Mark's Monastery: 1, The Isaiah Manuscript and the Habakkuk Commentary,* and *2, Manual of Discipline.* E. L. Sukenik published posthumously *The Dead Sea Scrolls of the Hebrew University* including plates and transcription of the *Second Isaiah Scroll, the Wars of the Sons of Light against the Sons of Darkness,* and the *Hymns of Thanksgiving.* For reports on the debates among scholars, and for convenient and competent translations of the major findings at Qumran the most useful books in English are those listed above by M. Burrows, and although they do not offer critical notes on the texts themselves, or give the column and line references, I have used them constantly. T. H. Gaster, *The Dead Sea Scriptures,* includes more material, in a livelier but rather free translation. For translations of the *Manual of Discipline* I am greatly indebted to W. H. Brownlee, *The Dead Sea Manual of Discipline, BASOR,* Supplementary Studies, Nos. 10–12, and to the parts of the *Discipline* scattered through the English translation of A. Dupont-Sommer's *The Jewish Sect of Qumran and the Essenes.* For other translations see W. H. Brownlee, "The Servant of the Lord in the Qumran Scrolls, II" *BASOR, 135* (1954). For translations of the *Habukkuk Commentary,*

W. H. Brownlee, "The Jerusalem Habakkuk Scroll," *BASOR,* *112* (1948) and further corrections in ibid., 114 and 116 (both 1949), and the parts scattered through A. Dupont-Sommer, *The Dead Sea Scrolls,* and *The Jewish Sect of Qumran and the Essenes.* For the *Hymns of Thanksgiving* see the two books by Dupont-Sommer just cited, and W. H. Brownlee's translation of Plate X of the *Megillot Genuzot,* Vol. 2, in the *Dead Sea Manual of Discipline,* p. 52. For the *Damascus Document* I have used the translation of R. H. Charles, *Apocrypha and Pseudepigrapha of the Old Testament,* Vol. 2 (Oxford, 1913), as also for references to *Jubilees, Testaments of the Twelve Patriarchs,* and *I Enoch.*

ABRAHAMS, I., *Studies in Pharisaism and the Gospels,* Ser. 2, Cambridge University Press, 1924.

ALBRIGHT, W. F., "Recent Discoveries in Palestine and the Gospel of St. John," in W. D. Davies and D. Daube, eds., *Background of the New Testament and Its Eschatology* (see below).

Antioch-on-the-Orontes, ed. the Committee for the Excavation of Antioch and Its Vicinity, Princeton University Press, 4 vols. 1934–52.

The Apocalypse of Abraham, ed. G. H. Box, Translations of Early Documents, Ser. 1, London, Society for Promoting Christian Knowledge, 1918.

The Ascension of Isaiah, ed. R. H. Charles, Translations of Early Documents, Ser. 1, London, Society for Promoting Christian Knowledge, 1917.

BACON, B. W., *The Gospel of the Hellenists,* New York, Holt, 1933.

BARTSCH, H. W., *Gnostisches Gut und Gemeindetradition bei Ignatius von Antiochien,* Beiträge zur Förderung christlicher Theologie, ed. P. Althaus, Reihe. 2, Sammlung wissenschaftlicher Monographien, Band. 44, Gütersloh, Werner, 1940.

—— ed., *Kerygma and Myth,* trans. R. H. Fuller, London, Society for Promoting Christian Knowledge, 1953.

BAUER, W., *Die Briefe des Ignatius von Antiochia und der Polykarpbrief,* Handbuch zum Neuen Testament, ed. H. Lietzmann, suppl. vol., *Die apostolischen Väter,* Vol. 2, Tübingen, Mohr, 1920.

—— *Rechtgläubigkeit und Ketzerei im ältesten Christentum,* Tübingen, Mohr, 1934.

BEURLIER, E., *Le Culte rendu aux empereurs romains,* Paris, Thorin, 1890.

—— "Le κοινόν de Syrie," *Revue numismatique,* Ser. 3, *12* (1894), 286–300.

BOUCHIER, E. S., *A Short History of Antioch,* Oxford, Blackwell, 1921.

—— *Syria as a Roman Province,* Oxford, Blackwell, 1916.

BOUSSET, W., *Hauptprobleme der Gnosis,* Göttingen, Vandenhoeck and Ruprecht, 1907.

BRÉHIER, E., *Les Idées philosophiques et religieuses de Philon d'Alexandrie,* Études de philosophie médiévale, Vol. 8, 2d ed. Paris, Vrin, 1925.

BROUGHTON, T. R. S., "Roman Asia Minor," ed. T. Frank, *An Economic Survey of Ancient Rome,* Vol. 4, Baltimore, Johns Hopkins Press, 1938.

BROWNLEE, W. H., "Biblical Interpretation among the Sectaries of the Dead Sea Scrolls," *BA, 14* (1951), 54–76.

—— *The Dead Sea Manual of Discipline,* BASOR, Supplementary Studies, 10–12, New Haven, American Schools of Oriental Research, 1951.

—— "The Jerusalem Habakkuk Scroll," *BASOR, 112* (1948), 8–18.

—— "John the Baptist in the New Light of Ancient Scrolls," in K. Stendahl, ed., *The Scrolls and the New Testament* (see below).

—— "The Servant of the Lord in the Qumran Scrolls, II," *BASOR, 135* (1954), 33–38.

BULTMANN, R., *Das Evangelium des Johannes,* Kritisch-exegetischer Kommentar über das Neue Testament, Abt. II, ed. H. A. W. Meyer, 12th ed. Göttingen, Vandenhoeck and Ruprecht, 1952.

—— "New Testament and Mythology," in H. W. Bartsch, ed., *Kerygma and Myth* (see above).

—— "Die religionsgeschichtliche Hintergrund des Prologs zum Johannes-Evangelium," in *Eucharisterion,* Vol. 2, ed. H. Schmidt (see below).

—— *Theology of the New Testament,* trans. K. Grobel, 2 vols. New York, Scribner's, 1951–55.

—— *Das Urchristentum im Rahmen der antiken Religionen,* Zurich, Artemis, 1949.

BURNEY, C. F., *The Aramaic Origin of the Fourth Gospel,* Oxford, Clarendon, 1922.

BURROWS, M., *The Dead Sea Scrolls,* New York, Viking, 1955.

—— *More Light on the Dead Sea Scrolls,* New York, Viking, 1958.

BUTLER, H. C., *Architecture and Other Arts,* Publications of an American Archaeological Expedition to Syria in 1899–1900, Pt. II, New York, Century, 1903.

BUTTERWORTH, G. W., "The Deification of Man in Clement of Alexandria," *JTS, 17* (1915–16), 157–69.

CAMPENHAUSEN, H. von, *Die Idee des Martyriums in der alten Kirche,* Göttingen, Vandenhoeck and Ruprecht, 1936.

CASEY, R. P., "Gnosis, Gnosticism and the New Testament," W. D. Davies and D. Daube, eds., *The Background of the New Testament and Its Eschatology* (see below).

CHADWICK, H., "The Silence of Bishops in Ignatius," *HTR, 43* (1950), 169–72.

CHARLES, R. H., ed., *The Apocrypha and Pseudepigrapha of the Old Testament in English,* Oxford, Clarendon, 1913.

CLARK, K. W., "The Gentile Bias in Matthew," *JBL, 66* (1947), 165–72.

CROSS, F. M., *The Ancient Library of Qumran and Modern Biblical Studies,* Haskell Lectures, New York, Doubleday, 1958.

CUMONT, F., *Études syriennes,* Paris, Picard, 1917.

—— "The Frontier Provinces of the East," in *The Imperial Peace* A.D. *70–192,* ed. J. B. Bury, S. A. Cook, M. P. Charlesworth, *CAH,* Vol. 11, Cambridge University Press, 1936.

—— *Les Religions orientales dans le paganisme romain,* Paris, Leroux, 1909.

CURETON, W., *The Antient Syriac Version of the Epistles of Saint Ignatius to St. Polycarp, the Ephesians and the Romans,* London, Rivington, 1845.

DAVIES, W. D., and DAUBE, D., eds., *The Background of the New Testament and Its Eschatology. In Honour of C. H. Dodd,* Cambridge University Press, 1956.

DELAFOSSE, H., *Lettres d'Ignace d'Antioche,* Les Textes du Christianisme, Vol. 2, Paris, Rieder, 1927.

DELAHAYE, H., "L'amphithéatre Flavien et ses environs," *Analecta Bollandiana, 16* (1897), 209–52.

DIBELIUS, M., *Die Geisterwelt im Glauben des Paulus,* Göttingen, Vandenhoeck and Ruprecht, 1909.

DIETERICH, A., *Eine Mithrasliturgie,* Leipzig, Teubner, 1910.

DINKLER, E., "Zum Problem der Ethik bei Paulus," *Zeitschrift für Theologie und Kirche, 49* (1952), 167–200.

DIO CHRYSOSTOM, *Discourses,* trans. H. L. Crosby, Loeb Classical Library, Vol. 4, Cambridge, Mass., Harvard University Press, 1946.

DODD, C. H., *The Apostolic Preaching and Its Developments,* 2d ed. New York, Harper, 1944.

—— *Gospel and Law, the Relation of Faith and Ethics in Early Christianity,* Bampton Lectures in America, No. 3, New York, Columbia University Press, 1951.

—— *The Interpretation of the Fourth Gospel,* Cambridge University Press, 1953.

DORESSE, J., "Trois livres gnostiques inédite," *Vigiliae Christianae, 2* (1948), 137–60.

DOWNEY, G., "The Gate of the Cherubim at Antioch," *Jewish Quarterly Review,* new ser., *29* (1938–39), 167–77.

—— "Imperial Building Records in Malalas," *Byzantinische Zeitschrift, 38* (1938), 1–15, 299–311.

DUPONT-SOMMER, A., *The Dead Sea Scrolls,* trans. E. M. Rowley, Oxford, Blackwell, 1952.

—— *The Jewish Sect of Qumran and the Essenes,* trans. R. D. Barnett, London, Macmillan, 1954.

DUSSAUD, R., "Note additionelle aux fouilles de Minet-el-Beida et de Ras-Shamra," *Syria, 10* (1929), 297–303.

Dussaud, R., *Topographie historique de la Syrie antique et médiévale*, Bibliothèque archéologique et historique, Vol. *4*, Paris, Geuthner, 1927.

Eucharisterion, Studien zur Religion und Literatur des Alten und Neuen Testaments, Hermann Gunkel zum 60. Geburtstage, ed. Hans Schmidt, Forschungen zur Religion und Literatur des Alten und Neuen Testaments, ed., R. Bultmann and H. Gunkel, Neue folge, 19 Heft, 2 Teil, Göttingen, Vandenhoeck and Ruprecht, 1923.

Evangelium Veritatis, ed., M. Malinine, H.-C. Puech, G. Quispel, Studien aus dem C. C. Jung-Institut, VI, Zurich, Rascher, 1956.

The Excerpta ex Theodoto of Clement of Alexandria, ed. R. P. Casey, Studies & Documents, ed. K. and S. Lake, Vol. 1, London, Christophers, 1934.

Eusebius, *Ecclesiastical History*, ed., H. J. Lawlor and J. E. L. Oulton, London, Society for Promoting Christian Knowledge, Vol. 1, 1927; Vol. 2, 1928.

Finkelstein, L., *Akiba, Scholar, Saint and Martyr*, New York, Covici Friede, 1936.

Fougères, G., "Koinon," *Dictionnaire des antiquités grecques et romaines*, new edition, Vol. 3, Pt. I, ed. C. Daremberg and E. Saglio, Paris, 1900.

Funk, F. X., *Patres Apostolici*, 2d ed. Tübingen, Laupp, Vol. 1, 1901; Vol. 2, 1913.

Gaster, T. H., *The Dead Sea Scriptures*, New York, Doubleday, 1956.

Genouillac, H. de, *L'Église chrétienne au temps de Saint Ignace d'Antioche*, Bibliothèque de théologie historique, Paris, 1907.

Goltz, E. von der, *Ignatius von Antiochien als Christ und Theologe*, Texte und Untersuchungen zur Geschichte der Altchristlichen Literatur, ed. O. von Gebhardt and A. Harnack, Band 12, Heft 3, Leipzig, Hinrichs, 1894.

Goodenough, E. R., *By Light, Light*, New Haven, Yale University Press, 1935.

—— "John a Primitive Gospel," *JBL, 64* (1945), 145–82.

Grant, R. M., "The Fourth Gospel and the Church," *HTR, 35* (1942), 95–116.

—— "The Odes of Solomon and the Church of Antioch," *JBL, 63* (1944), 363–77.

—— "The Origin of the Fourth Gospel," *JBL, 69* (1950), 305–22.

Guiraud, P., *Les Assemblées provinciales dans l'empire romain*, Paris, Imprimerie nationale, 1887.

Haddad, G., *Aspects of Social Life in Antioch in the Hellenistic-Roman Period*, Chicago University Press, 1949.

Harnack, A. von, *Die Chronologie der altchristlichen Litteratur bis Eusebius*, Geschichte der altchristlichen Litteratur, Pt. II, 2 vols., Leipzig, Hinrichs, 1897–1904.

—— *Die Zeit des Ignatius*, Leipzig, Hinrichs, 1878.

HARRISON, P. N., *Polycarp's Two Epistles to the Philippians*, Cambridge University Press, 1936.

HENNECKE, E., *Neutestamentliche Apokryphen*, 2d ed. Tübingen, Mohr, 1924.

HONIGMANN, E. "Syria," Pauly's *Real-Encyclopädie der classischen altertumswissenschraft*, 2d reihe, 8 halbbd., G. Wissowa, Stuttgart, 1932.

JAMES, M. R., trans., *The Apocryphal New Testament*, Oxford, Clarendon, 1924.

JONAS, H., *Gnosis und spätantiker Geist*, Göttingen, Vandenhoeck and Ruprecht, Vol. 1, 1934; Vol. 2, 1954.

———— *The Gnostic Religion*, Boston, Beacon Press, 1958.

JONES, A. H. M., *The Cities of the Eastern Roman Provinces*, Oxford University Press, 1937.

KAHRSTEDT, U., *Syrische Territorien in hellenistischer Zeit*, Abhandlungen des Gesellschaft der Wissenschaften zu Göttingen, Philologisch-Historische Klasse, neue folge, Vol. 19, Berlin, Weidmann, 1926.

JOSEPHUS, F., *The Jewish War*, trans. H. St. J. Thackeray, Loeb Classical Library, London, Heinemann, 1926–43.

KENNEDY, H. A. A., *St. Paul and The Mystery Religions*, London, Hodder and Stoughton, 1913.

KIRK, K. E., *Vision of God*, 2d ed. London, Longmans, Green, 1932.

KITTEL, G., ed., *Theologisches Wörterbuch zum Neuen Testament*, Stuttgart, 1933–.

KLEIST, J. A., *The Epistles of St. Clement of Rome and St. Ignatius of Antioch*, Ancient Christian Writers, Vol. 1, Westminster, Md., Newman Bookshop, 1946.

KNOX, J., *Philemon among the Letters of Paul*, Chicago University Press, 1935.

KRAELING, C. H., *Anthropos and Son of Man*, Columbia University Oriental Studies, Vol. 25, New York, Columbia University Press, 1927.

———— "The Apocalypse of Paul and the 'Iranische Erlösungsmysterium,'" *HTR, 24* (1931), 209–44.

———— "The Jewish Community at Antioch," *JBL, 51* (1932), 130–60.

———— *John the Baptist*, New York, Scribner's, 1951.

KROYMANN, E., ed., *Tertullian Adversus Praxean*, Sammlung ausgewählter kirchen- und dogmengeschichtlicher Quellenschriften, 2d ser., Heft 8, Tübingen, Mohr, 1907.

KUHN, K. G., "Die in Palästina gefundenen hebräischen Texte und das Neue Testament," *Zeitschrift für Theologie und Kirche, 47* (1950), 192–211.

———— "Die Sektenschrift und die iranische Religion," *Zeitschrift für Theologie und Kirche, 49* (1952), 296–316.

———— "The Lord's Supper and The Communal Meal at Qumran," in K. Stendahl, ed., *The Scrolls and the New Testament* (see below).

LAKE, K., *The Apostolic Fathers,* 2 vols., Loeb Classical Library, London, Heinemann, 1925.

LEBRETON, J., *Histoire du dogme de la trinité,* Vol. 2, 3d ed., Bibliothèque de théologie historique, Paris, Beauchesne, 1928.

LEBRETON, J. and J. ZEILLER, *The History of the Primitive Church,* 2 vols., trans. E. C. Messenger, New York, Macmillan, 1949.

LIDZBARSKI, M., *Mandâische Liturgien,* Abhandlungen der königlichen Gesellschaft der Wissenschaften zu Göttingen, Philologisch-historische Klasse, Neue Folge, Bd. 17, 1, Berlin, Weidmann, 1920.

LIGHTFOOT, J. B., *The Apostolic Fathers,* Pt. II, *S. Ignatius and S. Polycarp,* 3 vols., 2d ed. London, Macmillan, 1889.

———— *St. Paul's Epistle to the Philippians,* 8th ed. London, Macmillan, 1888.

LOEWENICH, W. VON, *Das Johannes-Verständnis im zweiten Jahrhundert,* Beihefte zur *Zeitschrift für die neutestamentliche Wissenschaft, 13,* Giessen, Töpelmann, 1932.

LOHMEYER, E., "The Right Interpretation of the Mythological," ed. H. W. Bartsch, *Kerygma and Myth* (see above).

LOISY, A., *Les Mystères païens et le mystère chrétien,* Paris, Nourry, 1919.

LOOFS, F., "Christologie," *Realencyclopädie für protestantische Theologie und Kirche,* 3d ed. *4, 27*

MALALAS, JOANNES, *Chronographia,* ed. L. Dindorf, in J. P. Migne, Patrologiae, Graeca, *97,* Paris, 1860.

MAURER, C., *Ignatius von Antiochien und das Johannesevangelium,* Abhandlungen zur Theologie des Alten und Neuen Testaments, ed. W. Eichrodt and O. Cullmann, Zurich, Zwingli, 1949.

MENSCHING, G., *Das heilige Schweigen,* Religionsgeschichtliche Versuche und Vorarbeiten, ed. A. Dietrich and R. Wünsch, Band 20, Heft 2, Giessen, Töpelmann, 1926.

MILIK, J. T., "Le Testament de Lévi en Araméen," *Revue biblique, 62* (1955), 398–406.

MOFFATT, J., *Grace in the New Testament,* New York, Long and Smith, 1932.

———— "Ignatius of Antioch—a Study in Personal Religion," *JR, 10* (1930), 169–86.

MOORE, G. F., *Judaism in the First Centuries of the Christian Era, the Age of the Tannaim,* 2 vols., Cambridge, Harvard University Press, 1954.

MOREY, C. R., "The Excavation of Antioch-on-the-Orontes," *Proceedings of the American Philosophical Society, 76* (1936), 637–51, and figs. 2–20.

———— *The Mosaics of Antioch,* London, Longmans, Green, 1938.

MOWRY, L., "The Dead Sea Scrolls and the Background for the Gospel of John," *BA, 17* (1954), 78–97.

The New Testament in the Apostolic Fathers, ed. by a Committee of the Oxford Society of Historical Theology, Oxford, Clarendon, 1905.

NORDEN, E., *Agnostos Theos,* Leipzig, Teubner, 1913.
—— *Die antike Kunstprosa vom VI Jahrhundert v. Chr. bis in die Zeit der Renaissance,* 2 vols., Leipzig, Teubner, 1898.
The Odes and Psalms of Solomon, ed. R. Harris and A. Mingana, John Rylands Library, 2 vols. Manchester University Press, 1916, 1920.
PREISKER, H., *Das Ethos des Urchristentums,* Gütersloh, Bertelsmann, 1949.
PREISS, T., "La Mystique de l'imitation du Christ et de l'unité chez Ignace d'Antioche," *Revue d'histoire et de philosophie religieuses, 18* (1938), 197–241.
PRENTICE, W. K., *Greek and Latin Inscriptions,* Publications of an American Archaeological Expedition to Syria in 1899–1900, Pt. III, New York, Century, 1908.
PUECH, H. C. and G. Quispel, "Les Écrits gnostiques du codex Jung," *Vigiliae Christianae, 8* (1954), 1–51.
PUECH, H. C., G. Quispel, W. C. van Unnik, *The Jung Codex,* trans. and ed. F. L. Cross, London, Mowbray, 1955.
RAMSAY, W. M., "Roads and Travel (in The New Testament)," Hastings, *Dictionary of The Bible, 5* (1904), 375–402.
REICKE, B., "The Constitution of the Primitive Church in the Light of Jewish Documents." in K. Stendahl, ed., *The Scrolls and the New Testament* (see below).
REITZENSTEIN, R., *Die hellenistischen Mysterienreligionen,* 3d ed. Leipzig, Teubner, 1927.
—— *Das iranische Erlösungsmysterium,* Bonn, Marcus and Weber, 1921.
—— *Poimandres,* Studien zur griechisch ägyptischen und frühchristlichen Literatur, Leipzig, Teubner, 1904.
—— *Die Vorgeschichte der christlichen Taufe,* Leipzig, Teubner, 1929.
REITZENSTEIN, R., and H. H. SCHAEDER, *Studien zum antiken Synkretismus aus Iran und Griechenland,* Studien des Bibliothek Warburg, 7, ed., Fritz Saxl, Leipzig, Teubner, 1926.
RICHARDSON, C. C., *The Christianity of Ignatius of Antioch,* New York, Columbia University Press, 1935.
—— "The Church in Ignatius of Antioch," *JR, 17* (1937), 428–58.
—— *Early Christian Fathers,* Library of Christian Classics, Vol. 1, ed. J. Baillie, J. T. McNeill, H. P. Van Dusen, Philadelphia, Westminster, 1953.
RIDDLE, D. W., *The Martyrs, a Study in Social Control,* Chicago University Press, 1931.
RIETSCHEL, G., *Lehrbuch der Liturgik,* 2 vols., Berlin, Reuther and Reichard, 1909.
ROWLEY, H. H., "Jewish Proselyte Baptism and the Baptism of John," *HUCA, 15* (1940), 313–34.
—— *The Zadokite Fragments and the Dead Sea Scrolls,* Oxford, Blackwell, 1952.

SCHENK GRAF VON STAUFFENBERG, A., *Die römische Kaisergeschichte bei Malalas Griechischer Text der Bücher IX–XII und Untersuchungen,* Stuttgart, Kohlhammer, 1931.

SCHLIER, H., *Religionsgeschichtliche Untersuchungen zu den Ignatius-briefen,* Beihefte zur Zeitschrift für die Neutestamentliche Wissenschaft, *8,* Giessen, Töpelmann, 1929.

SCHMIDT, C., and W. SCHUBART, eds., *Altchristliche Texte,* Berliner Klassi-kertexte, Königliche Museen zu Berlin, Bd. *1,* Heft 6, Berlin, Weidmann, 1910.

SCHULTZE, V., *Altchristliche Städte und Landschaften, III, Antiocheia,* Gutersloh, Bertelsmann, 1930.

SCHWEITZER, A., *The Mysticism of Paul The Apostle,* trans. W. Mont-gomery, New York, Holt, 1931.

SELWYN, E. G., *The First Epistle of St. Peter,* London, Macmillan, 1947.

SEYRIG, H., "La Triade héliopolitaine et les temples de Baalbek," *Syria, 10* (1929), 314–56.

SPINKA, M. and G. DOWNEY, *Chronicle of John Malalas, Bks. VIII–XVIII,* Chicago University Press, 1940.

STENDAHL, K. ed., *The Scrolls and The New Testament,* New York, Harper, 1957.

STRACK, H. L. and P. BILLERBECK, *Kommentar zum Neuen Testament aus Talmud und Midrasch,* 4 vols. Munich, Beck, 1922–28.

STREETER, B. H., *The Four Gospels: A Study of Origins,* New York, Mac-millan, 1925.

——— *The Primitive Church,* London, Macmillan, 1929.

SURKAU, H. W., *Martyrien in jüdischer und frühchristlicher Zeit,* For-schungen zur Religion und Literatur des Alten und Neuen Testaments, ed. R. Bultmann, new ser., Heft 36, Göttingen, Vandenhoeck and Ruprecht, 1938.

TARN, W. W., *Hellenistic Civilization,* London, Arnold, 1927.

TAYLOR, V., *The Atonement in New Testament Teaching,* 2d ed. London, Epworth Press, 1950.

THOMAS, J., *Le Mouvement baptiste en Palestine et Syrie,* Gembloux, Duculot, 1935.

TORRANCE, T. F., *The Doctrine of Grace in the Apostolic Fathers,* Edin-burgh, Oliver and Boyd, 1948.

VAUX, R. DE, "Fouilles au Khirbet Qumran," *RB, 61* (1954), 206–36.

VÖLTER, D., *Die ignatianischen Briefe,* Tübingen, Heckenhauer, 1892.

——— *Polykarp und Ignatius,* Leiden, Brill, 1910.

WAAGÉ, D. B., *Greek, Roman, Byzantine and Crusaders' Coins,* Antioch-on-the-Orontes, 4, Pt. II, ed. the Committee for the Excavation of Antioch and Its Vicinity, Princeton University Press, 1952.

WEBER, W., "Studien zur Chronik des Malalas," *Festgabe für Adolf Deiss-mann,* Tübingen, Mohr, 1927.

WESSELY, C., *Neue Materialien zur Textkritik der Ignatiusbriefe,* Sitzungsberichte der Kaiserlichen Akademie der Wissenschaften in Wien, Philosophisch-Historische Klasse, 172, Abh. 4, Vienna, Hölder, 1913.

WETTER, G. P., *Altchristliche Liturgien: Das christliche Mysterium*, Forschungen zur Religion und Literatur des Alten und Neuen Testaments, new ser., Heft 13, ed. R. Bultmann and H. Gunkel, Göttingen, Vandenhoeck and Ruprecht, 1921.

—— *Charis. Ein Beitrag zur Geschichte des ältesten Christentums*, Leipzig, Brandstetter, 1913.

—— "Eine gnostische Formel im 4. Evangelium," *ZNTW*, *18* (1917–18), 49–63.

WILAMOWITZ-MÖLLENDORFF, U. von, "Lesefruechte," *Hermes*, *37* (1902), 328–32.

WILDER, A. N., "Mythology and The New Testament," *JBL*, *69* (1950), 113–27.

WOODHOUSE, W. J., "Slavery (Roman)," *ERE*, *11* (1920), 621–31.

ZAHN, T., *Ignatii et Polycarpi, Epistulae, Martyria, Fragmenta*, Patrum Apostolicorum Opera, Fasc. II, ed. O. de Gebhardt, A. von Harnack, T. Zahn, Leipzig, Hinrichs, 1876.

—— *Ignatius von Antiochien*, Gotha, Perthe, 1873.

Index 1.   General

The references to contemporary scholars in the notes have not been indexed.

283

Index 2. Citations

Page numbers of the present volume are in italic type.

NEW TESTAMENT

OLD TESTAMENT

PHILO